Sociological Theory

Sociological Theory

Volume 1

From the 1850s to the 1920s

Richard Münch

Nelson-Hall Publishers
Chicago

Library of Congress Cataloging-in-Publication Data

Münch, Richard, 1945–
   Sociological theory / Richard Münch.
     p.   c.m.
   Includes bibliographical references and indexes.
   Contents: v. 1. From the 1850s to the 1920s.
   ISBN 0-8304-1255-7 (v. 1)
   ISBN 0-8304-1394-4 (case contains three volumes)
   1. Sociology—Philosophy. 2. Sociology—History. I. Title.
HM24.M838   1994
301'.01—dc20   92-39833
                                                                   CIP

Manufactured in the United States of America

10 9 8 7 6 5 4 3

CONTENTS

PREFACE

THESE VOLUMES have been written for students, teachers, scholars, and researchers. They emerged from many years of lecturing and teaching courses in sociological theory. I am therefore very much indebted to the many students who joined my classes and served as critical examiners of my presentation of sociological theories. They forced me first of all to make the greatest effort to present the theories in a way that allows students to understand their message and to critically discuss them. The reluctance of many theorists to do this leaves the teacher of a course in sociological theory with an enormous task. The favorable response of my students over many years of preparing presentations of theories in a teachable form has encouraged me to compile the results of these years of teaching in a textbook, which I hope will receive the same favorable response from many students in many theory classes.

These volumes have been written with the intention of providing texts for teaching sociological theory that overcome the weaknesses of those available to date. I endeavor to be more comprehensive in covering the whole development of sociological theory, from classical origins to contemporary debates. I have attempted to be less biased toward certain national and paradigmatical traditions in order to allow sociological theory to be taught on an international and pluralistic level. I have tried to present theories in a more systematically structured way, by revealing their core and their distinctive statements in order to allow easier access to their message. The theories are presented much more in discourse, mutually throwing light on their more obscure aspects and on their erroneous aspects. I hope teachers will find the book as helpful for teaching sociological theory as I did the materials that eventually constituted the book.

These volumes have also been written for scholars. This work is not simply a history of social thought, but a reconstruction and continuation of sociological discourse with the aim of advancing our theoretical knowledge to a new level: constructing networks of theories by way of interparadigmatical and intertheoretical discourse. I hope that many of my colleagues will join this enterprise.

These volumes have also been written for researchers. The state of theoretical knowledge is presented in a systematically structured way, which I hope invites researchers to work with that knowledge and to relate empirical research to theoretical questions more than has been usual up to now. Their reluctance to do so was caused to a not inconsiderable degree by the often very confusing writing style of many theorists. I have tried very hard to improve upon that style of writing theory.

This project has been written with the support of many people: students, assistants, colleagues, friends and family. Without their help the book would not have come to light. Many thanks to all of them. Special thanks go to Neil Johnson for working on the English language of this book.

For their assistance with references, preparing name and subject indices, and with word processing work, I wish to thank Susanne Gabele, Renate Kolvenbach, Christian Lahusen, Karin Rhau and Willy Viehöver. Special thanks also go to Michael Opielka for valuable comments in the final stage of working on the manuscript.

THE CLASSICAL period in the formation of sociology as a distinctive discipline ranges from the 1850s to the 1920s. This was the time when the founding fathers set the framework of sociology theory, each one from a very specific point of view and background. We will deal here with the contributions made by Herbert Spencer, Karl Marx, Vilfredo Pareto, Georg Simmel, Emile Durkheim, Max Weber, and George Herbert Mead.

I have ordered the approaches to social reality undertaken by these classics according to their theoretical core's location within the action space that represents the background to this whole reconstruction of sociological theories. Though all of them endeavored to cover the whole range of social action, they nevertheless started from certain fields where their major and unique contributions were located and stretched out to the other fields in a more or less biased or balanced way. The action space under consideration can be differentiated into four basic fields: the *economics of social action,* with its function of opening and adaptation to varying situations; the *politics of social action,* with the function of its specification and orientation toward goal attainment; the *structure of social action,* with the function of its closing and integration in an ordered system; and the *symbolics of social action,* with the function of its generalization and latent pattern maintenance within the framework of meaning (Münch, 1987a, 1987b).

In this perspective we will see how the different classics made their specific contributions to understanding and explaining the economics, politics, structure, and symbolics of social action, with a primary emphasis on one of the four fields and a secondary spreading out to the other fields of action.

Before we engage in studying the various contributions to forming sociological theory made by the classics, I will give an outline of the framework
that guides our investigation into the development of sociological theory.
I will point out the place of theory in sociology with an invitation to sociological discourse, a guideline for reconstructing the discourse of sociological theory, and an analysis of the structure and function of sociological
theory.

PART ONE

The Place of Theory in Sociology

ONE

INVITATION TO SOCIOLOGICAL DISCOURSE

SOCIOLOGICAL THEORY originated from different national origins and has developed within different national contexts, due to the persisting national organization of the training of sociologists. Nevertheless, international exchange has always contributed to the cross-fertilization of ideas in sociological theory. It has now become an international matter, due to the widely spread exchange between scholars (see Martindale, 1960; Aron, 1965; Nisbet, 1967; Mullins, 1973; Eisenstadt and Curelaru, 1976; Alexander, 1982–1983, 1987a, 1987b; Seidman, 1983; Collins, 1988; Fararo, 1989; Ritzer, 1988; Jonathan H. Turner, 1986; Wagner, 1984; Wallace, 1983; Giddens and Turner, 1987; Runciman, 1983, 1988).

However, this international character of sociological theory building is not sufficiently reflected in contemporary textbooks on sociological theory. They are still very much biased in line with the national origin of their authors. They have merit in themselves, but still call for more attempts to reach a level of presentation that is truly international in character. This text endeavors to come closer to that goal. The business of teaching and of advancing sociological theory needs to be elevated to this international level.

Sociological theory is a discourse that has a history, takes place in certain societal and cultural contexts, and develops according to the logic of rational criticism by continuously eliminating errors and improving arguments. It is a matter of discursive argumentation. Two forms of discourse occur in the field of sociological theory: one is the common undertaking of advancing theoretical knowledge, and the other takes the form of competition between divergent theories. Unfortunately, the texts available to date present sociological theory very much as a collection of pieces, of hypotheses

confirmed to a greater or lesser degree by facts. There is nothing wrong with
that, because sociological theory has to be broken down to that level; however,
it is not enough. What is lacking is the underlying argumentation and discursive context, in short, the meaning of sociological theorizing. This book
is an attempt at presenting the development of sociological theory as an
ongoing discourse between different competing paradigms and theories to
eliminate errors and to improve and to complete a framework, thus approaching a more valid position. By "paradigm" I mean a broader current of
thought with a common frame of reference, common basic concepts, ideas,
and premises. By "theory" I mean a more specific set of statements and
hypotheses on a specific object. Thus, one paradigm is generally the home
of a variety of theories.

The underlying basis of the outlined development is a continuation of
the debate on ever higher levels of completeness, on which ever finer biases
and errors become the objects of criticism and corresponding revisions aiming at the improvement of the paradigms and theories. It is the discourse
going on between the competing paradigms and theories that determines
their continuous improvement. In this way the paradigms and theories come
closer to each other, overlap, and cover a larger part of the reality of the
social world, but nevertheless continue to disagree and compete. However,
the points of disagreement and competition become ever finer over the course
of time.

This is what the progress of science is all about. Yet that is not to say
that every single step in sociological theorizing does indeed represent progress.
The history of sociological theorizing is full of steps that have proven fruit-
less and have forgotten the advances and errors made by predecessors, thus
moving backward and making old errors anew. An adequate reconstruction of the discourse of sociological theory has to notice where such backward steps and repetitions of old errors have occurred.

Sociology has accumulated an enormous amount of theoretical
knowledge over the past 140 years. Theoretical knowledge is not descrip-
tive; it is explanatory in character. It does not simply describe what happened in the past or what happens in the present but helps to explain why
things happen as they do and to predict which kinds of things will happen
when certain conditions pertain and to solve problems by telling us what
we should do in order to avoid, change, or bring about certain states of
affairs.

The accumulation of theoretical knowledge of this kind takes place in
a permanent discourse between competing paradigms made up of basic
world-views and competing theories comprising more specific sets of statements. Sociology is very much a discursive discipline. That means a great
part of the accumulation of its knowledge comes from this ongoing discourse, much more than in the natural sciences. In the natural sciences,

empirical research is by definition related to theory via experiment and thus has immediate effects on theoretical development. This is much less the case with the social sciences, where we have a large amount of empirical research without any relation to theoretical questions and a large amount of theoretical discourse without any relation to empirical reseach. However, theoretical progress depends on criticism. Because empirical research and theoretical problems are so weakly related, the mutual criticism of competing paradigms and theories is all the more important for eliminating errors and making progress (see Alexander, 1982–83, 1987a).

This is why any assessment of the state of theoretical knowledge in sociology has to identify and elaborate on the discourse of competing paradigms and theories in order to separate the truth content of theories from their erroneous content in the light of competing theories. Only in this way can we point out the aspects of social reality that are correctly explained and the aspects that are not correctly explained by a theory; and only in this way can we specify the conditions under which the application of a theory yields correct explanations and predictions of facts and correct solutions for problems. Inasmuch as there is an insufficient interrelationship between theory and empirical research, we receive most of the information about the errors of a specific theory by throwing the light of its competitors onto its darker aspects. Confrontation with competing theories opens our minds, helps to overcome theoretical prejudices, and sharpens our vision to allow us to discover the weak parts of our theories. Because this is so important for theoretical progress, we are very much in need of a comprehensive reconstruction of sociological discourse.

This book is such a reconstruction of sociological discourse. It presents the accumulation of theoretical knowledge in sociology as a discourse between competing paradigms and theories that works on eliminating errors by confronting theories with alternative views, statements, and hypotheses. This work cannot be done by presenting a simple history of social thought. More constructive work is necessary in presenting the theories often more precisely, and in a more consistent formulation, than their own authors did; they need to be built up much more around their core premises in order to give them a definite shape. This allows us to discover what a theory does say and what it does not say, what its unique contribution to our knowledge really is compared to the contributions of other theories. A theory that has no shape and does not close out any possibility but allows everything to happen cannot be criticized; it is composed of contradictory statements. This is why a reconstruction of theories that aims at advancing knowledge by criticism has to be more consistent than their authors were able to be.

A reconstruction of sociological theories with the aim of promoting progress in theoretical knowledge also has to involve new construction of these theories. This takes place insofar as the discourse in this book is conducted to a greater extent than it has been in reality, confronting theories with each other that have not been confronted to the same extent by their authors. Only in this way can we separate the truth content of a theory from its errors. In order to advance our knowledge of the development of the human personality, for example, it is helpful to throw the light of Durkheim's, Simmel's, Piaget's, and Mead's theories on each other, though these authors did not and were not able to discuss them with each other, with the exception of Piaget's critique of Durkheim's theory of morality.

By proceeding in this way this book tries to establish the discourse of sociological theory on a new level. This calls for comprehensiveness. Because sociological discourse has been conducted only partially, we are not in a position that allows us to leave our founding fathers behind to concentrate on contemporary discourse. Any presentation of sociological theory that does not include the theories of the classical period of sociology's foundation is unpardonably incomplete. The theoretical knowledge contributed by classics like Spencer, Marx, Durkheim, Weber, Pareto, and Simmel has not been preserved in the theories of later generations of sociologists. Theoretical development still requires work on the theories originally formulated by those classics, reworking and constructing them anew in the light of the ongoing discourse. Without such a continuity in our work we would forever be starting our enterprise from scratch, without making use of the capital accumulated by the founders of the enterprise. Sociologists who have not learned the lessons taught by sociological discourse from its very beginning remain half-educated and unable to do their job professionally. The same is true for all other stages of sociological discourse right up to contemporary debates. This is why we will cover the whole development of this discourse, from its classical origins in the 1850s to theoretical issues of today.

I have endeavored to present the discourse in such a way as to specify the truth content and the errors of the various theories involved in the debate. I have intended not simply to write a history of social thought but to advance theoretical knowledge. This advancement of knowledge leads to the construction of a network of sociological theory within which each specific theory occupies a distinctive core position from which its own network spans out into the areas where it interrelates and overlaps with other theories. The interweaving of that network is a new stage of contemporary theory development. There is a network of sociological theory evolving from our common undertaking of advancing theoretical knowledge, and at the same time there is a network of sociological theories that gives special emphasis to the differences between many competing theories that make up that network.

Such a program of advancing theoretical knowledge by way of interparadigmatical and intertheoretical criticism and by weaving a network of interrelated and overlapping theories clearly forbids any type of reductionism.

We need to discuss all the theories and even more, for the sake of competition and being able to form networks.

The advancement of theoretical knowledge in sociology has suffered for three reasons: too little interrelationship between empirical research and sociological theory, too little knowledge of competing sociological theories because of prejudiced preoccupation with a favorite paradigm and theory, and too little discourse and therefore too few opportunities to have one's eyes opened to one's own errors. Yet there can be progress in science only if we come to know our prejudices from the perspectives of competing paradigms and theories. And we can do that only if there is enough discourse between competing paradigms. Furthermore, we can eliminate theoretical errors only by making empirical statements that contradict our theoretical predictions inasmuch as empirical research is indeed related to theoretical questions. Here we need much more interrelationship in the future so that the task of eliminating theoretical errors no longer has to be nearly exclusively performed by interparadigmatical and intertheoretical criticism, as takes place here. It is unquestioned in the natural sciences that researchers relate their empirical research to theories and contribute to solving theoretical problems. Unfortunately, this is not the case in sociology. There is too much empirical research without relating it at all to theoretical questions.

It should be the obligation of every researcher to ensure that such a relation exists. A scientific discipline does not make progress by accumulating huge mountains of data if they have no relation to theoretical questions. Within a scientific discipline there is legitimacy of theoretical work without empirical research by way of intertheoretical and interparadigmatic discourse, though this cannot and should not be all there is. Empirical research cannot have legitimacy in a scientific discipline without any relationship to theoretical questions, because it does not advance generalized theoretical knowledge that can be applied to a greater variety of facts. Inasmuch as sociology seeks to be a scientific discipline devoted to the advancement of generalized theoretical knowledge, it will have to cut back the huge amounts of empirical research that have no relation to theoretical questions. When I lament the insufficient interrelationship between theory and empirical research, I have to say that this is by no means simply the fault of theorists who do not do their own empirical research. For reasons of labor division we cannot blame them for that. But we have to blame the many researchers who do not make enough effort to relate their research to theoretical questions, because their research could be scientific only to the extent that they did so.

The main intention of these volumes, then, is to make a forceful contribution to overcoming the outlined deficiencies. What we need is more training of sociologists in competing paradigms and theories, more training in interparadigmatic and intertheoretical criticism in discourse, and more training of researchers in theory. To be successful in that task we need a presentation of sociological theories that is comprehensive and makes the competing theories as comprehensible and distinctive as possible by reconstructing them from their core and by breaking them down to distinctive statements about social reality. These theories need to be presented in ongoing discourse by having light thrown on their darker aspects just as they throw light upon darker aspects of other theories. Finally, we need a formal framework that allows us to determine the distinctive position of individual theories within that framework and to interconnect them in a network of sociological theories.

Two

RECONSTRUCTING THE DISCOURSE OF SOCIOLOGICAL THEORY

IN RECONSTRUCTING the discourse of sociological theory over the past 140 years, I begin with a basic analytical differentiation of social reality and corresponding perspectives on that reality, that is, paradigms, into four areas or fields (Münch, 1982, 1984, 1986, 1987b, 1991; for translation, see 1987a, 1988; Aretz, 1990). These result from the cross-tabulation of the two basic dimensions of order/chaos in social reality: the complexity of the symbolic world (the number of imaginable symbols and meanings) and the contingency of action (the number of possible actions). The four fields are set out in figure 2.1 and are made up as follows.

A Framework for Reconstructing Sociological Discourse

A. Adaptation. The combination of high symbolic complexity and high contingency of action opens the space of action and encourages adaptation to varying situations. There are *many means* available for carrying out one action, and one means can be used for *many actions.* For example, the researcher may make use of many data to support one hypothesis and may use many hypotheses to explain one and the same fact. This is the area of markets, exchange, money, and freedom. The corresponding view of the world is provided by the economics of social action.

G. Goal attainment. The combination of high symbolic complexity and low contingency of action specifies the space of action and promotes goal attainment. There are *many alternative goals* imaginable for action, but any factual action has to make a choice of *one goal* (at least for the time it takes to carry out that action). For example, the leader of

Figure 2.1: The Action Space: Playground for the Discourse of Sociological Theory

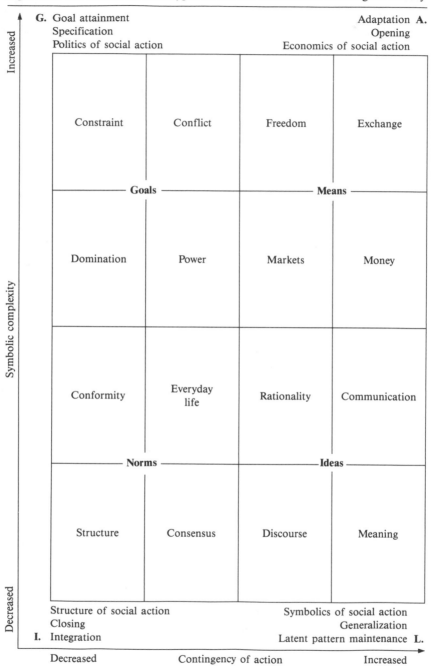

G. Goal attainment
Specification
Politics of social action

Adaptation **A.**
Opening
Economics of social action

Constraint	Conflict	Freedom	Exchange

— Goals — — **Means** —

Domination	Power	Markets	Money

Conformity	Everyday life	Rationality	Communication

— **Norms** — — **Ideas** —

Structure	Consensus	Discourse	Meaning

Structure of social action
Closing
I. Integration

Symbolics of social action
Generalization
Latent pattern maintenance **L.**

Increased — Decreased (Symbolic complexity)

Decreased — Contingency of action — Increased

a scientific research team selects one research object for the team, though a great many alternative research objects are imaginable. This is the area of domination, conflict, power, and constraint. The corresponding view of the world is provided by the conflict paradigm, which deals with the politics of social action.

I. Integration. The combination of low symbolic complexity and low contingency of action closes the space of action and furthers the integration of elements in a closed system. In the extreme case of closing there is *one norm* that allows the occurrence of just *one factual action*. For example, a scientific school has a small number of accepted methodological rules that precisely prescribe the correct way of conducting research. This is the area of structure, everyday life, consensus, and conformity. The corresponding view of the world is provided by the normative paradigm, which deals with the structure of social action.

L. Latent pattern maintenance. The combination of low symbolic complexity and high contingency of action generalizes the space of action and promotes the maintenance of latent patterns. In the extreme case of generalization there is *one basic idea* under which *many actions* can be subsumed. For example, a researcher is bound to search for the truth, but he or she can do so by carrying out many different forms of research. This is the area of discourse, communication, meaning, and rationality. The corresponding view of the world is provided by the symbolic paradigm, which deals with the symbolics of social action.

Some people are skeptical about the merits of such an attempt at constructing a basic framework for approaching reality. However, there is no alternative to such an approach. I have never met anyone able to approach reality without a preconception for ordering the chaos inherent in that reality. Whoever makes such claims takes his or her unconscious prejudices for facts. Since Kant's well-founded critique of such a claim in his *Critique of Pure Reason* (1781/1964a, translation 1952a), it should no longer be necessary to hear such claims, because "Concepts without intuition are empty, intuition without concepts is blind."

We have to construct a framework when we approach reality so that we can establish some order in that reality before investigating it. Such a framework is, in the first place, a formal apparatus of basic concepts with which we go on to build ever finer derived concepts and then statements about what happens under what conditions. The framework itself is not tested by empirical facts; only the statements we make using the concepts that make up the framework can be tested. However, the framework proves fruitful the more it allows any concept and statement to be translated into its language in order to make them comparable and to be able to confront them with each other. We need such a formal framework in order to bring divergent theories into competition with each other in a common arena.

The advantages of the framework outlined here are its comprehensiveness in covering the widest area of social reality and its ability to be broken down into ever finer fourfold differentiations in an infinite process of repeating the four-area schematization of reality. These facilities are preconditions for an unrestricted refinement of concepts and statements that allow us to capture reality with an ever more finely woven network of concepts and statements. The technique of forming concepts and statements is nothing but a parallel to the advantage of the endlessly repeatable row of basic numbers in mathematics, of which the binary system is the most simple one. Any acceptable criticism has to propose an alternative framework that allows us to cover wider and more finely graded areas of reality.

The Games of Sociological Discourse

The discourse of sociological theory can be conceived of as a game staged in an arena made up of the four different but interrelated fields of action outlined above. It is played with the instruments or pieces (concepts and statements) of the corresponding four basic paradigms. In such a game the winning player will be the one who manages to cover more parts of all four fields than any of his or her opponents. To do this, players may start out with the instruments of one paradigm. But, inasmuch as they play the game with other players covering other fields with their instruments and are not satisfied with occupying just one field or with pitting themselves against opponents operating in the same field, they have to equip themselves additionally with instruments that are adequate for operating in the fields outside their home base. As they do this, they are intermeshing a network of positions that reach beyond their home base right into the outside fields. The more this networking is established by different players, the more they construct overlapping networks. Thus, over time, we get an economic network that reaches from the field of money into the fields of power, consensus, and meaning, a conflict network that reaches from the power field into the fields of money, consensus, and meaning, and a symbolic network that reaches from the field of meaning into the fields of money, power, and consensus.

A player can start the game at different intermediate points among the four fields. A theorist may, for example, start out with the equipment of power but complemented by meaning, so that he or she plays the game primarily as a power struggle for meaning. The same player may add elements of consensus and money, so that he or she constructs a power/meaning network that also reaches into the fields of consensus and money, but with the leading role taken by power/meaning. Because it is mostly beyond the capacities of goal-directed action to play the game with many different pieces from the beginning, most players start out with a small number of pieces, or with one lead piece that is supported stage-by-stage by a number of followers in order to invade the foreign fields. This is why there are always those who play the game of sociological discourse with a different set of interrelated pieces occupying different parts of the action space. The best players are those who have organized their pieces in such a way that they control as much space as possible while maintaining their ties and a clear structure of command.

However, there are also players who do not set out to play the game across all fields, distributing their pieces across the whole action space. They prefer to concentrate on their home base and try to occupy this base exclusively. To do so they have to compete with their immediate opponents on that base, for example, by working out a finely graded theory of bargaining, and leave the other parts of the world to other theory players.

We can distinguish four basic types of player—home players, area players, cross-area players, and world players—in ascending order, as an ever greater part of the action space is covered. We will meet these different kinds of players in our exploration of sociological discourse. Correspondingly, we obtain four different types of theory networks: home, area, cross-area, and world networks. The discourse of sociological theory has accumulated overlapping networks of all four types.

The outlined game of sociological discourse, in turn, takes place on four different levels: national, international, periodical universal, and timeless universal. A national game is characterized by playing on the four fields and conceiving of them and the corresponding figures in a unique way. The international game puts all the players of a national game in one team that starts out on the international level only from a certain part of the action space, whereas the other parts are occupied by other national teams. In the periodical universal discourse, we have a game at a certain period of time in which players do not form a team with their national colleagues but with teammates from all over the world on the basis of paradigmatical affinity. In the timeless universal discourse, players with paradigmatical affinity form a team in a timeless game that spans the whole duration of sociological discourse from its beginning right up to the present day.

Let me illustrate what I mean by these four areas of sociological discourse. In the German national discourse we see Habermas with his symbolic team playing against Weber's conflict team. On the international level both form a symbolic team with a common heritage though differing positions to play against the normative team of Parsons and Merton from across the Atlantic. On the periodical universal level, Habermas joins Kohlberg in a symbolic team to play against the normative opponents Berger/Luckmann and Garfinkel. On the timeless universal level, Habermas and Piaget make up a symbolic team playing against Simmel and Pareto as a conflict team. It is important to observe the game on all four levels—national, international, periodical, and timeless universal levels.

The national discourse is relevant because sociologists are raised and primarily dispute within national traditions of thought. They learn their national masters in philosophy and social theory at school, whereas they learn the masters of other national traditions only secondarily. Thus, they cannot avoid thinking and arguing primarily in terms of their national traditions. If they do complement their thought by drawing upon other national traditions, this will occur at a later time in their life and on the basis of the national tradition thus far internalized. On the other hand, they communicate primarily with their national colleagues, and thus they mutually reinforce each other in speaking the same language (Lepenies, 1981; Genov, 1989; Krekel-Eiben, 1990). I distinguish four national traditions: British, French, German, and American discourse. Each centers around a unique "problematic" and has established a unique network of partly conflicting, partly interlinking paradigms.

Each national tradition plays the game in the four interrelated fields of action in a different way, with its unique language, starting the game from a specific home base and then moving into the other fields with the equipment constructed using the instruments applicable to its home base. Before it moves into other fields it needs to mobilize at least some of the equipment that is adequate for those other fields, but always in terms of its own home equipment (figure 2.2).

When we contrast the four national traditions, we find that the British game is primarily defined by traditional order accounted for by organicism as a paradigm, but as developments go on, this is complemented by playing individuality with liberalism, experience with empiricism, and class conflict with unionism. The French game is primarily a struggle for power, accounted for by vitalism but confronted by structure and structuralism, rationality and rationalism, spontaneity and existentialism. The German game is primarily a search for meaning, accounted for by idealism but sometimes ending up in conformity and historicism, alienation and materialism (Marxism), contradiction, paradox, and nihilism. The American game is primarily an exchange of goods and services accounted for by economism but is complemented by competition and instrumentalism, consensus and voluntarism, pragmatics and pragmatism.

Each national tradition plays the fourfold game with these different terms. The normative area, which is covered by "traditional order" and "organicism" in the British game, is covered by "structure" and "structuralism" in the French game, "conformity" and "historicism" in the German, and "consensus" and "voluntarism" in the American. The economic area, which is covered by "individuality" and "liberalism" in the British game, is

Figure 2.2: National Games of Discourse in International Context

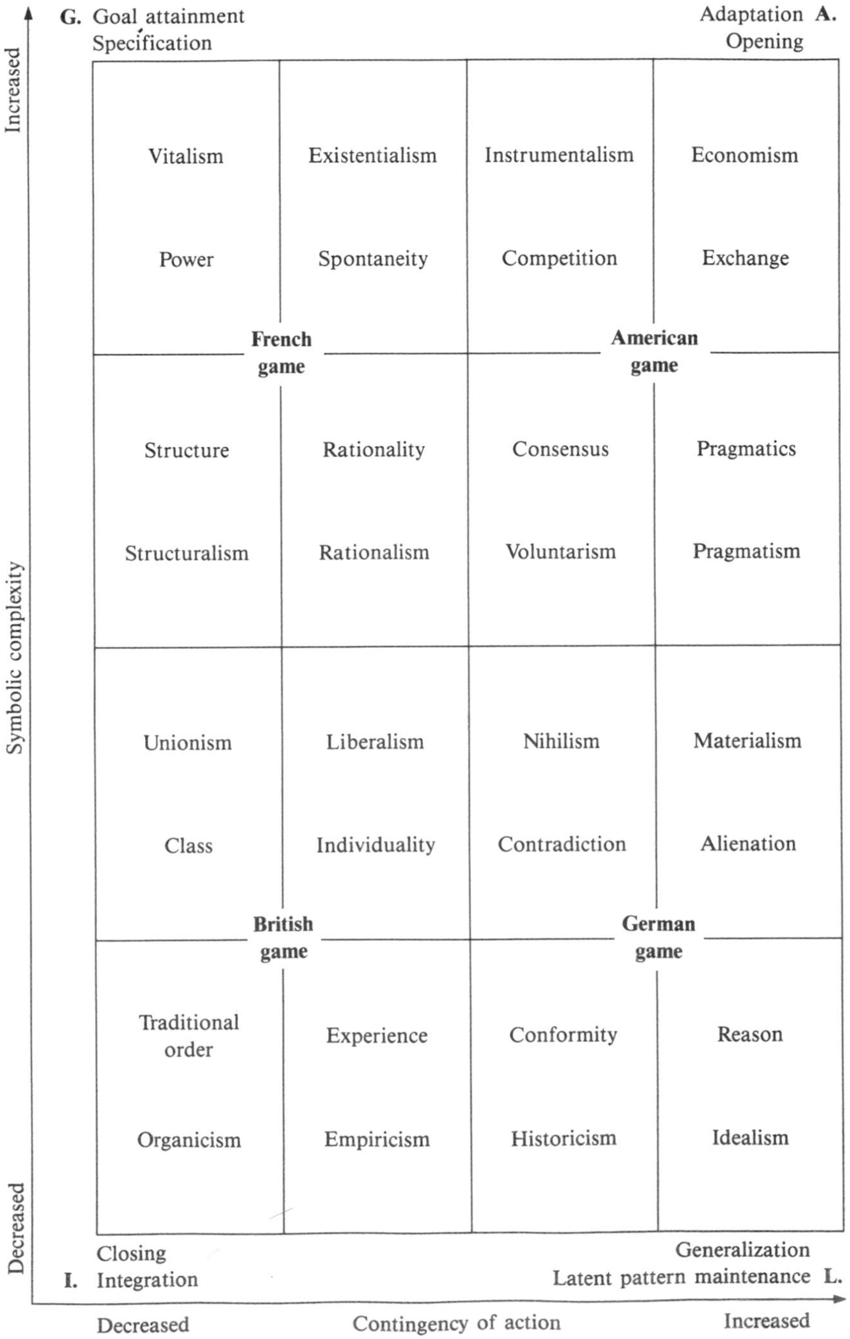

G. Goal attainment Specification			Adaptation **A.** Opening
Vitalism	Existentialism	Instrumentalism	Economism
Power	Spontaneity	Competition	Exchange
French game		**American game**	
Structure	Rationality	Consensus	Pragmatics
Structuralism	Rationalism	Voluntarism	Pragmatism
Unionism	Liberalism	Nihilism	Materialism
Class	Individuality	Contradiction	Alienation
British game		**German game**	
Traditional order	Experience	Conformity	Reason
Organicism	Empiricism	Historicism	Idealism
Closing **I.** Integration			Generalization Latent pattern maintenance **L.**

Increased — Symbolic complexity — Decreased

Decreased — Contingency of action — Increased

covered by "spontaneity" and "existentialism" in the French game, "aliena-tion" and "materialism" in the German, and "exchange" and "economism" in the American. The symbolic area, which is covered by "experience" and "empiricism" in the British game, is covered by "rationality" and "rational-ism" in the French game, "reason" and "idealism" in the German, and "prag-matics" and "pragmatism" in the American. The conflict area, which is covered by "class" and "unionism" in the British game, is covered by "power" and "vitalism" in the French game, "contradiction" and "nihilism" in the German, and "competition" and "instrumentalism" in the American. Thus we have a sociological discourse on the national level that approaches social reality with its unique language and paradigms and plays a unique game.

Next is the international discourse where different national teams, each with a common tradition but different positions, compete with one another. Then comes the periodical universal discourse carried out between teams, each with a paradigmatic affinity across national boundaries. Finally, we have the timeless universal discourse carried out between teams, each with a paradig-matic affinity across national *and* periodical boundaries. As this discourse goes on, we get an accumulation of ever more finely woven overlapping the-ory nets within and across national, periodical, and paradigmatic boundaries.

The Evolution of Sociological Theory in Discursive Games Since the 1850s

Looking at the evolution of sociological theory over the past 140 years, we can distinguish three periodical sections: the foundation period from the 1850s to the 1920s, consolidation and differentiation from the 1920s to the 1960s, and renewal and intermeshing since the 1960s.

The evolution of sociological theory got under way with its crystalliza-tion in the 1850s. This classical period of foundation lasted until about 1920. Characteristic of that time is the emergence of a specifically sociological approach to social reality, which interconnected divergent positions in a first network of sociological theory. Each classical author took a distinctive posi-tion in this classical discourse but also tried to a greater or lesser degree to expand his own field of vision to cover the other positions. Spencer started with a liberal economic paradigm but tried to reach out beyond the eco-nomic field. In his terms this meant combining liberalism with utilitarian-ism, organicism, and evolutionism. Marx started with a materialist-economic approach but extended this approach by elements of idealism, conflict the-ory, and structuralism. Pareto started with a conflict view but complemented that by elements of economic theory, organicism, and rationalism. Simmel's primary perspective was conflictual-paradoxical, but he related that to ele-ments of idealism, liberalism, and structuralism. Durkheim was first and foremost a structuralist but took over elements of idealism, economic liber-alism, and conflict theory. Weber made the most thorough attempt of this time to build an extended theory network, combining his idealist home base with conflict theory, economics, and structuralism. Mead's creation of what Herbert Blumer later called "Symbolic Interactionism" was shaped by combining behaviorism with pragmatism, evolutionism, and idealism.

The period from the 1920s to the 1960s was dominated by Parsons' massive attempt at working out the true synthesis. He progressed in this direction farther than everybody else, building a formal network that covered the whole action space. However, his overall distribution of formal figures was so widely spaced that he lost contact with some of them while concentrating on substantial work. This substantial work was characterized by playing the game from the normative-consensual home base, so that he really covered only those areas in the other fields that were located close to their boundaries with the normative-consensual sphere. In dealing with money, power, and meaning he was aware of their order-producing aspects. However, he also took this view as a member of the American team; that is to say, order for him was an outcome of the *voluntary* association of people sharing values and norms.

The other part of the development in this period was the reaction of other players against Parsons' attempts to monopolize the whole game. Their strategy became one of differentiation, that is, playing with those pieces that had been put aside by Parsons: power, money, and meaning. Thus, Berger and Luckmann on the one hand and Garfinkel on the other hand played the consensus game with pieces from the meaning game provided by German phenomenology. Coser and Dahrendorf played the power game, Homans and Blau played the money game, and Blumer and Goffman played the meaning game—all of them in different ways. The result of this differentiation of games was a rather separated consolidation of the corresponding paradigms and theories; however, they lost contact with the master and continued to play the game by themselves while the master was left in an exalted but distant position among the clouds. There was also little discourse between the power, money, and meaning players. They had lost their integrating master. Thus, in the 1960s we have a scene of differentiated, internally consolidated little paradigms and a loss of any attempt to intermesh them in a synthesizing effort. The progress that Parsons himself made toward the end of his life in the seventies was not recognized at that time (Wiley, 1985).

Since that state of the development of sociological theory in the 1960s, an enormous change has taken place. Since the mid-1960s we have had a renewal of sociological discourse that initially involved a further differentiation but then increasingly has developed an eye for competing paradigms. This has led to an international game that has exerted enormous pressure upon single paradigms and theories to enrich themselves and consequently to intermesh in order to cover a wider area in the action space. This is particularly true of the development in the 1980s, which led to a breakdown of former paradigm boundaries; we now live in a period of extensive and intensive intermeshing of theories to form ever wider-ranging and more finely woven nets.

Playing Different Games of Discourse

The discourse of sociological theory can be read on all the levels that I have outlined. However, in ordering that discourse in a sequence of chapters I had to make a choice. I decided in favor of the periodical presentation in universal terms. Three volumes correspond to periods of sociological discourse: the universal discourse of paradigms in the classical period of foundation from the 1850s to the 1920s; the universal discourse of paradigms in the period of consolidation and differentiation from the 1920s to the 1960s, where we have the establishment of the Parsonian monopoly that breaks down under attack from a variety of rebels, leading to a new differentiation of paradigms and theories; and finally the universal discourse of paradigms since the 1960s, with first ongoing differentiation but then growing attempts at intermeshing theories to form a network of sociological theories on a new level of theoretical progress. I discuss the various contributions to sociological theory at the time when they became part of sociological discourse, which does not mean that they are no longer parts of discourse at a later time. For example, I deal with Parsons' action theory and analytical functionalism in the section on consolidation and differentiation between the 1920s and the 1960s. However, after its decline in the 1970s, Parsonian theory has very much recovered and again become a major part of discourse in the 1980s.

The sequence of chapters does not close out a reading according to the other levels of the game. It is possible to select some home games, for example, games between interactionists like Blumer, Strauss, and Becker, all referring to their master Mead; or one can concentrate on area games, like the power game between various conflict theorists, or the money game between utilitarianism, exchange theory, rational choice theory, and Marxism, or the consensus game between structuralism, voluntarism, historicism, and organicism, or the meaning game between idealism, rationalism, empiricism, and pragmatism. In more specific terms one can look at the consensus game between Durkheim's structuralism, Parsons' analytical functionalism, Berger and Luckmann's phenomenology and Garfinkel's ethnomethodology; or one may take the meaning game between Habermas' discourse theory, different variants of symbolic interactionism, Goffman's frame analysis, and the cognitive-developmental approach of Piaget and Kohlberg. Likewise, the reader can follow the money game between Marx's historical materialism, Offe's theory of late capitalism, and Wallerstein's world systems approach on the one hand and the liberal views of Spencer's utilitarianism and evolutionism, Homans' theory of balanced exchange, Blau's theory of unbalanced exchange, and Coleman's rational choice theory on the other hand; or he or she may choose the power game of Pareto's elite theory, Simmel's theory of conflict, contradiction, and paradox, Coser's functonal conflict theory, Dahrendorf's theory of group conflict, the bargaining theory of Bacharach and Lawler, the interaction–ritual chains theory of negotiation of Collins, Touraine's dynamic action theory of conflict, Foucault's theory of the reproduction of structure and power, Bourdieu's theory of praxis, and Giddens' theory of structuration.

It is also possible to analyze games across the boundaries of specific areas, for example, between normativists and symbolists or conflict theorists and economists, in more concrete terms between phenomenologists and ethnomethodologists on the one hand and symbolic interactionists and discourse theorists on the other hand, or between Giddens' conflict approach and Wallerstein's economic approach.

Another way of reading these volumes is to look at world games between the basic economic, conflict, normative, and symbolic paradigms in terms of authors like Spencer, Marx, Pareto, Simmel, Durkheim, and Weber, or Parsons, Habermas, Luhmann, Offe, Wallerstein, Foucault, Bourdieu, and Giddens. Or again, one can confront the theories of identity formation formulated by Durkheim, Simmel, Mead, and Piaget.

One may also look at the national games, the British game of traditional order versus individuality, class conflict, and common sense; the American game of competition versus exchange, consensus, and pragmatics; the French game of power versus structure, spontaneity, and rationality; and the German game of reason and meaning against conformity, alienation, contradiction, and paradox. Finally, one can also confront the various national traditions with each other, thus reading Habermas, Bourdieu, Giddens, and Parsons against each other. Though I present the chapters in chronological order, I have kept in mind the various outlined levels of discourse and have tried to make apparent the national context of an author's contribution, its international standing, and its position in periodical universal and in timeless universal discourse. There is also reference to various home, area, cross-area, and world games. Thus, I leave it to the reader to make his or her own choice.

THREE

THE STRUCTURE AND FUNCTION OF SOCIOLOGICAL THEORY

WHY DO we need theory at all in sociology? This question leads on to an associated one, namely: What are the characteristic features of theory and what are the functions that distinguish it from other modes of "doing sociology"?

Why Theory?

First, why theory? People involved in the solution of everyday practical problems tend to mistrust theory. As a definitional term, it is opposed to practical knowledge that has grown out of day-by-day practical work. Theory is seen as being tremendously distant from the problems of such practical work. The term "theory" is sometimes used to label statements as mere speculations that have no confirmation in practical experience. Theory and knowledge of empirical facts are opposites: one is mostly a product of human fantasy, the other a product of involvement in practical work. There is a parallel opposition between theory and reality: theory as human speculation and reality as the world existing outside, which is independent of man's thinking.

If we label sociological work as theory, this bears the meaning of being remote from reality and from the practical affairs of everyday life. There is a tendency to consider theory as a product of the fantasies of purely intellectual minds captive within the walls of ivory towers. In sociology, pure theory is sometimes called "armchair sociology," suggesting a comfortable approach compared with the hard work involved in, say, field research, data gathering, and computer analysis.

The American way of life in particular is full of suspicion with regard to theoretical speculation. Tocqueville, in his famous account *Democracy in America*, which appeared in French in two parts in 1835 and 1840, observed that Americans had not developed a unique philosophy up to that time but that they proved to be masterful in the development of technological knowledge, which is useful for practical concerns. After Tocqueville published *Democracy in America*, a unique American philosophy did in fact emerge, but typically this philosophy is called pragmatism. It was founded on the works of William James, Charles Sanders Peirce, and John Dewey. The message of this philosophy is that our knowledge advances in the solution of practical problems. Beyond philosophy a pragmatic view of knowledge is a pervasive trait of American culture. Richard Hofstadter described the suspicion with regard to pure theory resulting from the emphasis on the practical use of knowledge in a well-known book entitled *Anti-Intellectualism in American Life* (Hofstadter, 1963).

This suspicion regarding theory does seem appropriate if we look at some examples of pure theory and research. A recent book on social systems by a leading theorist in German sociology, Niklas Luhmann (1984), was reviewed in the weekly magazine *Der Spiegel* under the heading: "Flight above the clouds" (Käsler, 1984). The review interprets the book as a game that is purely self-contained and self-related with its own interrelated concepts, creating and solving its own problems.

A second example comes from the natural sciences, from the field of physics. The Dutch physicist Simon van der Meer and his Italian colleague Carlo Rubbia, both from the European Organization for Nuclear Research in Geneva, Switzerland, were awarded the Nobel prize for physics in 1984. They discovered what are known as "W" and "Z" bosons, the existence of which was predicted by the theory of three other scientists, Weinberg, Salam, and Glashow, who won the Nobel prize some years earlier. The point of interest for our subject here is the characterization van der Meer (1985) gives of his work in an interview to the Dutch magazine *Holland Herald*. He says, "You could compare particle physics to astronomy. No one asks for a practical use in the study of galaxies, because they're too far away. The energies we produce and the machines we use are so completely out of scale with anything that's applied at the present that it's not easy to see how they could serve a practical purpose."

Nevertheless, the European Organization for Nuclear Research (CERN) had a budget of $280 million in 1984. In other words, the European countries cooperating in the organization spend a lot of money on research that has no practical application. Thus, there must be other functions that are fulfilled by pure theory and research and make them worth doing. And van der Meer does not leave the interviewer with a negative answer to the question of the practical use to which his discoveries can be put. He continues with a positive answer: "We try to prove theories which establish order in the situation as we know it." A few lines before that statement he tells the interviewer, "The reason why our discovery is of such great importance is that we were able to combine two of the four known fundamental forces of nature, which effectively simplifies the description of the world." What we can learn from van der Meer's answer is something peculiar to theory: it can establish order in the view of the world, and it does so by way of simplification. That is, theory brings order into the chaotic complexity of our situationally varying experience, and it accomplishes this task by way of discovering a latent structure that generally underlies the variety of facts that are observable on the surface of reality.

I will now approach this positive function of theory from the opposite direction, that is, from the appreciative view of theory and the critical view of practical experience. Europe, and in particular Germany, has a cultural tradition that is more favorable to theory and more suspicious of the truth that seemingly comes from the observation of facts. From Immanuel Kant we have inherited the famous phrase "Concepts without empirical intuition (observation) are empty phrases; empirical intuition (observation) without concepts is blind." We can extend it to the statement "Theory without experience is an empty phrase; experience without theory is blind." Kant not only repeats the distance of pure theory from reality by referring to it as empty but also warns us of the blindness of pure experience. This is an insight from his famous *Critique of Pure Reason* (Kant, 1781/1964a; for translation, see 1952a). He also wrote a small piece on the common phrase "This might be right in theory, but does not prove useful for practice" (Kant, 1793/1964f). In this piece he shows for the subject of ethics how practical action without the guidance of a theory of morals stumbles from one situation to the next without in any way being able to establish a continuing and predictable order of action. Again we discover the ordering function of theory as it was described by the natural scientist van der Meer.

With this insight of Kant's in mind, I would now like to ask: Is there any practical action at all without theory? My answer is quite definitely no. A reflection upon everyday action may prove the truth of this answer: How do we act in everyday life? We always act upon assumptions that an event of this or that kind will occur if we act in this or that way. That is, we assume a connection between a certain kind of action and certain kinds of events. I assume, for example, that dirty cups on my table will be transformed into clean ones if I ask my wife, Susan, to wash them in water. I know that from my experience in the past, and I generalize from this past experience to the present situation. I implicitly work on the assumption that whenever a dirty cup is put into water it comes out clean. This is an implicit theory insofar as it transcends the actual situation in time and space back to earlier situations and also forward to repeatedly new situations in the future.

But my action is not only based on such implicit theories on physical processes; it also relies on assumptions regarding the actions of other actors.

I suppose that asking my wife will motivate her to clean the cup. That is, I expect that my words will effect some reaction on her part. This, too, I generalize from past experience. I apply an implicit theory that tells me "Whenever I ask Susan in a certain way to clean my coffee cups, she will do that in a certain way." We can say that we come to such implicit theories through our practical experience.

Thus, there is an intimate linkage between theory and practice. Theory grows out of practice. But what happens if we step beyond the confines of our experience? If we do that, our implicit theories can soon turn out to be false and no longer useful. If I try to clean the ink-blots on my shirt with water, I soon realize that they will not disappear completely as was the case with the leftover coffee in my cup. If instead of my wife, Susan, I ask my son Marc to clean the cups, I realize that his reaction is completely different from hers. Even Susan may have changed her mind and may ask why I do not do the washing up myself. She could tell me that it is not a naturally given duty of hers to clean my coffee cups. If the material conditions (the ink-blots) and the cultural conditions (my wife's idea) of a situation change, my implicit theories, which I have generalized from my experience, do not provide successful predictions of events. Implicit theories that grow out of my experience are always bound to the particular circumstances (conditions) in which I live. Within the confines of these circumstances they provide correct predictions of events, but not outside of these circumstances. Our experience is always particularistic in character; it is bound to our own life-world. And if we generalize this experience to theories that state general relationships between certain kinds of events and actions, we commit the error of ethnocentrism. We confuse the particular life-world in which we live with the world as it is. We confuse that which is taken for granted in our life-world with the reality of the world as such.

Theory that grows only out of practical experience is always in danger of committing the mistake of ethnocentric generalization. Here again Tocqueville provides us with an interesting characterization of American pragmatic culture. He says, in *Democracy in America* (Tocqueville, 1835–1840/1986, translation 1969), that American thinking tends to consider particular features of American society as universal laws of society, particular views as universal ideas. And if we look at sociological theories we can discover the same tendency. American theories of modernization, for example, have treated the American road to modern society as the general road to modernity and the American institutions as the general form of modern institutions. These theories have been attacked because of their lack of sensitivity to the special circumstances of other cultures, for their ethnocentric generalization of a particular American experience to a general theory of modernization. This inclination toward ethnocentric theory building is an outcome of that very emphasis placed on allowing theory to grow out of practical

experience. We can say that the more theory seeks to be empirically concrete, the more it is in danger of the ethnocentric universalization of very
particular experiences.

An example of such a theory that is close to empirical observation is
the economic approach in sociology. It is commonsense knowledge that
actors seek rewards as results of their actions. This is corroborated by endless instances from personal experience. If we want children to help in the
household, we offer them money or we demonstrate our love for them; we
do the same when we want them to improve their grades at school. We offer
our partners in everyday discussions our interest in what they have to say,
expecting that they will repay us when we ourselves talk, and so on. It seems
that a hypothesis like "Whenever an action is expected to result in higher
rewards than an alternative action, it is preferred to the alternative" expresses
a universal law. But what happens when we step beyond the domain of our
particular economic common sense? What about people who maintain customs even if it costs them a lot of opportunities to obtain rewards they could
otherwise obtain? Take the Amish people in Lancaster County, Pennsylvania. They refuse to use modern technology in agriculture, and therefore they
live in poorer conditions compared to their neighbors who are not constricted
by such customs. In economic terms, we would have to expect a change in
customs if they are less rewarding with regard to other objectives people
have when they are compared to alternative ways of acting. If people do
not change their action in this way, they are refusing to calculate their action
economically: they do not compare their customs with alternatives from the
point of view of the rewards to be gained by attaining some other objectives. The customs are self-contained and self-evident objectives in their own
right, which are fixed and closed out from any economic calculation. The
customs themselves are pursued for their own sake and not because of other
resulting rewards. Thus, at least the customs as an objective in themselves
are not weighed up in economic terms.

The Elementary Function of Theory

It is clear, then, that we always work with implicit theories in everyday practical action. The assumptions we work with are implicit theories because
they are general in character, transcending the particular circumstances of
our experience. They state a relationship between actions and events that
is assumed to hold true beyond any one particular instance. They begin with
the introductory word "whenever." The *generalization* of knowledge is the
first and central function of theories. This generalization allows us to subsume very different particular instances of experience under a small set of
statements. Insofar as this is true, there is no practice without theory. But
theory bound to practice tends to take the particular for the universal. This

is one aspect of the blindness of experience without the conscious guidance of theory, as Kant put it; the stress here is on "conscious guidance." If we wish to avoid the failure of misplaced generalization from particular experience, we have to make theory construction a task for its own sake.

Here we touch upon the old philosophical problem of induction as it was stated by the Scottish philosopher David Hume in his works *A Treatise on Human Nature* and *Enquiries Concerning the Human Understanding and Concerning the Principles of Morals*, published in 1739 and 1777. Hume asks what would justify our assumption, having observed a sequence of two events, A and B, in which B always followed the occurrence of A in the past, that A always causes B. He says that it is nothing but habit that leads us to such an assumption and not a generally justified reason. As Karl R. Popper stated later in *The Logic of Scientific Discovery*, published in 1935, there is no general principle that would allow the induction from a hundred particular instances of a relationship between events A and B to the formulation of a general law that A always causes B. But Popper demonstrated that the reverse is possible: From one instance in which B does not follow A we can indeed logically draw the conclusion that the general formulation "B always follows A" is false. Thus Popper replaced the induction from a collection of particular instances and the method of verifying general hypotheses by citing such a collection of instances with the reverse principle of falsifying general hypotheses by explicitly looking for deviating cases. This by no means excludes the possibility that we might make observational errors, so we cannot be sure for methodological reasons that a falsification is indeed justified. But this does not change the fact that it is *logically* valid to conclude the falsity of a general hypothesis from one deviating case. As a result of this, we arrive at a different description of theory compared to the mere induction from particular experience. We must consciously face the fact that theory always transcends the limits of practical experience and should be constructed at least partly for its own sake and separately from practical experience.

This is where theory *per se* gains legitimacy (Parsons, 1937/1968: ch. 1). Theory can be constructed as a formulation that transcends commonsense practical knowledge from the beginning. Insofar as it reaches beyond the limits of practical experience it also explicitly provokes the testing of hypotheses outside our commonsense knowledge. On the one hand, then, a general theory covers more different situations in practice from the outset, while on the other hand, these situations can all serve as instances for testing a theory and therefore possibly falsifying it. Conscious theory-building aims at general knowledge that can be applied to different situations transcending every particular experience. Thus there is a greater chance that theory will fail as a result of deviating instances. And inasmuch as theories are continuously criticized by seeking such deviating instances we can hope that the surviving theories will approximate the truth more closely. Out of this emerges a clearer differentation of theory and reality compared to a particular commonsense knowledge. In the latter case we tend to confuse our limited commonsense knowledge with reality. In the case of greater differentiation between theory and reality, theory becomes more abstract, more general, and reality is everything in the world as it exists.

We thus can conclude that the first and central quality of theory is the *generality* of its formulations in distinction to the particularity of experience. A theoretical formulation remains the same throughout different situations; experience is particular and changes from situation to situation. This is one aspect of the *ordering function* of theory. It enables use to subsume a great many (as Kant put it: "manifold") events and corresponding experience under one general formulation. As distinct from theory, varying experience *opens* our knowledge and makes it innovative. Rules of thinking—that is, the rules of logic, of discourse, and of argumentation—*give our knowledge a regular order* that makes communication about knowledge predictable and easier than if there were no rules on which we could rely when communicating with other people. Technological models direct our knowledge to specific goals; they perform the function of the *specification* of knowledge.

The Elements of Theory and Their Specific Functions

Beyond distinguishing the generalizing function of theory as a general for-mulation of knowledge that transcends all particular instances of experience, we can also differentiate internal qualities of theories and corresponding functions. A theory starts with some *basic general (theoretical) concepts* that form a general framework or frame of reference for the process of discov-ery. More specific concepts are arrived at by specifying and combining these basic concepts. "Social interaction" as a basic concept of sociology, for exam-ple, is defined as a relationship between actors in which the actors choose (perform) their action according to their expectation of the actions, expec-tations, and reactions of the other actors. "Economic calculation" is a basic concept that means making a cost/benefit analysis of an action with a view to the help it will provide in attaining an optimum of goals. An economi-cally calculating actor seeks to realize a total set of goals to an optimum degree (not only one goal at the cost of other goals). "Exchange" is a specifi-cation of social interaction combined with economic calculation, which means that two actors adapt their action to the expected actions, expecta-tions, and reactions of others so that they draw an optimum of goal reali-zation from their interaction. In this way we have built a derived third concept out of the specification of a basic concept and its combination with another basic concept. The frame of reference made up of basic concepts performs the function of generalization, because we are able to subsume a lot of different specific concepts that relate different parts and aspects of reality to each other under a small set of general concepts.

The frame of reference guides the process of discovery, it is rather like a searchlight that illuminates a part of reality whereas those other parts not covered by the basic concepts remain in the dark. This does not mean that the conceptual frame of reference of a theory produces its own conforming reality. It only defines events relevant for the theory, either in the positive or negative sense. If we have a hypothesis that states, "Whenever actors enter into exchange they will change their action at a higher velocity than if they enter into traditionally based interaction," we look at those aspects of reality defined by the concepts of "exchange," "traditionally based interaction," and "velocity of change in action." We do not perceive whether the actors have a relationship of authority, love, or hate with each other and do not look at the amount of goal directedness in their action. Whether or not the above hypothesis is true, however, is a matter that remains to be tested. The selection of the relevant point(s) of reality does not automatically furnish the facts needed to confirm the hypothesis; it only provides facts that relate to the hypothesis either in a confirming or in a falsifying way. The searchlight character of a conceptual frame of reference means that those aspects of concrete reality between which a hypothesis assumes there is a definite connection are specially picked out. In this sense a theory always has an analytical character compared to the synthetic concreteness of immediate instances of experience.

The terms "analytical" and "synthetic" carry two meanings that have to be distinguished here. According to a distinction made by Kant, an *analytical statement* is proved to be logically true, independently of events in reality, whereas a *synthetic statement* can be proved to be true only by observing the reality to which it relates. While the first type of statement is always true, whatever happens in reality, the latter *can* at least be false. Let me give an example: A statement like "When the sunset is red, the next day may or may not be sunny" is always true and can be proven in strict logical terms, whatever happens in reality. It is an analytical statement. However, the statement "When the sunset is red, the next day will be sunny" is open to refutation; it is false if after a red sunset the next day turns out not to be sunny.

The meanings of "analytical" and "synthetic" with which we are concerned in the present account, however, are quite different ones. Concrete observed facts are synthetic in the sense that they always combine in a certain way, different aspects that are kept separate in theory in order to formulate relationships between them. Let us take an example: the success of two groups of students in an exam that allows them to collaborate. This is concrete action that synthesizes a lot of different aspects: the stratification of the groups according to grades, the originality or traditionality of their work, the conformity to or deviation from the questions formulated by the examiner, the degree of agreement within the groups on the answers to be given to the questions, the rapidity of incoming and outgoing ideas, the continuity of themes, the directedness toward certain specific answers to questions, and so on. This concrete action is precedented by a number of equally varied aspects of group action: competition within groups, the stability of the membership of the groups and their differentiation from other groups, the existence of a definite relationship of authority between groups and examiners, the cohesion of the groups, the closedness of groups toward their environment, the existence of long-term discussions, the existence of a leadership within the groups, and so on.

We cannot formulate a theory of group success that would tell us in one hypothesis the decisive cause of such a synthesized action. One group may profit from internal competition but lose because of its low cohesion, or another group may benefit from having strong leadership but lose out because of discontinuity in discussion. So we cannot predict the relative success of the groups through knowledge of one single factor. What we can do with theory, however, is to formulate more sharply differentiated relationships between analytically separate aspects of groups and group actions. Thus we may postulate "The stronger the internal competition in a group, the more it will be stratified in degrees," or "The stronger the group cohesion, the greater the agreement on answers to questions," or "The stronger the group leadership, the more its answers are directed to specific solutions." In this sense theory is analytical in its character and not synthetic or, as it is sometimes called, empirically concrete.

However, there is also a need for synthesis in theory on a higher level. A theory fulfills this function if it can integrate all concepts used in analytically differentiated hypotheses into a *framework of basic concepts* that are interrelated in basic statements (or hypotheses). That is, the framework of basic concepts must be complete so that every specific observation and every specific hypothesis can be formulated as part of the process of specifying and combining the basic concepts. Otherwise, we are left with certain residual categories, that is, the concepts that are used ad hoc for specific problems but that are not integrated into the theoretical system. If, for example, we were to start with "exchange" as the basic concept for social interaction, the observation of interaction following a stable pattern independent of any benefits or costs accruing to the actors would force us to explain it using a variable such as the actors' commitment to a tradition, and the term "tradition" would not be an integral part of the conceptual frame of reference. In the same way the ad hoc hypothesis to the effect that "The stronger the commitment to a tradition, the less change occurs in action" would not be a part of the theoretical system. Theoretical progress would go in the direction of including the residual categories and ad hoc hypotheses in a new comprehensive theoretical system. In this way we reestablish the *consistency* of our knowledge. Every observation can once again be formulated within the same system of basic concepts and can be explained by the same system of hypotheses.

I said the conceptual frame of reference fulfills the function of generalization within theory. Other functions that we can distinguish from this are those of opening, closing, and the specification of theory.

A theory becomes a closed system if every hypothesis is ordered in an *axiomatic system* made up of first premises and derived secondary, more specific hypotheses. A hypothesis formulates a relationship between two events: "Whenever A, then B." A premise is a general statement of this kind. An example of such a premise might state "The stronger the cohesion of a group, the stronger its consensus on norms." A derived secondary premise would be a hypothesis like "The better the members of a discussion group like each other, the more they will agree on the kind of sanction to be applied against anyone deviating from a norm." In this case the concepts (terms) used in the second hypothesis are specifications of the more general concepts (terms) in the first. Liking each other is interpreted as a specific instance of cohesion, agreement on sanctions as a specification of consensus on norms. The criterion for the closedness of a theoretical system is the *absence of contradictions.*

For example, we may have two hypotheses, one of which states "The more frequently an activity has been rewarded in the past, the more frequently it will be chosen in the future," whereas the other might state "The more frequently an activity has been rewarded in the past, the less frequently it will be chosen in the future." These two hypotheses contradict each other. In this case our knowledge is not ordered. We want to know which of the two is true or how they can be reconciled. For example, we can formulate a more general hypothesis that "The greater the reward minus costs, that is, the greater the profit an activity promises, the more it will be chosen." In the light of this hypothesis we can see that frequency of past rewards can affect the expectation of future rewards either in a positive or in a negative sense. The level of past rewards may diminish the value of each additional unit of reward because these may have little to add to the effect of the existing total reward and may even prevent an actor from obtaining other kinds of rewards. Economists know this phenomenon as the law of diminishing returns (marginal utility). If, for example, we have just had lunch, we will probably no longer be hungry and will have nothing to gain by eating another sandwich, especially if it keeps us away from our sociology studies. On the other hand, past experience of reward resulting from a certain kind of activity motivates us to expect further rewards from the same activity. Thus, it is the mere expectation that becomes stronger; yet, if combined with the experience of satiation, the mere expectation of rewards will not provoke the relevant action. Indeed, "eating" in the case just illustrated is no longer a reward at all. It may become a punishment for someone already full if he or she has to eat more. Our more general profit expectation hypothesis reconciles the contradiction between the two hypotheses as they were formulated initially. We have to reformulate them in one proposition as follows: "The more an action has been rewarded in the past and the less it led to the satiation of a corresponding need, the more frequently the action will be chosen in the future." In this way we have ordered our knowledge by eliminating a contradiction. This ordering function of an axiomatic system is an important part of a general theory. Another aspect of this ordering function of the axiomatization of hypotheses is the inclusion of ad hoc hypotheses so that they become part of the overall theoretical system.

Quite another function of theory is its *specification* in solving technological problems theoretically. In this case we construct a technological model. We may, for example, be interested in enhancing the quality of grades achieved by a group of students. We might apply the hypotheses of a theory in order to tackle the problem. In pressing for a solution, we may state that we have to enhance competition, cohesion, continuity in discussion, and the leadership of the group in order to better its success. As long as this technological advice leads to success, the theoretical model is corroborated. That is, *technological success* is the criterion for *theoretical problem solution*.

Finally, a theory is *opened* to varying experience insofar as we formulate hypotheses and apply them to certain singular circumstances in order to *explain* or *predict* an effect that is purported to flow from those circumstances. We may take the hypothesis "The stronger the cohesion of a group, the stronger its consensus on means" and compare groups differing in cohesion, predict different degrees of norm consensus, and observe the outcome. Here, the observation of reality decides on the validity of a hypothesis as a part of the theory. The criterion is *withstanding the severe tests of reality*. Here the door is opened for experience and innovations that may lead to a collection of falsifying instances for a theory, to so-called anomalies. These anomalies urge us to revise the hypotheses and possibly the conceptual frame of reference as it is no longer capable of including (internalizing) residual categories in the theoretical system (figure 3.1).

Figure 3.1: Functions and Criteria of Knowledge

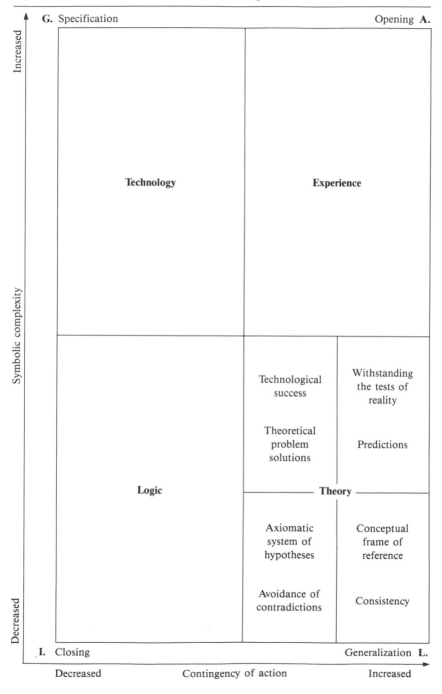

PART TWO

The Economics of
Social Action

FOUR

FROM UTILITARIANISM
TO EVOLUTIONISM: HERBERT SPENCER

HERBERT SPENCER was born on April 27, 1820, and raised within a radically liberal political context in Derby, an old county town that had become a medium-sized industrial center. After finishing his education he first worked as a railway engineer, but then became increasingly involved in radical liberal politics. In 1848 he moved to London and was appointed to a post with *The Economist*. This is the time when he began his scholarly writing with *Social Statics* (1851/1970) and a series of articles, particularly on population, progress, and the social organism. He became a reputable and influential scholar. In 1873 he published *The Study of Sociology*; from 1897 to 1906, *The Principles of Sociology* appeared in eight parts. At the end of his life his reputation was declining. He died on December 8, 1903.

Of the founding fathers who shaped the emergence of sociology as a distinctive scientific discipline the English scholar Herbert Spencer represented most vigorously the liberal economic view of society. He combined the philosophical utilitarianism of his British compatriots Jeremy Bentham (1789/1970) and John Stuart Mill (1861/1974) with the organicism and evolutionism blossoming in his own days because of the striking success of Darwin's evolutionary theory in biology. Spencer was a scholar who covered the fields of philosophy, biology, psychology and sociology. His sociology is thus part of a broader system of thought that is committed to the idea of the unity of the sciences in their convergence in an evolutionary model. We begin our analysis of Spencer's thought with an outline of the Anglo-Saxon tradition of individualism and utilitarianism in which his thought is rooted.

The Anglo-Saxon Tradition of Individualism and Utilitarianism

The human individual is an independent, rational being capable of rationally calculating his or her behavior so that the applied means will ensure the best outcome in terms of costs and benefits. The individual can and will do what is most beneficial for him or her. Society, on the other hand, is nothing but an association of independent individuals in a free contract. Such a free contractual association is most beneficial for everybody, because everyone can profit from anyone's individual achievements, and everyone can rely on the order guaranteed by their contractual association. There is no source for this order other than the free contractual association of independent individuals nor any source of benefits other than the achievements of individuals. Neither God, nor tradition, nor the power of the Crown can create such an order if it is not based on the achievements of individuals and on their free contractual association. Powers other than the individual have to be conceived of as being immediately linked to the achieving and associating individuals in order to guarantee a social order that is beneficial for everybody. God wants the individual to be free and self-responsible; tradition gives him or her the right to be so. The monarch has to accept this right, because he or she has been placed in that representative position only by the free agreement of individuals.

This view of the individual and society is common today but is nevertheless a very distinctive view, rooted in a specific tradition of thought: the Anglo-Saxon liberal school of thought as it emerged with the liberal movement in seventeenth-century Britain. That was the century in which the power of the monarchy was broken, establishing government as nothing but a governing committee elected by and responsible to freely associating, independent individuals. Even apologists of monarchical absolutism like Thomas Hobbes (1588–1679) were forced by this movement to derive absolutist rule from the contract made by freely associating individuals (Hobbes, 1651/1966). Hobbes was no longer able to refer to God or to the tradition of the monarchy in order to provide legitimation for monarchical sovereignty. According to his argument the lack of such a sovereign political power in the so-called state of nature leaves individuals with no device for guaranteeing their natural rights. Individuals' actions are guided by their passions and their prudence. The fact that everybody acts in this way guards nobody against the appetites of others. Thus, everyone has to safeguard him- or herself against such appetites. The only means that appear to provide that safeguard are force and fraud in an attempt to forestall infringements by others against one's person or property. Yet, because everyone behaves in this way, a war of all against all develops, with everybody afraid of everybody else. In this situation individuals realize that it is against their own interests to go on with such a state of nature and that it would be more useful for everybody to conclude a contract with one another in which each gives away his or her individual power, transferring it to a sovereign power. The latter is then responsible for maintaining the civil order that guarantees the rights of individuals. Individuals have no right to resist sovereign power as long as it guarantees that civil order. This is Hobbes' legitimation of abolutism in terms of the utility calculation of individuals who associate under a free contract. Hence, he used the vocabulary of individualism to legitimize absolutism.

A much more consistent theory in terms of individualistic utility calculations was developed a generation later by Hobbes' younger colleague John Locke (1632–1704). Locke (1690/1963) is the first major theoretician of liberalism. For Locke, too, society is nothing but an association of freely contracting individuals. However, these individuals do not need any superior power that goes beyond their association in society itself. Locke draws a much less disastrous picture of the state of nature than Hobbes. Individuals are capable of regulating and coordinating their behavior by themselves, and infringements of their person or property can be avoided to a large degree. They are guided by identical interests in safeguarding both person and property. Building a political society by association is only a further step toward more securely guaranteeing personal and property rights against any individual violator, not a leap from universal struggle to peace, as in Hobbes' social theory. Normally, individuals do not fear each other but have in common the fear of infringements by outsiders. This is why they associate and build a political society that elects a legislative body and a government and establishes an independent judicial power. The division of powers between these governing bodies is a guarantee against any misuse of power and serves to maintain the rights of individuals. Moreover, it is the convergence of individuals' utility calculations on how to safeguard their rights regarding their personal lives and property that leads individuals to associate and to build a political society in a free contract. This is Locke's legitimation of a liberal political society in terms of the utility calculations of individuals.

Locke's theory of liberal society is both a reflection and a legitimation of a rising society that was increasingly based on economic market transactions between individuals who were freely concluding contracts and on freely elected government with divided powers. This was a unique development in history. The bourgeois movement collaborated successfully with the established aristocracy in its economic enterprises, in its struggle against monarchical absolutism, and in its advocacy of the rights of the individual with regard to personal life and property. This was indeed a society that rested much more upon the free contractual association of individuals than had any national society before. It transferred the civic association of the medieval cities to the national level. Anglo-Saxon social theory carried this individualistic view of society on into the eighteenth and nineteenth centuries, centering on the utility calculations of freely contracting individuals (Schneider, 1967).

David Hume (1711–1776) argues in his moral philosophy that there is no morality and no justice that is not rooted in utility (Hume, 1739/1978,

1777/1980). He writes that the property of a human being and its rightful use are defined by statutes, customs, and precedents of different kinds. What makes them all obligatory is that they promote the interest and happiness of human society. Because society is the sum of individuals, everyone's interest and happiness must be served by such rules, otherwise they would not be felt to be obligatory. Hume denies that there is an unavoidable conflict between the interests of different individuals. He says the human individual has not only egoistic desires but also social desires, namely, a sentiment for others. This is why individuals will be able to reach common definitions of right and wrong in terms of everybody's utility. Rules that are detrimental to some people will not be approved by others because of their sentiment for those who might be harmed; they, too, are hurt by the damage done to others. Furthermore, everybody has the desire to gain others' approval, and this is mostly done by giving social services. That makes doing good for others useful for everyone, because it also conveys social approval.

Adam Smith (1723-1790) is famous for his economic theory of the wealth of nations in which he praises the useful effects of the free market system on human society and hence for every single individual (Smith, 1776/1937). As purchasers, we all benefit from the competition between producers, who have to serve us better if they want to increase their profits. This effect of market competition leads Smith to his famous phrase that the market turns private vice (the desire to make a profit) into public good (the creation of wealth) like an invisible hand. In his theory of moral sentiments, he argues that the individual is guided not only by egoistic desires but also by social sympathy, which prevents him or her from unrestrictedly pursuing egoistic interests at the cost of other people. Thus, the egoistic pursuit of interests would also hurt those who engaged in it, because it runs counter to a fundamental need (Smith, 1759/1966).

Jeremy Bentham (1748-1823) and John Stuart Mill (1806-1873) elaborated on the approach to human behavior, moral order, and society in terms of utility as they built up what came to be called utilitarianism.

Bentham (1789/1970) devoted a long treatise to the principle of utility, pointing out its general validity in accounting for any type of human conduct ranging from the most egoistic to the most altruistic forms of behavior. He said that every human action is guided by the pursuit of pleasure and the avoidance of pain. To the extent that individuals achieve this, they attain happiness. Actions are calculated by individuals in terms of their usefulness for promoting that happiness; that is, benefits and costs are weighed against each other, and the action chosen is that which yields the greatest gain in terms of benefits less costs. This is action according to the utility principle. And because Bentham defined community as the sum of individuals associated as members of that community, the utility principle also defines whether any act, organization of action, law, or political measure is good or bad for society. Anything that increases the amount of pleasure and/or decreases the amount of pain among society's members is defined as good, while anything that exerts effects in the opposite direction is bad. He introduced the principle of the greatest happiness of everybody whose interests are involved in an action or a proposed measure. Whatever action one carries out, whatever measure a government implements, whatever rule one applies will be the more useful for the community the more it increases the happiness of everybody affected by that action, measure, or rule. There is no social good that cannot be defined in terms of the happiness of individuals promoted by that good. Society is a composition of individuals and has to be organized so that it works for the happiness of these individuals. Social norms and moral rules are not abstract obligations imposed on the individual without consideration of their happiness but are instruments for promoting the happiness of as many individuals as possible.

Bentham's utilitarianism gives individualistic social theory an explicitly universalist turn. Society is still nothing but the sum of individuals; however, what is done by various bodies within society—the government, courts, moral codes—is accounted for not in terms of individual utilities in individual situations but in terms of the utility of everyone affected by that action. However, it is not some abstract common good from which this criterion is derived but the increase in pleasure and decrease in pain for every individual affected. This is a universalist individualism. For society to have a moral order it has to take into account that everybody's individual utility is positively and not negatively affected.

John Stuart Mill (1861/1974) elaborated on Bentham's universalist individualism when he explicitly addressed the problem as it was raised by the German philosopher Immanuel Kant (1724–1804). According to Kant (1788/1964d), no individual benefit can be enough to make a rule binding for everyone—which is a feature of moral rules—because what is beneficial for one individual is painful for another, or what is beneficial for an individual at a certain place and time is painful at some other place and time. Thus, only a rule that is valid independently of any utility outcome for individuals can be binding for everyone. Kant, therefore, formulates the abstract categorical imperative as a criterion of any moral rule: Only a rule that can be made a universal law can also be binding. This is the case only if everybody consents to this law completely of his or her own free will, guided by nothing but reason. This is why Kant says freedom and moral law are mutually linked. Only a free individual can follow a moral law, and only if he or she does so on the basis of reason will he or she really be free.

John Stuart Mill accepts Kant's statement that a rule can be morally binding for everybody only if it can be adopted as a universal law by every human being. However, he objects that this remains a rather empty phrase unless it is filled out by referring to the collective interest of individuals (Mill,

1861/1974:308). The collective interest is the sum of individual utilities affected by a law. Only a moral law that serves the happiness of everybody can be binding. In this way, Mill reformulates Kant's universalistic theory of morals in utilitarian terms. For Kant, a moral act results from an abstract duty imposed by the validity of a universal law and disregards any individual benefits and costs. This is the essence of its universal binding quality: that it is independent of individual costs and benefits. For Mill, a moral act requires motivation, and this can only come from an individual's desires. An individual cannot be motivated to carry out a moral act if he or she feels no desire to do so; and he or she will feel such a desire only if the act promotes his or her happiness. Only if an action promotes the happiness of everyone will it also be binding for everyone. The same is true for any criterion of justice. Whatever is accepted as just by everybody can be so accepted only because it promotes everybody's happiness.

This is Mill's transformation of Kant's moral universalism into a universalist utilitarianism that is nevertheless based on individualistic foundations, because it is still the sum of *individual interests* served by a rule that makes it morally binding. As far as Kant is concerned, it is his abstraction from any individual interests that allows him to state a truly universalistic morality; yet this remains empty in substantial terms. For Mill it is simply the addition of all individual interests that gives universal validity to moral rules, in this case more concrete rules, but mostly rules that would change in their substance with changes in situations. Because society is based on the free association of individuals, it can only work according to the desires that motivate these individuals. This is the basic message of utilitarian social theory as it emerged in the Anglo-Saxon social and cultural context.

Utilitarian social theory flourished in the nineteenth-century Anglo-Saxon social and cultural context when sociology took shape as a distinctive scientific discipline. The scholars who framed sociology and were educated in this context did so in individualistic and utilitarian terms. In dealing with social development they were also fascinated by the success of Darwinian evolutionism in biology. What they created was very much a combination of philosophical individualistic utilitarianism with biological evolutionism. A further source of their thought was the French Saint-Simonian and Comtian positivism and organicist evolutionism. However, they did not share the French emphasis on the predominance of the social organism over the individual but conceived of the emerging society much more in individualistic terms. This is the approach to building sociology as a science of society as it became established in Anglo-Saxon culture by scholars like Herbert Spencer (1820–1903) in England or William Graham Sumner (1840–1910) and Lester F. Ward (1841–1913) in America (Hofstadter, 1959, 1963; Hinkle, 1980).

Sumner (1906/1940) pointed out the evolution of folkways and mores in the struggle for survival of human individuals based on the principles of pursuing pleasure and avoiding pain. Folkways evolve as initial regulation mechanisms for human conduct as better adaptations of means to ends. A strain of consistency in human conduct serves to coordinate these folkways. Sentiments of solidarity emerge in groups, because they safeguard individuals against external enemies. These sentiments sustain the folkways. The more norms serve the welfare of the whole society, the more they will be firmly established as mores. To cater to the need to adapt to changing situations, conventions are built up. They provide the resources for the evolution of new folkways and mores. In this evolutionary process norms undergo a steady change toward being ever better adapted to the environment. Sumner sees the developing liberal market society as society's highest form with the highest adaptive capacity. He says it works on the basis of antagonistic cooperation.

Lester F. Ward (1883/1902, 1903/1925, 1906) also conceived of human behavior as determined by the principle of pursuing pleasure and avoiding pain. Social development is an outcome of the individual's search for pleasure and avoidance of pain in the struggle of existence. Evolution, however, is characterized by a growing antagonism between individuals' desires in their existential struggle and the survival of the human race itself. This conflict is the originating cause of the evolution of social structure in the form of institutions such as religion, morals, law, and the state. These institutions evolve out of a synergetic process coming from the conflict between individual desire and the survival of the human race. With this statement Ward lays much more emphasis on the order-preserving function of social institutions for liberal society than do most of his liberal colleagues. However, in true individualistic-utilitarian terms he saw them evolving from the individualistic struggle of existence. What he called synergy—the force that transforms the conflict arising from the antagonism between individual desires and the survival of the human race into useful social institutions—is a *deus ex machina*, a lucky stroke of fate that reconciles the individual's desire for pleasure with the advancement of the human race. Like Adam Smith's invisible hand of the market, it turns private vices into public good.

This is the intellectual context within which Herbert Spencer (1851/1970) developed a grand theory of the evolution of liberal market society on the basis of the individual's struggle to maintain his or her existence. We will deal with Spencer's theory in more detail in this chapter because it was the most fully developed and most influential at the time.

Methodology

Spencer presented his methodology in *The Study of Sociology* (1873/1908). He was convinced that society needs sociology, because it is the science of sociology that can point out the laws of social development. Sociological knowledge warns not to have the illusion that political decision making can do away with any evil. Politics can shift the evil's expression but not its amount, because the latter depends on the state of fitness of the human individual for the condition of existence on the stage of social evolution, which proceeds in a much slower process. Sociology tells us something that we do not get from the study of history, which tells us stories about kings but nothing about the natural evolution of society, about social progress. To inform us about this process is the task of sociology.

Spencer conceived of society as a social organism. Nevertheless, he argued for methodological individualism, which means the whole of the social organism must be regarded as a result of the working and interdependencies of its parts, namely, human individuals.

Spencer was aware of certain difficulties in practicing social science: Social phenomena are very often not directly perceivable; habits of thought determine the observation of facts; the observer is part of the phenomenon that he or she studies; facts that are embedded in very different social and cultural contexts have to be compared; the course of social change cannot be determined by observing only a small part of that process; measuring other persons' actions by one's own standards leads to misconstructions; the future social state cannot be understood from the viewpoint of currently existing society; the very slow process of transformation cannot be observed easily; and the complexity of sociological conceptions makes them difficult to understand.

Moral Philosophy

Spencer's *Social Statics* (1851/1970) sets out the foundations for his integration of a utilitarian ethic with the idea of evolution. He starts by discussing a common objection to Bentham's utilitarian moral principle of the greatest happiness of everybody. According to this objection everybody can understand this principle in a different way; thus, it has no definite meaning. Spencer argues that this is a natural outcome of the changing constitution of the human individual in his or her phylogenetic and ontogenetic development. The human being is not uniform in character. Because the constitution of the human individual develops in interaction with the environment, different meanings of the principle of happiness are a natural outcome.

Spencer goes on to assert that every evil will necessarily disappear as the human individual evolves to attain a better state of fitness for the environmental conditions of his or her life. In proving this assertion, he says that every evil comes from a failure of the individual's constitution to adapt to the external conditions of his or her existence. Evil is imperfection, and this in turn is unfitness for the conditions of existence. This unfitness means having faculties either in excess or in deficiency. In the case of faculties in excess, conditions do not demand that they be fully exercised, whereas those in a deficient state are required to be exercised more than is physically possible. However, it is an essential principle of life that faculties that are not exercised will diminish, whereas those that are excessively exercised because of demand by external conditions will grow. Therefore, excess faculties disappear and deficient faculties develop up to the point where there is no longer any excess or deficient faculty, and the human individual then lives in a state of perfect fitness for his or her conditions of existence. All imperfection will disappear, and with it, all evil. Because immorality is part of evil, all immorality will also disappear. The final emergence of the ideal, morally perfect, and happy human individual is thus not just a hope but a logical necessity. Progress comes about not by accident but in accordance with a logical rule. The only drawback is that the human individual has a long way to go in this natural process of adaptation to the conditions of his or her existence.

We have to note here that the principle of decrease or growth in faculties according to their exercise required by the external conditions of existence is the evolutionary law that was formulated in biology by Lamarck (1815-1822). According to Lamarck, organisms develop traits by way of exercise and pass them on to their offspring. This principle was replaced by Darwin's (1888) principle of natural selection: organisms do not develop traits by exercise, but those organisms that accidentally acquire the traits by birth are therefore better suited to the environment, making it more likely that they will survive and pass on their traits to their offspring. The same criticism has to be made against Spencer's Lamarckian idea of evolutionary adaptation of the human individual to his or her conditions of existence.

Looking for a first principle of ethics, Spencer starts

> . . . from the admitted truth, that human happiness is the Divine will. (Spencer, 1851/1970:75)

Then he argues that happiness is a state of due satisfaction of all one's desires. Desires, however, can be satisfied only through the exercise of the human faculties. Therefore, the due exercise of human faculties is a precondition of happiness. Because God wants human beings to be happy, He also wants them to exercise their faculties. However, it is the human being's duty to obey God; therefore, it is his or her duty to exercise his or her faculties. It is contrary to God's will not to exercise one's faculties. In order to do that, however, one must have freedom of action. Without enough scope for action it is impossible for the human individual to exercise his or her faculties. Because God wants the individual to be happy, He also wants him or her to be free; that is, He intends each person to have a right to liberty. Every human has this right, but that means that a necessary condition for its exercise is that every human respects all others' rights to liberty. Every individual has the right to exercise freely his or her faculties inasmuch as this is compatible with the same free exercise of faculties by every other individual.

Social Evolution

Distinguishing social dynamics from social statics, Spencer (1851/1970:409–76) says that social statics deals with the conditions, that is, the equilibrium of the perfect society, whereas social dynamics is concerned with pointing out the forces that advance society toward this state of perfection. The perfect moral state of society is not eternally given but the outcome of an immensely long process of evolution from lower to higher stages of development. The perfect state of society is a state where every human individual exercises his or her faculties to the fullest degree in liberty insofar as this is compatible with every other individual's exercise of his or her faculties. It is a state that attains the fullest degree of individuation and that corresponds to the utilitarian moral principle of the greatest happiness of everybody. It is a state of society that requires individuals with highly developed moral character who are capable of freely choosing the right ways of exercising their faculties without interfering with any other individual's exercise of his or her faculties.

Evidently not everybody and not every human race has fulfilled this requirement from the beginning of human history and to the fullest degree. It is much more an outcome of an evolutionary process according to which, in the long run, the human race will be made up of those individuals who are best fitted to the moral state of society. History is therefore a long process of eliminating those living beings and human races and individuals who are not fit to meet the growing demands of the moral state. Systems of authority, domination, coercion, and militancy are an inevitable force by which humankind moves toward the final moral state on earlier levels of evolution. They serve as educational institutions for training those moral qualities that make the individual capable of self-discipline in carrying out his or her right to liberty in the final stage of evolution. Suppression and war serve as means of educating or eliminating those people who are not or not yet adapted to higher moral life by their constitution. Therefore, domination, militancy, and suppression as features of primitive and traditional societies must not be morally condemned from the point of view of modern liberty, but have to be conceived of as preconditional stages on the way to modern liberty. We cannot expect that human beings who have been accustomed to suppressing other species or other human beings or who have been accustomed to being suppressed could adapt to the final social (moral) state in a matter of days. A slow, gradual granting of liberties is necessary to adapt the human individual step by step to this higher stage of social evolution.

With the arrival at this moral state there is no longer any need for coercive institutions. The state as an agency of external constraint will be reduced more and more to the role of a guardian of human liberties and will finally disappear. Ever greater liberties of free trade, free press, universal suffrage, and so on can be granted, because individuals adapted to such liberties will then exist. Progress toward the moral state of liberty is a necessary outcome of this evolutionary process.

What then are the laws that bring about this progress? Spencer's answer to this question refers to population growth and to the change from incoherent homogeneity to coherent heterogeneity. Population growth is not a dangerous phenomenon for the survival of humankind—as was asserted by Malthus—but has positive effects for the upgrading of its adaptation (Spencer, 1852/1972a). Any excess fertility that goes beyond the existing means of satisfying needs exerts pressures for faculties to be increased and also for the improvement of cooperation and for a decrease in fertility. Families and races who do not meet these conditions will die out. Those who improve their faculties and cooperation for higher rates of production and reduce their fertility will survive. Thus, population growth contributes to the growth of human faculties and cooperation and to the selection of ever better adapted human beings.

Dealing with progress, Spencer (1857/1972b) states that it has one formal feature throughout all areas of human life, in organic life as much as in social and cultural life. This feature is the transformation of an incoherent homogeneity to a coherent heterogeneity, which is the general pattern of evolution as Spencer (1862/1904:291, 438) understands it. That process entails the functional differentiation of systems into interdependent parts. The development of organic life from lower forms to higher forms and from the embryonic state to the fully developed organism corresponds to this pattern. The same is true for the individual and for society. Primitive society is composed of family groups that are very similar to each other and that live scattered over a certain area. They all do the same things, and this makes them similar in themselves. However, they live mostly from their own work and resources and do not exchange very much. This makes them incoherent. On the other hand, the more different families specialize in the production of particular things, the more dissimilar they become, but the more they are forced to get things they cannot produce themselves by entering into exchange with other families. In this process, their interdependence and their coherence grows. The society is more heterogeneous in character but also more coherent.

The law that explains this development from incoherent homogeneity to coherent heterogeneity states:

> Every active force produces more than one change—every cause produces more than one effect. (Spencer, 1857/1972b:47)

Spencer illustrates the increasing heterogeneity of society produced by the multiple effects of one cause with the following example: One member of a tribe may turn out to have an extraordinary aptitude for making weapons, which up to now every individual man has made by himself. Because his fellows see the superiority of this man's weapons, they are inclined to have him produce their weapons for them. Inasmuch as that man has the unusual faculty of making weapons and likes doing this, he will provide the weapons if he is rewarded by his fellows. This is a first specialization of function, which is steadily built upon as the corresponding division of labor goes on. The weapon maker may further improve his faculties in this regard, while the other men will lose their weapon-making faculties more and more. Other effects will occur; for example, barter for the exchange of goods will be established. The weapon maker will take from his clients in exchange for his weapons those goods that they can produce. This gives an incentive to everybody to specialize in his own best faculties. Thus, further specialization takes place, gives rise to still further specialization, and so on. Another example given by Spencer to illustrate his law of progress explaining progressive differentiation is the introduction of the locomotive and the many effects that this generated: a railroad system, legislative acts, construction work of many different kinds, new organization of business and communication, and so on. These examples show that the growing division of labor also leads to interdependence, exchange relationships, and integration of specialized families and individuals who previously led separate lives.

Society that develops according to the law of progress, therefore, develops like an organism that has several qualities similar to those of biological organisms in addition to traits that are dissimilar but of less importance. The similarities are these (Spencer, 1860/1972c):

1. They start life as small aggregations and grow immensely in mass.
2. They start with simple structures, if any, to then build up increasingly complex structures.
3. They start with little interdependence among constituent parts to develop increasingly more interdependence among them.
4. The life of the organism continues to exist beyond the life of its constituent parts.

The differences are these:

1. There is no specific external form to society, which is of less importance, because this is also true of the lower living systems.
2. The living tissues of organisms form a continuous mass; the living elements of society do not. However, the lower divisions of organisms are not far from this quality of society.

3. The living elements of organisms are fixed in their place; those of societies aren't. However, in their public capacities in contrast to their private ones, the individual members of society are also not much more mobile than the living elements of organisms.
4. In society every member has feeling; in organisms, only particular parts have feeling. However, in the lowest animals feeling is also distributed all over the system.

Spencer continues his argument by referring to further analogies: Society differentiates into classes like the different layers of organisms. It differentiates into parts that fulfill specific functions, as is the case with organisms. The circulation of commodities corresponds to blood circulation. Both need channels of communication. Representative bodies are the nervous system of society.

The Principles of Sociology (Spencer, 1897–1906/1975) elaborates the ideas developed in the earlier writings in detail, with lots of descriptions of facts gathered. *The Principles of Sociology* studies:

1. the progressive modifications to their general environment effected by the action of societies,
2. the growing size and density of the social aggregate,
3. the increasing interdependence between the whole of society and its constituent parts, and
4. the growing interdependence between societies.

The evolution of society is given impetus by these interdependencies. Sociology investigates how the fitness for social cooperation develops in this evolutionary process. The object domain, then, is the evolution of institutions performing functions of coordinating human action. The family is the first of these institutions. It performs the function of making the growing child fit for cooperation. Ceremonial institutions, like ritual dances, are primitive forms of social control that precede the civil forms. Political institutions develop in order to coordinate collective action and to direct it to common ends. Ecclesiastical systems establish social bonds. Religion gives a sense of the providence of the divine being, which is expressed in the process of evolution.

Social evolution proceeds toward increasing differentiation by way of the economic division of labor and of the compounding of political aggregates within a higher-order political system via military conquest or confederation. The latter process starts with simple societies of one political aggregate and moves on to compounded societies with two or more formerly independent political aggregates compounded within one political system under one political head. The next step of political evolution is the compounding of two or more such compounded systems under a still higher political head, and so on.

The major transformation that was occurring during Spencer's time, according to his own view, was the decline of militancy or of military society and the rise of industrial society. Militancy is the characteristic feature of traditional society. Here, every social action is based on status-relationships between unequals or equals; action is coordinated through constraint exerted by a centralized political and military authority. This is a necessary stage of social evolution as long as there are races, groups, classes, and individuals who are not adapted to a higher form of the social state, where coordination is based on voluntary associations between individuals. The latter type of coordination characterizes industrial society. Here, social differentiation grows to an unprecedented degree. Decision making can be decentralized and left to ever smaller entities and to individuals. Specific interaction proceeds on the basis of contracts between free and equal individuals, who conclude contracts on the basis of individual choice. They associate voluntarily in the exchange of goods and services.

The development of an individual's faculties converges with that of other individuals and with a progress of the whole system to higher levels of satisfaction of desires, thus with progress toward the greatest happiness of the greatest number. The state disappears, because individuals will have learned to exercise their faculties without interfering in how others exercise their faculties. Orientation toward one's own happiness coincides with an orientation toward the happiness of other individuals. Egoism and altruism are two sides of the same coin under these conditions. In striving for their own happiness, individuals at the same time contribute to the happiness of others, for example, via exchange of goods, and are well aware of the rights of the others to the same happiness. Individuals act according to the universalist utilitarian principle of the greatest happiness of everybody.

However, as Spencer emphasized ever more the older he grew, this process of evolution toward the final social state is a very slow one that also undergoes partial detours and regressions. Yet, as he puts it, only a gradual but continuous granting of the corresponding liberties of free trade, free press, separation of state and church, and universal suffrage can in the long run nurture the kind of individuals who will fit into such a social state. That is, the exposure to such a social state step by step brings about those characters and selects those characters that are best suited to that social state; individuals gradually learn that it is in their own interest to respect everybody else's rights of liberty, because otherwise their own exercise of this right would be jeopardized by the same interference from others. Egoism and altruism converge in this process. Spencer was engaged in arguing for the expansion of liberty in Britain throughout his life in order to bring about this social state. He was convinced that England was farthest developed in this respect and had the best preconditions for such an expansion of liberties.

In his critique of socialism Spencer pointed out that socialism not only abandons economic liberties but also establishes an all-embracing industrial subordination of the workers to a strong, centralized, militarylike regimentation (Spencer, 1897–1906/1975: vol. 3, part 8). Spencer's involvement in political debates shows that he conceived of the future social state not just as an inevitable outcome of social evolution but also as a valued state for which one has to argue and to help provide the right preconditions. Thus he did not believe completely in the working of social evolution independently of man's will as his theory claims.

Summary

Methodology

1. Sociology is of practical use for society because it informs us about the laws of social development.
2. Whereas the study of history tells us stories about kings, sociology informs us about the natural evolution of society.
3. Society is a social organism, but one that is determined by its constituent elements, that is, by human individuals, in its working and development.
4. Sociology has to be aware of specific difficulties deriving from the complexity of its object domain.

Moral Philosophy

5. The utilitarian moral principle of the greatest happiness for everybody has different meanings according to the constant modification of the human individual's constitution in the evolutionary process.

The Evanescence of Evil

6. Every evil originates in the individual's imperfection in the sense of nonadaptation to the conditions of existence due either to excess or to deficient faculties.
7. Because excess faculties are exercised less and deficient faculties are exercised more in the process of adaptation to the environment, imperfection and thus evil will tend to disappear the longer evolution goes on.

The First Principle of Ethics

8. God wants each human being to be happy. Happiness is a state of due satisfaction of desires, which requires the full exercise of one's faculties

in liberty. Thus, everybody has the duty and the right to be able to fully exercise his or her faculties in liberty. Because any one individual can have this only to the degree to which he or she is not hindered by anyone else, it is also everyone's duty to respect other individuals' rights of liberty in exercising their own faculties.

Social Evolution

9. The perfect social state of society is a state in which all individuals have the liberty to exercise their faculties to the fullest degree without interfering in each other's liberty.
10. The perfect social state of society is the ultimate outcome of a long evolutionary process.
11. Authority, domination, coercion, militancy, and war fulfill the function of educating or extinguishing those living beings, races, societies, groups, and individuals which/who are not adapted to the conditions of existence and have lesser faculties.
12. The processes of exercising faculties and of extinction give rise to individuals possessing the qualities that, in the long run, are adapted to the perfect social state and are higher physical and moral faculties.
13. The higher the stages reached by evolution, the more the granting of increasing liberties of free property ownership, free trade, free press, the free exercise of religion, and universal suffrage will set the conditions to which the higher human beings will adapt still further in order to bring about the perfectly moral human being who self-responsibly exercises his or her liberties.
14. With the attainment of the perfect social state, the state first will be reduced to the role of a guardian of liberties and then will eventually disappear.

The Laws of Progress in Evolution

15. Excess fertility leads to efforts to improve faculties and cooperation and to reduce that fertility; it also leads to the selection of those families and individuals who act in this way, thus achieving adaptation to increasingly complex conditions of existence. Population growth therefore pushes social evolution toward higher levels of perfection.
16. Social evolution starts from incoherent homogeneity and proceeds toward coherent heterogeneity, that is, toward the progressive differentiation of interdependent and integrated parts of one whole.
17. Every active force produces more than one change; every cause produces more than one effect.
18. Every initial act of specialization causes an endless chain of further specializations and a corresponding division of labor.

19. The farther the division of labor becomes, the more interdependence and exchange, and hence integration between differentiated parts, will occur.

Society as an Organism

20. Societies, like organisms, start life as small aggregations and grow immensely in mass; they start with simple structures or none at all and then build up increasingly complex structures; they start with little interdependence between parts and develop ever more interdependence between them; finally, they continue to exist beyond the life of their constituent parts.

21. Societies, like organisms, are differentiated into classes or parts fulfilling specific functions; they have a circulation of commodities like a bloodstream, and channels of communication and governing bodies as nervous systems.

22. Unlike organisms, societies have no specific external form, do not constitute a continuous mass, have elements without any fixed place, and also have elements that are all capable of feeling. However, the differences are not always very great, depending on which societies are compared with which organisms.

23. Social evolution involves the progressive modification of the environment effected by the action of societies, the growing size and density of the social aggregate, the increasing interdependence between the whole of society and its constituent parts, and the growing interdependence between societies.

24. Social evolution brings about the differentiation of institutions that fulfill specific functions: the family prepares for cooperation; ceremonial institutions exert primitive social control; political institutions direct collective action toward common ends; ecclesiastical institutions establish social bonds; and religion gives a sense of the divine being's providence finding expression in the process of evolution.

25. Social evolution proceeds from simple societies to increasing division of labor and the compounding of political aggregates on increasingly higher levels.

26. Social evolution proceeds from primitive societies with an incoherent homogeneity to military societies with centralized authority, constraint, and status relationships, and then to industrial societies with decentralized decision making, liberty, and contract-based relationships.

Critical Assessment

Spencer's strongest argument is his explanation of the economic dimension of social development: the division of labor involving a growing differentiation of the population into heterogeneous but interdependent parts exchanging commodities with each other. If people learn that they can make a better living by specializing in the production of specific goods and services and exchanging them for all the different things they want afterwards, they will indeed do so, which leads to a level of specialization from which any return to less sophisticated levels would be more costly, but changes toward even further specialization would be more profitable.

Thus, under the external pressure of scarcity caused by population growth, individuals who strive for a better living and who calculate in economic terms specialize and hence initiate the process of the division of labor. They apply the best means in order to attain an optimum level of need satisfaction. That means they strive to satisfy as many desires as possible to the highest possible degree. They are not oriented to the satisfaction of one single desire, for example, maintenance of their independence, but to the satisfaction of many different desires, which makes them much more flexible in their actions but also forces them to mobilize as many resources as possible to use them for the satisfaction of as many desires as possible. This is their specific economic orientation in distinction to an actor who is oriented to the realization of one single end, or to conforming to norms that prescribe what means may be used, or to maintaining consistency with general values that close out the striving for specific ends and/or the application of specific means. Individuals who are oriented in these noneconomic ways will not be apt to learn and to specialize as quickly as Spencer presupposes with the economically calculating actor in mind. Individual actors who have only the one single aim of living from their own products, who are committed to preserving the production techniques of their ancestors, or who want to maintain the traditional identity of their family will not participate in the process of specialization simply because this offers a better living in terms of material products. They do not calculate their actions economically.

One could argue, though, that if only some actually initiate the process of specialization and the pressure from population growth increases, only those who have specialized and hence participated in the process of dividing labor will survive. This is an explanation of the growing division of labor as resulting not from learning and economic calculation but from natural selection. At least part of Spencer's theory of the growing division of labor can be read in this sense. Thus, he formulates what Emile Durkheim, the French classic, took up as an explanation in his own study on the division of labor. However, this explanation is feasible only to the extent that there are established markets and that success in the market is the criterion by which the human individual makes his or her living. What we still lack is an explanation of how markets are established. One explanation could be that societies that have established markets do better in the political struggle between societies. This, however, is not wholly correct, because societies may well concentrate on establishing the highest possible level of physical force, with less emphasis on markets. That means they are more centralized than market societies and much quicker at decision making and collective action, which makes them superior in the political struggle to market societies with more decentralized decision making. Therefore, the establishment of markets is not an advantage in all cases in the struggle between societies; decentralized market societies may be extinguished by centralized, military ones.

We cannot explain the growth of markets in societies all over the world by their evolutionary superiority in the struggle between societies. More causes are needed to explain the growing division of labor and corresponding markets. There must be a growth in the scope of one political authority or cooperation between various political authorities in order to regulate expanded exchange under one jurisdiction. There must be a transformation of solidarity, a shift from the particularistic solidarity of primordial groups (families, clans) to the universalistic solidarity of all those involved in market exchange, which presupposes the breaking down of boundaries of solidarity and the establishment of a common morality. There must be a dissolution of the distinction between in-group morality and out-group immorality, and general value must be placed on the rational and instrumental mastery of nature and the world and on active intervention in the world, and that world must be transformed rather than passively accommodated to as it exists. There must be value placed upon work rather than work being devalued in comparison to a life of distinction or viewed as penance for one's sins. These are presuppositions for the establishment of a progressing market economy that do not come about automatically just by the combination of learning and economic rationality or external selection.

Spencer's economic evolutionary explanation for the progressing division of labor and the establishment of a capitalist market economy is much too narrow in character to give us the capability to cover the various noneconomic preconditions for such an economy. A look at Emile Durkheim's study on the transformation of solidarity with the growing division of labor shows us that we have to complement such an explanation by a theory of the formation of normative structures. A look at Max Weber's comparative studies on world religions and the rise of rational capitalism tells us how indispensable a detailed reconstruction of the cultural foundations of this process is for an appropriate explanation. A look at Pareto's theory of the dynamics of power systems tells us more about the contribution of this factor to historical developments. And Marx's radical economic view demonstrates that the expansion of the capitalist market economy does not lead ultimately to the social state of universal liberty but if left to itself will eventually result in alienation and the establishment of an uncontrollable power over the human being and in irreconcilable class antagonism. Not one of these important aspects of the progressing division of labor with the establishment of a capitalist economy comes to light in Spencer's economic evolutionary theory, which is devoted to the appraisal of economic liberty as the final state of highest morality.

There are further shortcomings connected with Spencer's liberal economic evolutionism. He declared the disappearance of evil and the growth of happiness as an inevitable outcome of evolution, but this is simply wishful thinking. Durkheim emphasized, contrary to Spencer, that the progressing division of labor by no means increases happiness. It intensifies competition for scarce resources, breaks up traditional bonds, means people often have to suffer failure, and increases frustration because desires grow faster than the means for satisfying them. These effects of the growing division of labor bring with them a lot of unhappiness. The growing rates of suicide that accompany the growing economy and its upswings and downswings are evidence of this unhappiness. From Max Weber's cultural studies we can derive the proposition that the continuing intervention in the world by modern man, which is exemplified by a growing economy, produces a new, artificial world that is full of new evils. This is an endless and inescapable process. Spencer's own law that one cause always has multiple effects could be applied to explaining this feature of modern societies, but Spencer himself did not apply the law to such an explanation.

According to Spencer, the final social state of an industrial society based on individual liberty and mutual respect of liberties, contract, and decentralization is an inevitable outcome of natural evolution. However, militant societies are well capable of defeating their enemies in the struggle for survival. Contrary to Spencer's assumption, it is improbable that the more liberal societies would survive if there were no factors at work other than simply physical selection in the struggle for survival. Physical and moral selection do not coincide in any respect as Spencer presupposes.

It is also improbable that individuals initially would be educated or selected to a higher moral state by the coercive force of militant societies, yet after that simply by the granting of liberties in industrial societies. Achieving a state of moral self-responsibility is a very long process that has its roots in Judeo-Christian religion and underwent a process of secularization and universalization in the Enlightenment. This process proceeds on the level of moral discourse and of socialization and has to be approached on this level, as it was by Durkheim in his sociology of morality, opening up insights that were extended by Mead, Piaget, Kohlberg, and others. Max Weber pointed out the unique roots of such moral self-responsibility in Judeo-Christian culture.

Spencer's evolutionary theory suffers from its too narrow economic and naturalistic conception. Evolution is seen as an automatic, natural process in which society is economically upgraded via the division of labor, which then brings about all the amenities of greater liberty and a higher morality. Our critical discussion of his theory has proved this claim to be much too far-reaching. What Spencer is able to explain is only a small part of the progressing division of labor and nothing beyond that. Even this process can be explained only in its purely economic dimension and not in the dimensions of political regulation, solidarity structures, and cultural legitimation. What goes beyond the progressing division of labor — and Spencer makes such claims — requires even more explanations in terms of factors of political regulation, solidarity structures, and cultural legitimation. In order to get to these dimensions of social development, we have to go on to the works of Marx, Pareto, Durkheim, Simmel, Weber, and Mead.

Further Developments

Herbert Spencer did not create a school of thought. However, his major views have found their way into various kinds of sociology. Utilitarianism has been revitalized enormously in recent years. Evolutionism was taken up again in new versions of evolutionary theory like Talcott Parsons's and Niklas Luhmann's theories of socio-cultural evolution. Functional differentiation as a master scheme of societal development has been reworked by Luhmann. A new presentation of Spencer's sociological theory was recently made by Jonathan H. Turner (1985).

FIVE

THE CONTRADICTIONS OF CAPITALIST DEVELOPMENT: KARL MARX

KARL MARX was born on May 5, 1818, in the small city of Trier in the Rhenish Province near the French border. His father and mother originated from old Jewish families. His father was the first in the family to work in a secular profession as lawyer and head of the bar. Young Marx began to study law at the University of Bonn at the age of seventeen. He moved to the famous University of Berlin in 1836 and was then very much influenced by the idealist dialectical philosophy of Georg Wilhelm Friedrich Hegel, who had died before Marx came to Berlin but whose influence was still prevalent at that time. Marx joined the left-oriented Hegelians, young philosophers like Bruno and Edgar Bauer and Max Stirner, and switched from law to philosophy. After graduating with a dissertation on the natural philosophies of Democritus and Epicurus in 1841, he left Berlin with few professional prospects. Because of his left-liberal stance he had no chance of being appointed to an academic position.

After a short time at the *Rheinische Zeitung,* a Cologne newspaper that was then suppressed by the Prussian government, and after marrying his young love, Jenny von Westphalen, in 1843, Marx moved to Paris and became a socialist under the influence of the French reformist and socialist philosophers, particularly Fourier, Proudhon, Blanc, Cabet, Saint-Simon, and Blanqui. It was then that he began his life-long friendship with Friedrich Engels, son of a Rhenish textile manufacturer, and wrote with him the early manuscripts on philosophy and political economy including *The Communist Manifesto,* which appeared in 1848. In the meantime he had been expelled from Paris for political reasons and had moved to Brussels.

In 1848, when the revolution broke out, Marx went to Paris and then to Cologne in order to edit the *Neue Rheinische Zeitung.* After the collapse of the revolution, Marx stayed for a short time in France, where he was obliged to move to a distant province. He finally settled down in London in 1849 where he stayed for the rest of his life, living a life in poverty with his wife and children, two of whom died of malnutrition. He had no job besides writing for the *New York Daily Tribune* for ten years and mostly lived from the money sent by his friend Engels. He joined the First International at that time and was visited by socialists and social democrats from all over Europe for his advice. After being admitted to the reading room of the British Museum in June 1852, Marx spent most of his time studying there and writing his famous *Capital*. In 1881 his wife died, and a year later his eldest daughter died. He himself died on March 14, 1883.

The German Tradition of Idealism, French Socialism, and the British Political Economy

The rise of capitalism is part and parcel of the rise of modern society. It brought a dynamism of change to modern society that is unprecedented in history. The effect of capitalism and its laws of development on modern society are the basic concerns of Marx's theory of modern society.

Marx drew the major elements of his theory from three divergent sources: British political economy, French socialism, and German idealism. From British political economy he took the concern with the laws of capitalist production, distribution, and consumption; from French socialism, the concern with looking for a society that would be able to overcome the contradictions, conflicts, inequalities, and irrationalities of capitalism; and from German idealism, particularly from Hegel, he took the understanding of historical development as a dialectical and ultimately meaningful process.

Three principles of Hegel's (1770–1831) philosophy make up the starting point for Marx's theory of society: the philosophy of history, dialectics, and idealism (Hegel, 1964–1971).

History has meaning. This is what the philosophy of history wants to reveal. History is not just a collection of accidentally occurring events without any detectable meaning but rather the contrary. The task of the philosophy of history is to uncover this meaning. The first feature of this meaning is direction. History proceeds not in a completely accidental way but in a certain direction. The origin of this claim to meaning including direction in history is the fact that humans can progress beyond simple responses to stimuli by virtue of their ability to interpret stimuli and and events, to interpret the world using language.

Interpretation is a process of understanding the meaning of an object under consideration. The human being who looks at history tries to understand its meaning. He or she wants to know what happened and why. Thus the human being constructs systems of explanation for the world and its history. He or she develops theories about the world and its history. For these theories to be understood they have to be internally consistent, otherwise nobody would know what is really claimed. Inasmuch as a pluralism of theories exists, they can contradict each other. Understanding and explaining the world rightly necessitates resolving such contradictions in an endless process.

On the other hand, there are the factual events of the world and its history. Theories and factual events can be in disharmony. Resolving such contradictions between theories and facts becomes a major task toward understanding and explaining the world. Resolving contradictions between theories and between theories and facts becomes the main task for finding meaning in the world and its history.

This is the way in which the construction of human knowledge proceeds, aiming at understanding and explaining the world and its history, thereby constructing meaning. History has meaning here in this sense: Human knowledge does not proceed in accidental ways but develops in evolutionary steps in which the internal contradictions between theories and external contradictions between theories and facts are resolved. To the extent that knowledge makes such progress, the human being uncovers meaning in the world and its history and builds up meaning in his or her knowledge of that world.

However, the human being is capable of raising questions not only about what happened and why it happened but also about what should happen and why it should happen. In answering these questions he or she establishes systems of norms and values that define right and wrong and ideal and perfect states of the world. Inasmuch as a number of such norms and values are formulated, contradictions between them occur. In order to understand and know what is right and wrong and what is a perfect state of the world, the human being is then preoccupied with resolving these contradictions and attaining more generally valid systems of norms and values.

When a person is confronted with the factual world, contradictions abound between norms and values on the one hand and the factual events in the world on the other. In order to maintain meaning the human being is forced to work at resolving these contradictions, otherwise he or she would no longer know and understand what is right and what is wrong. However, in distinction to his or her knowledge of facts, this resolution of contradictions does not work in the direction of progressively moving knowledge closer to the world; rather, it works the other way around, of progressively moving the world closer to systems of norms and values. Thus, the human agent does not just *uncover* a hidden meaning in the world but intervenes in the world and *constructs* meaning in that world. This means that, in the endless process of resolution, the two kinds of contradictions work together. Resolving contradictions between norms and values necessitates the development of more generally valid systems of norms and values. There is a direction in their evolution that approaches ever higher levels of scope and validity. On the other hand, the resolution of contradictions between this evolving system of norms and values and the factual world necessitates moving the world so that it approaches this system in an endless process. Because it is in the nature of human thought to fail, to raise questions, and to proliferate alternatives, and in the nature of norms and values to exist separately from the factual processes of the world, this process is endless.

The philosophy of history is concerned with answering the questions of meaning in history. It is a secularized version of religious theodicy, which raised and answered the same question in religious terms (Weber, 1920–1921a/1972a: 244–54). According to such religious theodicy, the apparent inaccessibility of the world to human understanding and its apparent irrationality and injustice are resolved when they are seen in terms of religious salvation. The Hindu belief in retribution and reincarnation is a belief that explains away every particular injustice and irrationality by attributing rationality and justice to the whole system of endless retribution of actual behavior in later reincarnations. The Buddhist entering Nirvana has left behind all irrationality and injustice in the actual world. The Christian belief in salvation by Jesus' return to the world explains away actual irrationalities and injustices by the final destruction of this world and the construction of the new world.

The philosophy of history in Hegel's sense is a secularized version of religious theodicy, because it claims a factual evolution of the world toward a higher state of reason. Inasmuch as knowledge approaches the world and the world approaches an ever more generally valid system of norms and values, the reasonable becomes real and the real becomes reasonable, as he put it. According to Hegel this is a factual process leading to the final state, in which reason and reality are reconciled. His philosophy of history is a secularized theodicy, because it claims that this reconciliation is an inevitable final state of history leading to secular salvation.

In making that claim, Hegel undoubtedly went much too far. Nevertheless, there is a kernel of truth in his thought. It is that kernel which had been much more clearly stated by the more cautious Immanuel Kant (1724–1804), the other great German philosopher who preceded Hegel. According to Kant (1781/1964a, 1784a/1964b, 1784b/1964c, 1788/1964d, 1790/1964e, 1793/1964f, 1795/1964g, 1964h; for translation, see 1952a, 1952b, 1952c, 1972, 1974) there is a difference between moral reasoning and factual history that can never be finally resolved. Moral reasoning can serve only as a measure for evaluating and correcting behavior and thus the course of history. It is a necessary critical instrument that can be used in order to intervene in the world and to work toward bringing the world closer to the standards of morality. This, however, is a never-ending process, which always has to fight against all factual motives for erring from the standards of morality. Only insofar as moral reasoning is firmly institutionalized in society, for example, in institutions like the U.S. Supreme Court, can we assume that reality moves a step further toward reason and morality. It is this minimal type of Kantian critical philosophy of history that is still feasible, but not Hegel's secularized theodicy. Also still feasible is a metaphilosophy of history that explains the feasibility of a philosophy of history as set out in the preceding argumentation.

The argumentation I have outlined entails all three principles of Hegel's philosophy: history has meaning, proceeds in dialectical steps, and is the work of the objective spirit. History has meaning because it is guided by the human construction of meaning in procedures of forming theories about the world and in procedures of constructing systems of norms and values; one process brings reason closer to reality, the other, reality closer to reason. This procedure is a dialectical one. The moving force in history is the dialectics of resolving contradictions. The essentially human capability of imagining very different statements about the world and systems of norms and values leads inevitably to contradictions; the separation between thought and reality also inevitably leads to contradictions between the two. Contradictions, however, result in a loss of meaning, because the human mind is disoriented. This exerts pressure to seek the resolution of these contradictions by reaching higher levels of statements and systems of norms and values that are capable of embracing the truth and excluding the falsity of the contradictory statements, norms, and values. This is the process by which a more generally valid synthesis is formed on a higher level of knowledge reaching beyond the contradiction between thesis and antithesis. Thus, the intrinsic human capacity to raise questions and the intrinsic human need to understand the world and thus to construct meaning are the driving forces of the dialectical process. This is what is right about Hegel's dialectics.

However, what is wrong with Hegel's dialectics is his claim that the process will eventually come to a halt when the highest synthesis has been reached in absolute knowledge and in the subsumption of the contradictions of particularistic interests in civil society under the synthesis of a state committed to the general interest. According to Hegel, knowledge proceeds in a dialectical turn from the primitive unity of experience and reality in primitive thought to the separation between thought and reality in positive science, which is known as the state of alienation between consciousness and reality. Reality appears as something that is unfamiliar to the human consciousness. This is the antithesis of positivist thought to the thesis of primitive experience. Positivist thought is itself characterized by the contradiction between thought and reality. This double contradiction finds a resolution in the synthesis of the absolute knowledge of Hegel's philosophy, in which thought and reality are reconciled on a higher level. The corresponding dialectical process of human organization starts with the thesis of primitive unity and moves toward the antithesis of contradictory civil society based on the conflict between different interests, which is replaced by its subsumption under the general interest of the state.

What is wrong with Hegel's dialectics is its idea of convergence in the fulfillment of meaning in history. This convergence is untenable on the straightforward grounds of the following human properties: the ever-present chance of being wrong in one's statement and claims; the ever-present possibility of raising questions and criticizing claims to knowledge; and the unbridgeable gulf between thought and reality. These very human properties make dialectics a never-ending process, far from achieving its end in some absolute knowlege.

According to Hegel's third principle, the principle of idealism, the evolution of human society in history is a process that is guided by the logic of reasoning and meaning construction. In his terms the development of knowledge and society is the work of the objective spirit. Here, too, we find a secularized theodicy in Hegel's philosophy. Whereas in religion God directs the fate of the human race, it is the objective spirit that performs this work in Hegel's philosophy. This is certainly untenable, because we cannot assume that the objective spirit is an almighty power that eventually directs human history toward a reconciliation between reason and reality.

Nevertheless, there is a kernel of truth in Hegel's principle of idealism. He states in this principle that culture is a reality *sui generis* that develops according to its own laws and has effects on the development of human knowledge and society. The essential law of the cultural process is the dialectics of evolving internal and external contradictions, which call for attempts to resolve them by formulating more generally valid statements, norms, and values, and for attempts to bring knowledge closer to reality and bring reality closer to norms and values. Thus, there is a developmental logic of cultural systems and a pressure to bring cultural systems and reality closer to one another. For knowledge, this is a pressure to eliminate errors; for reality, this is a process of eliminating deviations from valid moral knowlege, as derived from the process of eliminating errors in such knowledge.

Whenever history is not just an outcome of coincidence but can be moved toward a closer consistency with moral ideas, it is because of this developmental logic of moral reasoning and because of the pressure it exerts for the transformation of society. However, the realization of moral ideas needs institutions that provide for the transmission of moral knowledge into society. The U.S. Supreme Court is such an important institution. Whenever we claim the chance for the human species to make history according to principles of reason, we presuppose the working of a developmental logic of reasoning, which proceeds according to its own criteria independently of individual decisions. This is the kernel of truth that we can take from

Hegel's idealism; it is a truth that Kant keeps within its outlined limits in his critical philosophy. However, because Marx learned more from Hegel than from Kant and falls into the fallacies of Hegel's untenable claims, it is necessary to discuss Hegel's philosophy in order to understand Marx (1843/1956, 1844/1968, 1845/1969, 1852/1960, 1859/1961, 1867/1962, 1885/1963b, 1894/1964; Marx and Engels 1846/1969, 1848/1959a; for translation, see Marx 1963a, 1967, 1971a, 1971b/1981; Marx and Engels 1947, 1959b).

Historical and Dialectical Materialism

Marx, in his own words, turns Hegel's philosophy of history and his dialectics upside down (Marx 1844/1968: 511–12, 571–74, 584–85); he turns Hegelian historical and dialectical idealism into Marxian historical and dialectical materialism. Whereas, in Hegel's terms, the historical and dialectical evolution of humankind is the work of the objective spirit, or in other words the work of a developmental logic of reason, in Marx's terms, it is the work of humankind's labor in order to make a living in relation to nature, or in other words the work of a developmental logic of how humankind copes with scarcity in order to secure the material preconditions of life. In this approach, Marx retains Hegel's dialectics and his notion of a philosophy of history, but replaces idealism with materialism. History is still not an accidental process but a development that has meaning and that leads to a final state of reconciliation between reason and reality, thereby undergoing a dialectical process starting from the primitive unity of humankind, evolving to a state of alienation, where humankind is in a contradictory state with nature and with itself. This calls for a new synthesis on a higher level (Marx and Engels, 1846/1969).

For Marx the original unity of primitive man entails an original communism, which he says was broken up by the expansion of economic production and trade, leading to the establishment of ancient, slave-holding society. The contradiction between slave and slave-holder is later replaced by a societal type that is slightly more integrated: feudalism. In this society master and servant are obligated to each other in bonds of support and service; nevertheless, the society is split into these two classes. The expansion of economic production and trade with the rise of industrial capitalism produces a society ruled by the laws guiding industrial capitalist production, distribution, and consumption, which is in a state of alienation and is split into the classes of capitalists and wage-laborers. The alienation and contradictions of this capitalist society are overcome by the new synthesis of communist society, where humankind controls the economic process and classes dissolve.

It is not the work of the objective spirit, as Hegel claimed, but the work of humankind toward materially securing its very existence that is the driving force behind its own dialectical and historical evolution. According to Marx (1859/1961, 1844/1968; Marx and Engels, 1846/1969), humankind produces and reproduces itself in material work. People necessarily relate to nature by developing technology, that is, productive forces, in order to extract resources from nature and to process them into products for securing human life. At the same time, people relate to each other in the production, distribution, and consumption of these products; they enter into relations of production, out of which productive forces are developed. Relations of production are the institutional framework of human labor, embracing property rights, class-relations, work organization, institutions of contract, trade relations, patent rights, and so on. Both the productive forces and the relations of production make up the economic substructure of society, which is the material basis on which the legal, political, and intellectual superstructure become established. As Marx states, the economic substructure determines the nature of the superstructure in the long run, though there are admittedly dialectical repercussions from the superstructure to the substructure. The superstructure provides institutional order and legitimation for the economic substructure. The development of the productive forces is the major innovative force in this historical process. They always develop faster than the relations of production. Therefore, at some time the relations of production will no longer encourage their development but will constrict it. This is the time when the productive forces come into contradiction with the relations of production. This contradiction initiates a period of crises resulting in a revolution that transforms the relations of production and with them the legal, political, and intellectual superstructure.

The technology of industrial capitalism partly developed within the traditional feudal relations of production and became a force able to break its constrictions and to establish free labor, free contract, and free disposal over one's private property as the new framework of capitalist society. However, the more capitalism develops on a large scale, the more private ownership becomes a fetter for technology developed on such a large scale that its further development needs collective organization. This is the contradiction in developed capitalism that leads to crisis and revolution, bringing about the collective organization of production, distribution, and consumption. This is the contradiction between productive forces and relations of production in developed capitalism.

Alienation in Simple Commodity Production

Embodied in this historical process is the process of alienation in work (Marx, 1844/1968; Marx and Engels, 1846/1969; see Mészáros, 1970; Israel, 1971). Marx distinguishes two levels of alienation: alienation in simple commodity production and alienation in extended commodity production. In general, alienation means that the human worker, by processing natural resources, creates an artificial world of productive forces and relations of production, which breaks up his or her original primitive unity with nature where he or she lived simply from the products of nature but without intervening in nature. In that original state of primitive society, people not only live in unison with nature but also share a primitive unity with each other. They commonly share production, distribution, and consumption. The more humankind develops technology, the more the economic process becomes an artificial world in itself. Division of labor and, along with it, trade and the exchange of products emerge. In this process human beings are separated both from nature and from each other and lose power over their production, distribution, and consumption of products, which now proceed according to their own laws. This is a threefold process of alienation from nature, one's fellows, and the products of one's labor. Productive forces, relations of production, and one's fellows appear as strange, independent powers. This process of alienation proceeds with the development of commodity production.

On the level of simple commodity production (Marx, 1867/1962: 161–66), independent owners of commodities have to enter into exchange, because the division of labor makes their living dependent on exchange. Whereas in primitive production and consumption the value of a product is defined by its utility for satisfying one's needs, in processes of exchange a separation between a commodity's value in use and its value in exchange emerges. The commodities are exchanged according to the laws of the market, not according to the use-value for individual purchasers and not according to their needs. The market is blind with regard to the needs of single purchasers. Whether one is very much or very little in need of a product does not change its price, because price is based on exchange value.

What then is the basis of that exchange value? According to Marx (1867/1962: 49–160), the utility of a commodity for individual purchasers does not explain the relative stability of prices regardless of the needs of different purchasers: Everybody has to pay the same price. What he provides as an explanation is the labor theory of value, which he draws from the British political economist David Ricardo. According to Marx's labor theory of value, it is the amount of time needed on the average to produce a commodity, at a certain level of technological development in a society that determines its exchange value. This is always the same throughout society, regardless of the different needs of individual purchasers, and explains the relative stability of this value even though needs vary greatly.

In relating the exchange value of commodities to labor-time embodied in the products, all commodities can be compared according to a single standard measure. We can say, for example, that one jacket has the value of 20 yards of linen; in this case, the jacket appears in what is termed the value-form, while the linen is in the equivalent form, serving as an expression of the jacket's value. The emergence of money makes one commodity, namely money, the universally used equivalent form for expressing the value of any commodity. Money allows an enormous expansion of economic production, distribution, and consumption by fulfilling three functions: it serves as (1) a measure of value, (2) a means of payment, and (3) a store of value.

Commodities are exchanged according to the law of commodity production. The exchange of products can no longer be determined by the needs of individual human beings; it is simply inaccessible to the individual variation of needs and particularly inaccessible to need for help. Commodity exchange proceeds according to its own laws, not according to individual needs or moral standards. In expanding commodity production humankind has built up a system of economic production, distribution, and consumption that proceeds according to its own laws and establishes a power over humankind rather than being mastered by humankind itself. Humankind has lost control of its economic production and reproduction and instead is controlled by that process. In his earlier writings, partly produced with Friedrich Engels, Marx calls this alienation resulting from the division of labor, without explaining that process by the so-called contradiction between the use value and exchange value of commodities. Marx developed the latter explanation after his extensive study of British political economy. He then no longer made systematic use of the Hegelian notion of alienation, but he meant the same when he spoke of "commodity fetishism" (Marx, 1867/1962: 85–98). Humankind, in the processes of economic production and reproduction, establishes a system that exerts a power over people similar to that of a fetish, which itself is the product of religious thought. Humankind has forgotten that these powers are the products of its own activity.

Alienation in Extended Commodity Production

In simple commodity production the level of production remains affiliated with the traditional standard of living of people according to their membership in a particular estate in society. The artisan produces as much as he or she has to in order to get the money needed to buy all the commodities that correspond to his or her traditional standard of living. Artisans themselves regulate the area in which they are entitled to sell their products via a system of guilds. Master and servant are mutually obliged to provide service and support. Production, distribution, and consumption proceed in the series: commodity → money → commodity; the producer sells his or her products on the market and receives money to buy those products he or she needs according to his or her standard of living.

This traditional regulation of commodity production radically changes with the establishment of extended commodity production, beginning with major changes, called original accumulation by Marx (1867/1962: 161–91, 741–88). Here, money is turned into capital; production and selling are freed from traditional constraints. There is no guild to restrict competition, no traditional constraint on standards of living, and no mutual bond between master and servant. The owner of the means of production is free to do as he or she likes with his or her property. Masses of peasants are expropriated, stripped of any means of production, and provide the labor power for industrial capitalism. The worker no longer has a bond with a master but has to sell his or her labor power on the labor market. Labor power itself becomes a commodity. Freed from any constrictions, the production process becomes an aim in itself, namely the expansion of production and the realization of its results in further increasing production.

The agent of this process is no longer the traditional artisan or manufacturer working in order to uphold a traditional standard of living but the capitalist who works for nothing but profit. The capitalist starts with a certain amount of money, buys resources, machines, and labor power as commodities, and processes them into a commodity, which he or she sells on the market in return for money. The process begins with money, turns that into comodities, and turns them back into money. This process would be meaningless if the result were not a growth of money extracted from that process. Making more money than was originally invested in the production process becomes the single aim of capitalist production. This is profit-seeking as the central element of capitalist production involving the endless accumulation of capital as a process that takes place for its own sake.

What are the specific conditions that allow the accumulation of capital according to Marx (1867/1962: 192–355, 531–56, 591–740)? Here, he makes use of his labor theory of value in a very specific sense. The difference between the exchange value and the use value of labor power as a commodity becomes the basis for the exploitation of workers and for the accumulation of capital. The value of labor power is the time needed to produce all those commodities, including food, clothing, housing, and the education of children, which are needed to reproduce the workers' and their offsprings' labor power at a certain level of production in society. This may require, say, eight hours' work per day. The capitalist buys a worker's labor power at this price. However, he or she may make use of the worker's labor power for twelve hours a day. The extra four hours then represent surplus labor provided by the worker. This is the source of the capitalist's surplus. He or she can increase this surplus by increasing the number of hours worked per day, which is absolute surplus, or by expanding productivity through technological rationalization, which is relative surplus. The capitalist invests money for resources, machines, and labor power and receives money on the market for all these investments plus the commodities produced during the four hours of surplus labor. This difference between invested capital and realized capital on the market is profit. Thus, the accumulation of capital results from the exploitation of the worker in those four hours of surplus labor. This appears to be just in terms of the system of commodity production, because the worker is paid for the exchange value of his or her labor power.

The Contradictions and Crises of Capitalist Development

This process of accumulation of capital is marked by a double contradiction. First, there is the contradiction between societal, cooperative, collective production and private appropriation of profit, which is paralleled by the conflict between wage laborers and capitalists. This double contradiction contains the alienation of wage labor and capital. On the one hand, ever more privately appropriated capital is accumulated, which becomes concentrated in ever fewer hands, namely, large-scale corporations, involving a centralization of the production process. On the other hand, the wage-laborer is impoverished at least relatively, because he or she can never earn beyond the limits of his or her reproduction costs within this system of commodity production. Labor produces huge amounts of capital, yet this manifests itself as an alien power exploiting and constraining it. Society is split into the two antagonistic classes — capitalists and wage laborers. Alienation reaches its highest level.

The tendency toward sharpening the antagonism between wage-labor and capital is accompanied by temporary crises of overproduction and the resulting destruction of capital and a tendency toward falling profit rates, leading to a slow-down in investment. The capitalist enterprise is damned to make ever better use of its invested capital by increasing productivity via technological rationalization. This, however, steadily increases the part played by "constant" capital invested in machines and decreases the part played by "variable" capital invested in labor power. However, because labor power is the only source of surplus, the corresponding rate of profit goes down. This leads to a slow-down in investment and in technological progress. On the other hand, replacing labor power by machines builds up an industrial reserve army that contributes to keeping down the price of labor power but also keeps down the purchasing power of the working population. Production, though, tends to increase, and because of this, periodical overproduction occurs, leading to the collapse of capitalist enterprises and to destruction of capital. Together with the slowing down of technological progress, this contributes to the breakdown of capitalism.

This truly fateful process is accompanied by the intensification of class struggle resulting from the parallel structural contradiction between collective production and private appropriation of profit. The structural contradiction is the origin of capitalism's rational organization of the single enterprise but irrational organization of the whole economy, leaving the economy to the chaotic struggle in the market place. This is the origin of capitalism's fateful development toward ever more acute crises. The structural contradiction, however, finds a specific expression in class antagonism between labor and capital, making labor the revolutionary force that takes the lead in overthrowing a capitalism plagued by ever more severe crises. In this process the centralization of production binds ever broader masses of workers together and encourages their class communication, organization, and class consciousness, turning a pure category of a class "in itself" into the real community of a class "in and for itself," which is conscious of its position and role in society.

In this process, the proletariat becomes the bearer of reason in history, overthrowing the ailing capitalist system in order to build a new society of communism in which economic production, distribution, and consumption are organized by society as a collective, according to proper plans and on a new level of technology, thus resolving the contradiction between collective production and private appropriation of products and the antagonism between classes. Capitalism's steps toward centralization of production and concentration of capital make it easier to fully turn the economic process into a rational collective organization.

Summary

Historical and Dialectical Materialism

1. The more humankind engages in economic production, distribution, and consumption through the input of labor, the more humankind will reproduce itself and the more it will produce forces and relations of production as an artificial world between itself and nature, breaking up its primitive unity with nature and alienating people from nature, from the economic process, and from themselves.
2. The more the economic substructure of productive forces and relations develops, the more a legal, political, and intellectual superstructure will evolve from that substructure, providing institutional order and cultural legitimation of the economic substructure.
3. The greater the tendency of productive forces to develop faster than the productive relations and the more generally they do so, the more the productive relations change from promoting to constraining their development, leading to a contradiction between productive forces and productive relations.

4. The more the contradiction between productive forces and productive relations sharpens and the more it is paralleled by the antagonism of classes, the more a revolutionary epoch will develop, leading to a transformation of the economic substructure and, at whatever rate of change, to the transformation of the corresponding superstructures.

Capitalist Development

5. The more primitive collective organization of the economic process is replaced by simple commodity production, the more the economic process operates according to its own laws, independently of subjective needs and moral claims, and exerts an alien power on people, but nevertheless remains regulated by traditional constraints.
6. The more extended commodity production is established, the more capital accumulation will guide the economic process as an aim for its own sake.
7. The more capital accumulation becomes an aim for its own sake and is accompanied by the liberation of the economic process from traditional constrictions, making the free use of private property, free labor, and free trade into the basic institutions, the more capital accumulation will result from the difference between the exchange value and use value of labor power and the difference between necessary and surplus labor, which constitute the source of absolute and relative surplus and hence profit.
8. The more capital accumulation proceeds, the more the contradiction between collective production and private appropriation of profit will sharpen.
9. The more the contradiction between collective production and private appropriation of profit sharpens, the more the constraint of the self-realization of capital will enforce technological rationalization.
10. The more technological rationalization advances, the more the constant and unproductive capital of machines will increase and the variable and productive capital of labor power will decrease.
11. The more variable capital decreases relative to constant capital, the more the profit rate will go down.
12. The more the profit rate goes down, the more crises of investment and technological progress will occur.
13. The more variable capital decreases, the greater will be the industrial reserve army.
14. The more capital accumulation is pushed forward, thus leading to increased production, and the larger the industrial reserve army grows, the more the gap will increase between production and consumption involving periodic overproduction.

15. The more overproduction occurs, the more capitalist enterprises will collapse and the more capital will be destroyed.
16. The more capital accumulation develops, the more privately appropriated masses of capital will abound and the more the worker will become relatively impoverished.
17. The more privately appropriated masses of capital abound and the more the workers become impoverished, the more class antagonism between workers and capitalists will sharpen.
18. The more capital is accumulated, the more capital will be concentrated in ever fewer hands and the more production will be centralized and collectively organized on a large scale.
19. The more production is centralized and collectively organized on a large scale, the more the communication, organization, and class consciousness of the workers will increase and the more the collective organization of production and appropriation of products will become possible.
20. The more crises of investment and technological progress increase in severity, capitalist enterprises collapse (with the resulting destruction of capital), class antagonism sharpens, workers' communication, organization, and class consciousness expands, and the collective organization of production and appropriation of products is made possible, the more likely it will be that capitalism breaks down in a revolution to be replaced by the collective organization of production and appropriation of products in a classless communist society, in which humankind again holds control over the economic process and its fate.

Critical Assessment

Marx is certainly right when he criticizes Hegel's idealist notion of humankind's evolution and when he turns our attention to the processes of the material production and reproduction of human life. The technology of productive forces in particular is a paramount dynamic force that permanently precipitates change in the organization, that is, in the relations of production, and in the corresponding institutional and cultural framework. It is true that technological innovation is faster than institutional change and that technological development comes into contradiction with the institutional framework the faster it develops. This calls for a new correspondence between technology and institutional order, whether this be the regaining of institutional control over technology or a change in institutions in order to promote technological development.

The greater rapidity of technological innovation compared to the innovation of the institutional framework thus is a cause of periodic contradictions calling for a realignment of technology and institutional order. This structural contradiction becomes even more virulent the more it is paralleled by conflict between classes. In pointing to this process Marx reveals a major dynamic force in historical development. This is the true element in his historical and dialectical materialism.

However, his argument goes wrong the more he seeks to replace Hegel's idealistic philosophy of history by a materialistic philosophy of history. Here he falls into the trap of claiming meaning for a naturalistic process determined only by material dynamic forces. Why should this technological dynamics lead to a final state of reconciliation between reason and reality? Why should it proceed in a reasonable way at all? Whereas Hegel consistently claims that the developmental logic of reason moves toward higher levels of reconciliation between reason and reality the more it is the driving force in history, Marx claims such a reasonable logic for the material forces in the economic process, which is a contradiction in itself.

According to Marx, the economic forces develop a chaotic dynamism, so that they do not lead society consistently toward a specific end. Nevertheless, he claims such a direction for the historical process. This contradiction in his theory is the sacrifice he has to make for turning Hegel's idealistic philosophy of history into a materialistic one, thereby attributing meaning to meaningless phenomena. Or, in other words, Marx retains elements of Hegel's idealism without solving the corresponding problems. Otherwise he would have to assign procedures of rational argumentation and discourse a much more crucial status in historical development than that of an appendix to the economic substructure of society. This is the reason why he cannot answer the question of the conditions under which human society would develop in the direction of bringing reason and reality closer to each other. Rather than answering this question, he claims that such a closing of the gap between reason and reality is a naturalistic process of historical development. Marx, who was trained in the philosophy of German idealism but turned to British political economy while he was studying in the British Museum, was not able to combine these two opposing systems of thought in a consistent and tenable way.

What is right and what is wrong with Marx's general theory of historical and dialectical materialism is also right or wrong with his particular theory of capitalist development. He points out the dynamics of commodity production and capital accumulation, demonstrating how they establish an economic process that proceeds according to its own laws and exerts a constraining power on humankind, independent of and contrary to needs and moral standards. He shows how production becomes a process for its own sake and involves crises of overproduction, capital destruction, technological stagnation, class antagonism, concentration of capital, and centralization of production as capitalist accumulation expands and covers the whole of society and finally the world in a process in which everything is "commodified." These are major insights into the essential dynamics of capitalism.

However, some of his specific explanations are flawed and have to be replaced by more tenable explanations. Thus we can explain the working of market exchange and its inaccessibility to subjective variations of needs and moral claims much better by the laws of supply and demand than by Marx's labor theory of value. We also have to call Marx's law of the tendency toward a falling profit rate into question, because increasing productivity resulting from technological rationalization increases *relative* surplus, which therefore works against falling profit rates. In both cases, Marx is inclined to use the labor theory of value to claim that the worker alone is the source of capital accumulation. His labor theory of value functions as a moral legitimation for claiming the proletariat's historical mission in turning the private appropriation of profit into the collective appropriation of products. These are, however, minor defects in Marx's theory of capitalist development.

More important defects begin with Marx's claim that he predicted the breakdown of capitalism and its transformation to communism. This is an attempt to slip a particular theory of the inner dynamics of capitalist production and appropriation of profits into the shoes of a philosophy of history that are much too big for it. Nothing allows us to attribute such a developmental logic to dynamic forces that have no meaning in themselves. The explanatory and predictive value of Marx's theory has been tremendously contradicted by the actual development of modern society, whether in the context of a capitalist or a socialist economy. The reason is a lack of concern for the independent working of noneconomic forces. Marx commits the mistake of turning an analytical construction of the working of economic forces into an empirical factual prediction based on that economic process and treating all other phenomena as dependent upon it. This is what gave rise to the failure of the Marxist project, both in theory and in practice.

The error of disregarding the working of noneconomic forces begins with Marx's account of original accumulation as the starting point of capitalist development. The original accumulation of capital in the process of expropriating peasants and of commercializing agriculture in England undoubtedly contributed to the economic beginnings of capitalism. However, this is only one factor in a much more complex process. Without the formation of strong nation states in Europe, without the backing of trade and industry by a system of civil law, and without the establishment of the work-ethic by Puritanism, no capitalism would have developed in Europe. Because such a unique convergence of different causes came about, Europe became the center of capitalist development. Outside of Europe all the material preconditions also existed, but not the legal, political, associational, and cultural preconditions. Therefore, no rational capitalism emerged outside Europe.

What is true for the emergence of capitalism holds true for its development. It is inseparably interrelated with different noneconomic institutions in a very complex way and not only shapes these institutions by its dynamics but also is framed by these institutions. Political intervention, the labor movement, the rise of the welfare state, the broadening of education, the rise of cultural standards of living, the working of the legal system in controlling capitalism, and the expansion of citizenship rights all exerted their own influence on capitalist development so that it did not completely correspond to Marx's derivation from its internal dynamics. Class compromise, rising standards of living, the broadening of education, a progressive shift from manufacturing to service industries, political guidance of the economy, and the welfare system have brought forth a complex system that no longer corresponds to the picture of capitalism drawn by Marx.

On the other hand, the failure of Marxism in the socialist societies of the Soviet and Chinese types indicates the defects of Marxism with regard to its assumptions about resolving the contradictions of capitalism by socialism and, later on, by communism. The irrationalities produced by the market in capitalist societies, that is, by private appropriation of products leading to private and uncoordinated decisions on investments, are minor ones compared to the irrationalities of socialist production involving technological stagnation, the lack of coordination and flexibility, permanent crises of supply, and a chronically low level of availability for many important goods. The populations of these societies have long since lost their confidence in the "rationality" of that system.

The flaw in Marxist theory that is responsible for these practical defects is its lack of concern for the specific contributions of specific institutions to the overall working of society in a complex system of interrelated institutions. Replacing a capitalist economy with a state-regulated socialist economy leads to a society that is ruled by an authoritarian state with no access to the benefits of a capitalist economy. Such a replacement replaces not only the capitalist economy as such but also its interrelationships with a democratic state, a welfare system, an educational system, and a legal system, which make up a complex set of interrelated institutions fulfilling specific functions that cannot all be carried out by one institutional synthesis. The socialist authoritarian state is the last embodiment of the Hegelian dream of synthesis. For the population of countries with this system the dream has long since turned into a nightmare. The perversion of Marxist social theory into a political ideology is finally due to Marx's claim that there is a unity of theory and praxis (see Mannheim, 1936). Only their differentiation will allow Marxian social theory to regain the respected status in the spectrum of theories that it truly deserves.

Further Developments

Marx's theory has stimulated a large number of interpretations and Marxisms of various kinds according to the divergent traditions of thought that influenced Marx. The first of these is Marxist political economy, which was established in orthodox form in the Soviet Union. In a more sophisticated form it developed particularly in Anglo-Saxon Marxism (Anderson, 1974; Baran and Sweezy, 1966; Burawoy, 1979; Wallerstein, 1974, 1979, 1984; Roemer, 1982). Lenin (1917, 1920, 1927, 1955) laid the foundations for orthodox Marxism. In contrast to Lenin, the Marxist Revisionism of Kautsky (1910, 1918, 1922, 1927) and Bernstein (1906, 1907, 1969) called the economic determinism of the orthodoxy into question and attributed a much more vital role to the democratic state in reforming capitalism and moving it closer toward the goal of socialism (Bryan S. Turner, 1986). The Hungarian Marxist Georg Lukács (1923/1968; for translation, see 1971) turned back to the Hegelian dialectics in dealing with phenomena like the fetishism of commodities and class consciousness. He arrived at a complex view of the dialectical relationship between economy, politics, social structure, and cultural ideas. The Italian Marxist Antonio Gramsci (1932/1975, 1971) did the same when he developed his notion of hegemony as cultural leadership exercised by the ruling class. The second tradition is Marxist class conflict theory, which is most influential in Anglo-Saxon and Scandinavian Marxism. It concentrates on class struggle and assigns the state a special role on the site of this conflict (Miliband, 1982; Rex, 1981; Elster, 1985). The structuralist version of Marxist class conflict theory is the domain of French Marxism (Althusser, 1965; Poulantzas, 1968; Bourdieu, 1979). The third form of interpretation is Marxist praxis philosophy, which became prominent in the regime-critical Marxism of Yugoslavia and Hungary (Djilas, 1957; Markovic, 1968, 1979; Stojanovic, 1973; Heller, 1976) and also in reference to American pragmatism (Bernstein, 1971, 1985; Joas, 1980; Honneth and Joas, 1980; Kilminster, 1979) and French structuralism (Castoriadis, 1987). The fourth is Marxist critical theory, which was created by the so-called Frankfurt school and revitalized the hermeneutic and Hegelian elements in Marxian theory (Adorno, 1966/1973a; Horkheimer and Adorno, 1947; Habermas, 1981; Offe, 1972, 1984).

PART THREE

The Politics of Social Action

SIX

THE DYNAMICS OF POWER SYSTEMS: VILFREDO PARETO

VILFREDO PARETO was born in Paris in 1848 to a French mother and an Italian father, a marquis. He died in 1923. Pareto was bilingual and lived his life in Italy and in French-speaking Switzerland. He studied mathematics, physics, and engineering sciences at the University of Turin, worked as an engineer, but became more and more attracted by political matters and economics. In 1893 he was appointed to a chair in political economy at the University of Lausanne, from which he retired finally in 1911. Pareto's economic writing is still a fundamental building block of modern economics. Most famous is "Pareto's law of income distribution." According to Pareto, an optimum of income distribution exists either when no shift of income is possible that will make *everyone* better off or when those who would gain by such a shift are unable to compensate the losers sufficiently to repair their situation while still enhancing their own.

While he was teaching at Lausanne, Pareto turned more and more to sociology. He devoted most of his time to writing his great work, *The Mind and Society: A Treatise on General Sociology*, a book 2000 pages long, which was published in Italian in 1916. This book is one of sociology's classic works, though it has been much less influential than the works of Marx, Durkheim, and Weber for several reasons: the formal character of the book, its length, and the fact that it is filled with many different insights from different disciplines and with many different formalizations. Also, it is written in the language of natural science, which is not very attractive to the hermeneutic currents in social science. Another reason is that Pareto is thought to have an elitist view of society, which provokes rejection from the standpoint of humanitarian motives (Pareto, 1901, 1902–1903, 1916, 1921; for a translation, see Pareto, 1917–1919, 1935, 1968).

The Italian Tradition of Machiavellism

Of the classical founders of sociology, it was Vilfredo Pareto who placed in the foreground the dynamics of gaining and losing power as a determining force of social development. It is with Pareto's work that we get the best insight into the argumentation in terms of power dynamics of a sociological theory.

The study of society in terms of conflict and power politics was established in the history of Western thought by the Italian Renaissance political analyst Niccolo Machiavelli (1469–1527). Italy was not a unified society until the 1860s. Its history is framed by the permanent struggles between the princes of small states, between city states, and between the princedoms and the city states. War, conquest, and defeat were the common experience for centuries.

This is the social context in which Machiavelli's political theory emerged and to which it was applied. There was no firmly established organic social order, no common belief, no complementary exchange on which social life could rely. Any established order was based on the intelligent use of power and was always in danger of being displaced by some external or internal enemy. In his book *The Prince* (1532/1979), Machiavelli gives an analysis of various situations in terms of what would be the best strategy and tactics in order to maintain power or to gain it by overthrowing another set of forces. He asks, for example: How should the divided parties be treated in a city a prince has just conquered — should one reconcile them, collaborate with one, or do away with both of them? How should a prince treat a victorious army leader? How can a conspiracy of citizens be made successful? And, how can a prince guard against such a conspiracy?

Machiavelli studies a great number of such situations in order to find out which strategy by a given actor will have which consequences. His book *The Discourses* (1531/1984), which he wrote at the same time and after *The Prince*, also entails a lot of such strategic analyses of political situations. Machiavelli always starts with the assumption that two or more actors come into conflict with each other because they have mutually exclusive goals, mostly aimed at maintaining or winning power positions; he also assumes that they are willing to apply any means available in order to attain their goals. Machiavelli points out which strategy will have which effects for one or the other party's chances of maintaining or winning power — like an analysis of possible strategies for chess players in certain situations.

Machiavelli distinguishes two basic qualities of actors in the political game: *virtù* and *fortuna*. *Virtù* is the capacity of an actor to act powerfully on the basis of some firm principles that enhance his or her reputation with followers, other people, and opponents. *Fortuna* is fate, or fortune. A successful political actor needs both of these or at least some minor compensations like courage to make up for *virtù* or luck alone.

Machiavelli enquires into the successful strategies for establishing power firmly in different situations: in cases of inherited power, in states founded as a result of annexation, in states with their own laws before their conquest by an external power, in cases of conquest by one's own weapons and by *virtù*, in cases of conquest by other parties' weapons and *fortuna*, when a prince comes to power by criminal means, when the prince is a popular leader, and when the state is ruled by religious leaders. He also analyzes how a prince should relate to followers, other people, and opponents: how to relate to troops and mercenaries, to auxiliary, and to one's own armies, how to perform one's military duties, when to be generous or mean, when to be cruel or lenient, whether it is better to be loved or to be feared, how far one should keep one's word, the necessity to avoid hate and scorn, the usefulness of fortifications, how to acquire a good reputation, how to treat secret ministers, how to safeguard against flatterers, why the princes have lost power in Italy, what is brought about by *fortuna*, and how to safeguard against it. These are the many situations of the power game for which Machiavelli provides strategies for successfully winning and maintaining power.

One can imagine that the continued splitting of Italy into small states and city states with a history of permanent conquest and loss of power and also submission to foreign powers contributed to the relevance of Machiavelli's thought for centuries. This was still true for the nineteenth century when Pareto's thought took shape: It is borne out particularly by Gaetano Mosca, who published his political theory of the interrelationship between the ruling and the ruled classes in 1884, well before Pareto published his theory of the circulation of elites (Mosca, 1884). Mosca was outraged that Pareto had stolen his idea, but Pareto put the theory of the struggle between ruling and opposing elites and their relation to the masses on more general ground and gave a more precise analysis.

The Machiavellian tradition is most apparent in Pareto's approach. Conflict and power are the central phenomena that determine what goes on in social life. However, Pareto went beyond the original boundaries of Machiavellian thought, due to the influence of Anglo-Saxon economic theory and Darwinist evolutionism as represented by Herbert Spencer, and of French rationalist positivism as represented by Claude-Henri de Saint-Simon and by Auguste Comte. The French tradition made Pareto's work much more systematic than allowed by the Machiavellian analysis of innumerable situations, and it opened his work to the possibility of incorporating the function of sentiments and solidarity bonds for the maintenance of social structure and for collective action. The Anglo-Saxon tradition opened his eyes to the dynamics of differentiation, though he finally rejected the feasibility of a Darwinist theory of social development and its linking to the idea of progress. In Pareto's view of permanent power struggle there was no chance for teleological progress by society to higher levels of morality, but only the replacement of one ruling elite by another. Though Pareto incorporated elements of French organic structuralism and Anglo-Saxon economism, the power struggle remained the predominating force in history and shaped his view of the elements of sentiments and solidarity and of the economic division of labor. He did not fully give those elements a status and logic in their own right.

Methodology

As a trained physicist and a working political economist, Pareto was very much committed to the ideals of positive science, which he called logico-experimental science (Pareto, 1916; translation 1917–1919, 1935: chs. 2, 3). The natural sciences provided the model for his understanding of sociology. According to this view, sociology has to proceed from facts via induction to general analytically abstracted laws, which then have to be proved again by facts. Precise definition of concepts, analytical separation of items under investigation from concrete reality, the formulation of general laws, and their confirmation by the facts are the main tasks of a logico-experimental science.

Logical and Nonlogical Action

Pareto's entrance to sociological analysis is the differentiation between logical and nonlogical conduct (Pareto, 1916; translation 1917–1919, 1935: chs. 2, 3). In a general sense, the former conforms to the standards of logico-experimental science, whereas the latter does not. In logical conduct the actors apply theories that are or can be proved according to the standards of logico-experimental science; in nonlogical conduct actors apply theories that cannot be proved according to these standards. An engineer who constructs a machine according to the laws of physics confirmed by physical science acts logically. He or she relates the means to an end logically according to objectively validated knowledge. His or her subjective view coincides with the objective view of any observer who would represent the accumulated knowledge of science. The Greek sailors who offered a sacrifice to Poseidon in order to have a safe voyage were convinced of the effective relationship between the sacrifice and a safe voyage and the other way around. Thus, in their subjective view, they performed a logical action, but this cannot be proved from the viewpoint of an objective observer who applies today's scientific knowledge. From the objective scientific point of view it is nonlogical in character.

Logical action does not by any means fill the greater part of human conduct. It is mostly restricted to the areas of rational economic calculation and scientific investigation. The greater part of human conduct is nonlogical in character. Because the two are not concrete entities but analytical aspects of concrete action we can even say that every single action entails logical and nonlogical elements. As Pareto puts it, there is no society that rests exclusively on reason. The entrepreneur's calculation of profit may be based purely on scientifically proved knowledge; his or her devotion to making a profit, however, does not fit this requirement. It may be motivated by a religious belief in proving oneself to be righteous or by a belief in being elected to lead other people. These beliefs may be wrong or may be just unprovable according to the methods of logico-experimental science.

Last but not least, every action is guided not only by knowledge, scientifically adequate or inadequate, but also by ultimate ends that are not themselves related as means to further ends. The entrepreneur's devotion to religious salvation or to leadership may be ends in themselves. Why he or she has chosen these ends cannot be proved by any logical relationship to other ends. Thus, they lack scientific proof. The entrepreneurs' devotion to religion or leadership, therefore, introduces a nonlogical element into his or her conduct. We can say that any action needs such an orientation to an ultimate end; otherwise, it would not have a direction that made it distinct from any other action. Thus, every action needs nonlogical elements in order to really take place. Nonlogical action performs a useful function for the individual and for society, namely, a function of orienting action to individual and common ends. It is, therefore, important to study its internal structure, its preconditions, and its consequences.

As Pareto states, there is an unfortunate tendency in philosophy and the social sciences to deny the importance of nonlogical action. This has led to attempts at explaining away its occurrence or importance and rationalizing nonlogical actions, either by denying their occurrence or by giving seemingly rational grounds for them, or by closing them out from investigation because they have no relation to progress.

Nonlogical action is seldom acknowledged as such but is backed up by grounds of justification. It is usually accompanied by enormous efforts to give reasonable grounds for that action (Pareto, 1916; translation 1917–1919, 1935: ch. 4). Many such attempts refer to certain entities that transcend experience and empirical observation. References to God, reason, a natural order, natural rights, morality, and justice are of this nature. They describe either entities that cannot be observed or that are so loosely defined that everybody can understand them in a different way. Because God is not an observable entity we do not know whether He has given certain commands. Commitment to such commands cannot be proved as right behavior in the name of God by the methods of logico-experimental science. Nevertheless, it is a common justification of human conduct that is nonlogical in character. Terms like *nature, natural order, natural rights, reason, morality,* and *justice* are so loosely defined that everything can be justified in their name. No precise correspondence between them and any specific action can be formulated. Thus, no claim at all of an action to represent these values can be proved as scientifically correct.

The triumph of science has outdated the traditional justifications of nonlogical action by references to entities that transcend experience. This does not mean, however, that nonlogical action has been left to itself. Attempts at justifying nonlogical action are as effective as before. Their nature has changed. They now appear in the guise of logico-experimental science. However, because nonlogical action cannot be proved by real science, these justifications work as pseudo-scientific theories (Pareto, 1916; translation 1917–1919, 1935: ch. 5). The theories of Liberalism, Marxism, and Social Darwinism are most influential in determining the actions of historical actors, of the bourgeoisie and the working class, and they work very much in the way of pseudo-scientific theories. They provide justifications for the commitment to capitalism or socialism in terms of theories that argue scientifically but cannot be completely proved by scientific methods. They entail partly scientifically proved statements but combine them with disproved statements and also with unprovable statements. Thus, the commitment to capitalism or socialism is not really proved by scientific theories; it is therefore nonlogical in character. This does not mean, however, that such theories are useless. They are useful for human conduct and society because they bundle human beings together under a common faith, give guidance to their actions, and lead societal development toward common ends. They function as ideologies in the struggle of developing society. Without such ideologies society would lose guidance and direction and would be helplessly exposed to situationally varying external selection. Ideologies thus fulfill a necessary function for society.

Sentiments, Residues, and Derivations

Pareto, then, is interested in the roots of nonlogical conduct. Such conduct is characterized by a stable commitment to certain ends that cannot come from logico-experimental scientific knowledge. Such knowledge tells us what is so and why that is so but cannot tell us what we should do. It leaves us without guidance and direction. But what are the elements that give our action a stable commitment to certain ends? Pareto's answer connects the organic substrata of the individual with the collective organization of social life and its cultural legitimation: sentiments, residues, and derivations (Pareto, 1916; translation 1917–1919, 1935: chs. 6–11). Pareto says that nonlogical action is guided by theories that are composed of a stable element and a varying element. The stable element is called a residue; the variable element is called a derivation. The residue is, in turn, linked to sentiments; it is a manifestation of sentiment. An example of a residue is the Christian commitment to righteous behavior that resists temptation. The Baptists place the baptism of adults in the center of their religious rituals. The effect of this ritual is to strengthen the commitment to righteous conduct in the name of Jesus Christ. This is the collective origin of the residue of righteous Baptist conduct. The involvement of the human body in this ritual stimulates the individual's sentiments. The Baptist has a morally clean feeling after the ceremony. He or she feels good in behaving righteously and bad in behaving sinfully. Observing righteous behavior stimulates his or her approval; observing sinful behavior stimulates his or her disgust. This is the interrelationship between sentiments and residue. The sentiment is the feeling of good and bad, approval and disgust; the residue is the commitment to righteous behavior.

Where is the derivation involved in this nonlogical action? It is the explanation the Baptist applies in legitimating the specific actions in the ceremony and in legitimating the residue. The Baptist says that the water into which he or she is immersed has a morally cleansing effect. This legitimates the special conduct in the ceremony. And the Baptist says that God wants us to obey His commands. This is his or her legitimation of the residue of righteous behavior. These derivations are variable in the sense that there can be many different devices applied in rituals aiming at a moral cleansing of the soul besides immersing oneself in water, for example, anointing the body with oil or some other substances, and many different grounds for righteous behavior besides God, for example, reason or the order of nature.

This is why the residue of righteous conduct, the general form of the cleansing ritual, and the corresponding sentiment of moral approval and disgust are considered as stable, and the derivation giving grounds for a residue and a specific cleansing ritual as varying in character. Sentiments, residues, and derivations are interlinked in this way in every nonlogical action.

Sentiments, residues, and derivations and their interlinkage perform important functions for society (Pareto, 1916; translation 1917–1919, 1935: ch. 11). Residues commit the individual to specific actions and ends. Inasmuch as they have origins in common rituals they direct action to common ends. Sentiments provide organically rooted motivation of the individual to act in specific ways. Inasmuch as they are linked to residues rooted in common rituals, sentiments motivate action that contributes to common ends. Derivations give residues and sentiments and therewith the commitment to specific ends and the motivation to realize them a broader cultural legitimation and an adaptation to different situations. Without the assistance of derivations, residues would degenerate into blind conduct; without support from sentiments, they would ossify into empty ceremonies.

Pareto distinguishes six classes of residues and four classes of derivations. The classes of residues are the following:

1. Instinct for combinations. This residue encourages innovation. It is the basis of skepticism and speculative economic entrepreneurship.
2. Group-persistences (persistence of aggregates). This residue commits the individual to social relationships, to family, groups, social class, and places, to values, norms, and persons. It is the basis of faith and a rentier-mentality in economic activity.
3. Need for expressing sentiments by external acts (activity, self-expression). This residue places the expression of the self at the center of human activity.
4. Residues connected with sociality. These residues bind the individual to society via conformity, pity, and repugnance of suffering, self-sacrifice for the good of others, and concern for superiors, inferiors, and the group.
5. Integrity of the individual and his or her appurtenances. This residue secures the dignity of the individual.
6. The sex residue. This residue attributes an erotic element to social activity.

The four derivations are the following:

1. Assertion. Here assertions of facts and/or sentiments provide justification for action.
2. Authority. Here reference to an individual, a number of individuals, tradition, usages, and customs and to divine beings or personifications provide justifications for action.
3. Accords with sentiments or principles. Here justification of action is provided by its accordance with sentiments, individual or collective interests, and juridical, metaphysical, and supernatural entities.
4. Verbal proofs. These are justifications of action that make use of terms with indefinite, vague, and multiple meanings, metaphors, allegories, and analogies.

For a society to develop in a balanced way the distribution and intensity of the different residues must be balanced. A predominance of the residue of innovation subjects society to dynamic transformations, however, without any constant direction. A predominance of the residue of persistence gives society a constant guidance and direction, but with the lack of any flexible change. This is a combination of the functions of latent pattern maintenance and collective goal attainment. A predominance of the residue of sociality makes for a close integration of society, but with the complete constriction of any individual and particular aspirations. A predominance of the residues of self-expression, individuality, and sex places the individual over society so that its integration and persistence is endangered. Thus, we can group Pareto's six residues into four classes with four different functions: adaptation, latent pattern maintenance, integration, and goal attainment on the collective and individual level. The derivations perform the same functions on the collective level: assertion provides adaptation, authority provides collective goal attainment, sentiments and principles provide integration, and verbal proofs provide latent pattern maintenance.

The Dynamics of Gaining and Losing Power

The development of society is determined first of all by its division into an elite and a nonelite (the masses) (Pareto, 1916; translation 1917–1919, 1935: ch. 12). A member of the elite is anyone who excels in a certain quality, good or evil: wealth, military strength, education, artistic capacities, knowledge, virtue, criminality, and other qualities. The elite is always a small minority. It can also be divided into the governing elite—those who govern society politically—and the nongoverning elite—those who do not participate immediately in this government. It is Pareto's central assumption that the elites never hold their position forever in society, but necessarily decline sooner or later and are replaced by a new elite, which again will necessarily decline in order to be replaced by the next elite, and so on. This is his statement of the rise and fall of elites as a basic cyclical process of historical development:

> Hence—the history of man is the history of the continuous replacement of certain elites: as one ascends, another declines. (Pareto, 1901; for translation, see 1968:36)

During normal periods of the predominance of a certain elite, there is a continuous circulation between the members of the elite and the masses. As some climb up to join the elite, others go down to join the masses. The rise, maintenance, and fall of a ruling elite, with which we shall be dealing in the following pages, is accompanied by a specific variation of the residues of combination and persistence. An elite group that comes to power does so because it is strong in the residue of persistence. That means it has a strong faith in certain ideals, a strong commitment to common ends and to the group, and is prepared to apply force in order to realize its ideals and common ends. It is a strong, forcefully acting group. The use or threat of force contributes particularly to its successful establishment in the struggle with the old declining elite. What makes the rising elite successful is the intimate linkage between faith, commitment, and the application of force. A strong belief in its ideology disposes the rising elite to using force in order to realize the ideology. The rise and establishment of an elite is the time of the "lions" who are strong in the residue of persistence and fight for their common concern.

The more the elite becomes established as the ruling elite in society, the more the conditions for maintaining power have to be met, which are different from the conditions for rising to power. Maintaining power by running the government requires other qualities, namely, technical knowledge, intelligence, situational tactics, negotiation, brightness of intellect, innovation, ruse, cunning, and even sometimes fraud and deceit. These are the qualities covered by Pareto's residue of combinations. The more this residue is demanded in running the government, the greater will be its part in the ruling elite and the more it will displace the residue of persistence. The ruling elite has to solve this problem of running the government by ruse by turning more and more to the residue of combinations and by recruiting persons from the masses who excel in these residues. In this way more and more residues of combinations predominate in the ruling elite and replace those of persistence. The lions are replaced by a new species: the "foxes."

Even though this shift toward the residue of combinations within the ruling elite helps it to run the government, it nevertheless has detrimental effects on the maintenance of power by the existing elite against the opposition of a potentially rising new elite. With the replacement of the residue of persistence by the residue of combinations, the faith in ideals and the commitment to common ends and to the group begin to fade away. The ideals, ends, and group solidarity that originally constituted the strength of the elite are forgotten. Many of the new bright members of the elite do not even know them, nor do they feel any commitment to these ideals, common ends, or to the group. The exercise of power then becomes an end in itself and is no longer guided by strong faith and commitment to ideals and common ends. The egoistic satisfaction of needs begins to prevail over a faithful and forceful government. The satisfaction of appetites and interests motivates toward the exploitation of the weak; fraud and deceit begin to replace any rightful exercise of governmental power. There is no longer an orientation to the future or a plan-based organization of government in order to realize ideals and common ends. Instead, an addiction to the satisfaction of appetites and interest in the immediate present predominate.

In the economic sphere a parallel process goes on. Here the elite is divided into the *"rentiers"* who save money and the entrepreneurial innovators and speculators who invest that money. The *rentiers* are people with strong residues of persistence; the entrepreneurial innovators and speculators are strong in residues of combination. The established ruling elite needs money in order to run the government and therefore supports the dynamic economic growth initiated by the innovative speculators. This contributes to a growth of the residues of combination in the economic elite. Fewer people save money; many more people spend money. The immediate satisfaction of appetites and interests predominates over the long-run saving of money, which then is less available for investments reaching much farther into the future. Short-lived interests displace long-term planning. In this process, the economic resources — namely, savings — burn out sooner or later so that the resources for running the government become smaller and smaller, which in turn means that the governmental elite will be even more inclined to exploitative action against the weak and poor. The parallel process in the economy contributes its part to the decline of the ruling elite.

The decline of faith in the ruling elite is paralleled by a rise of skepticism on the ideological level. People strong in the residue of combination do not believe in ideals but conceive of themselves as guided by scientific knowledge and interests, which makes them skeptical about the legitimation of ideals. With this growing skepticism the legitimation of the original faith that provided the strong basis of the ruling elite becomes more and more weakened up to the point where the elite no longer believes in its original ideals. This is the point at which the old elite is totally weakened and becomes open to the language of the opposition, which speaks for the weak and the dispossessed. The opposition makes its claims to power in the name of humanitarian ideals, speaking in the name of the whole society. Because of their lost faith in their own ideals, members of the old elite become vulnerable to the attacks of the opposition and take up its humanitarian ideals. In doing so they dig their own graves, because there is no longer any reason for them to be placed in positions of power.

Thus, the old elite commits suicide from two sides: first, from the side of the growing reckless exploitation of the weak in order to satisfy short-sighted appetites and interests; second, from the side of taking up the ideals of the opposition. Loss of faith in ideals is the cause for both aberrations, and that originates from a shift of the residues from persistence to combination.

A further implication of this transformation taking place within the ruling elite is its declining courage and ability to apply force in response to attacks and violations of social order. Its weakness even endangers the maintenance of social order. Because ruse prevails in running the government and because the ruling elite has lost belief in its own original ideals, it does not know what it stands for and thus is no longer committed to its ideals and ends to the extent that it has the courage of its convictions and applies force against attacks and violations of its order. There is no longer any faith, and therefore no need to apply force in the name of such a faith. The ruling elite becomes more and more divided into the selfish exploiters of power and the disappointed humanitarians. Some of the latter even leave the ruling elite and join the opposition. Thus, the decline of the old elite is caused by three immediate factors: (1) reckless satisfaction of appetites by the exploitation of the weak, (2) weakening faith, and (3) declining courage in applying force to defend its power.

With the old elite weakened in this process, there is ample room for a new elite to grow. The growing reckless satisfaction of appetites and interests, corruption, fraud, and deceit, and the exploitation of the poor call for an opposition that builds up resistance against this decadent leadership. This opposition speaks in the name of the exploited weak and poor and even in the name of the whole society. It speaks for a better society. The leaders of this opposition make up the rising elite and include speakers who came from the masses and humanitarian speakers who left the old ruling elite. The old elite's growing inability effectively to resist violations of social order by the application of force even places the rising elite into the position of restoring social order.

The rising elite becomes the reservoir of residues of persistence. People strong in combinations and ruse have continuously climbed up to the ruling elite, whereas people strong in persistence are concentrated in the new oppositional elite, which grows from the masses. These are people who have a strong faith in their ideals, a strong commitment to their common cause and ends, and a strong solidarity to their group. They know what they stand for and are prepared to fight for their cause and even to apply force in order to realize their ends. This makes them strong enough to overthrow the weak, declining elite and finally to take over the position of a new ruling elite.

However, after the new elite has put itself into power it will inevitably undergo the same process of decline. Belief in the future realization of universal ideals and concern for the weak and poor and for the whole society will inevitably fade away and be replaced by the short-sighted satisfaction of appetites and interests. Skepticism and cynical exploitation of power positions will replace faith up to the point where the time is again ripe for the replacement of this decadent elite by a new ruling group. The loss of faith in the bourgeois elite and the growing faith in socialism in the masses together with this inevitable process of decadence within the ruling elite is the reason why Pareto predicts on the one hand the victory of socialism as the replacement of the ruling bourgeois elite by a ruling socialist elite and also the failure of socialism as an ideal, because it will undergo the same process of degeneration as every ideal in history has done.

Summary

We can summarize Pareto's central ideas in the following statements:

Methodology

1. Sociology has to be conceived as a logico-experimental science that proceeds with precision in defining its concepts, empirical reference of concepts, analytical abstraction from concrete reality of items to be investigated, induction from facts to the formulation of general laws, and the confirmation of these laws by new facts.

Logical and Nonlogical Action

2. Action can be logical or nonlogical in character (or action has logical and nonlogical aspects).
3. Logical action applies knowledge that conforms to the standards of logico-experimental science; nonlogical action does not conform to these standards.
4. No action, no society rests exclusively on reason.
5. Nonlogical action performs a useful function in giving the individual and society guidance and direction toward ends.
6. Philosophy and the social sciences often falsely deny or rationalize nonlogical action.
7. The more nonlogical action is supported by reference to entities that transcend experience or by pseudo-scientific theories, the more firmly it will be established.
8. References to transcendent entities and pseudo-scientific theories function as ideologies that give society and individuals guidance and direction toward ends.

Sentiments, Residues, and Derivations

9. The most stable guidance and direction is given by residues, which are linked to sentiments and derivations.
10. The more action is determined by residues like the Christian commitment to righteous behavior, the residues are locked up by rituals that are oriented to the establishment of that attitude, the rituals involve the sentiments of the individuals and connect them with the residue, and the ritual and residue are founded upon derivations, then the more emotionally anchored, firmly established, collectively binding, continuously justified, and situationally adapted the guidance and direction of action toward specific ends will be.
11. Sentiments give action motivation, residues give it stable orientation, and derivations give it continuity and adaptability to changing situations.
12. Residues can be differentiated into six classes: (1) combinations, (2) persistence, (3) self-expression, (4) sociability, (5) individualism, and (6) eroticism.
13. Derivations can be differentiated into four classes: (1) assertion, (2) authority, (3) accords with sentiments and principles, and (4) verbal proofs.
14. In order to develop overall, society needs a balance of residues and derivations.
15. Combinations provide adaptation, persistence provides latent pattern maintenance and collective goal attainment, sociality provides integration,

and finally self-expression, individualism, and eroticism provide individual goal attainment.

16. Assertion provides adaptation, authority provides collective goal attainment, accord with sentiments and principles provides integration, and verbal proofs provide latent pattern maintenance.

The Dynamics of Gaining and Losing Power

17. Every society is divided into a minority elite and a majority nonelite (the masses).

18. The elite is divided into a ruling and a nonruling elite.

19. The development of society is determined by the endless rise and fall of elites.

20. The stronger a nonruling elite is in residues of persistence and the more it is committed to a common cause and apt to fight for its aim, being willing to apply force if necessary, the more it is likely to overthrow the ruling elite and rise to power.

21. The more a newly established ruling elite turns to running the government, the more it will be in need of residues of combinations.

22. The more the need for residues of combinations is met by a newly ruling elite by shifting to this residue and by recruitment of new able members from the masses, the more the residue of persistence will be replaced by the residue of combinations.

23. The more the residues of a ruling elite shift from persistence to combinations, the less members will be committed to their common cause, the more they will be engaged in the short-sighted satisfaction of appetites and interests, the less they will be oriented to planning the future, the more they will lose their faith in their common cause and will be vulnerable to attacks from the opposition and open to its humanitarian ideals, and the less they will be apt to defend their power by applying force.

24. The more members of a ruling elite are engaged in the selfish addiction to appetites and interests, the more recklessly they will exploit the weak and the more they will provoke the protest and resistance of the nonruling elite and of the masses and their leaders.

25. The more the "foxes" prevail in the ruling elite, the stronger will be the demand for sudden growth.

26. The more the speculators predominate over the *rentiers* in the economy, the faster will be its short-term growth, but the more the resources for long-term growth will burn out.

27. The more the economic resources for long-term growth burn out in the economy, the less resources it will provide for government in the long run.

28. The less resources are provided by the economy for government in the long run, the more the ruling elite will turn to the exploitation of the weak.
29. The longer the ideology of the ruling elite is in power, the more its false claims will be revealed by scientific criticism.
30. The more the false claims of the ruling class's ideology are revealed, the more members of the ruling class will lose faith in their own ideology.
31. The more members of a ruling elite are open to the humanitarian ideals of the opposition, the less members will resist its attacks and the more they will turn to the opposition and serve as its leaders.
32. The more the ruling elite provokes the protest and resistance of the masses, the more members looking for a new faith it loses to the opposition and the less apt it is to defend its position by using force, the more likely it is to be overthrown by a newly rising elite.

Critical Assessment

Pareto's general sociology demonstrates forcefully the place and determination of the nonrational elements of human action. In his theory of sentiments, residues, and derivations he points out their concerted effects on action: motivation, commitment to ends, continuity, and adaptation. His residues and derivations cover the whole field of social action: adaptation, goal attainment, integration, and latent pattern maintenance. Thus Pareto approaches a comprehensive sociological theory in its formal exposition.

However, his approach is much too biased toward dealing with the nonlogical elements of action as deviations from the standards of positive science. Though he emphasizes the useful function of the nonlogical for giving guidance and direction to individuals and society, he does not completely understand the nature of the nonlogical elements of action in themselves, independent of their deviation from the standards of positive science. Because he measures nonlogical action with the standards of positive science, the production of the nonlogical elements of action appears as a deficient aberration from scientific method. This however, limits considerably the view on the internal processes by which the nonlogical elements of action are produced. What receives a full treatment as production and transformation of solidarity, consensus, and morality in the work of Durkheim appears as a residue rooted in the linking of ritual and sentiments and thus as something that deviates from the standards of positive science in Pareto's work. Therefore, Pareto is unable even to ask the important questions of the transformations of solidarity structures and morality that accompany the development of society and that get a much more adequate treatment in the work of Durkheim. Pareto's theory of residues addresses the same subject as Durkheim's theory of the social fact, of solidarity and morality, but it does not provide insight into its internal structures and processes that could compete with Durkheim's achievements.

The same is true of Pareto's theory of derivations. This theory addresses the problem of the legitimation of social action and social structure, a problem closely investigated by Max Weber. However, Pareto's treatment directs our attention mainly to the deviation of derivations from the standards of scientific explanation instead of looking at them in their own right in analyzing their structures, processes, and functions for society. This is where we have to work out the role of ideas and their involvement in the legitimation and criticism of social action and social structures. Pareto's treatment cannot even approach the level reached by Max Weber, who concentrated on this subject matter.

Here we have to reject Pareto's treatment of processes of legitimation and criticism as nonrational deviations from the standards of positive science. Pareto falsely enshrines the rationality of positive science as comprehensive rationality, which it simply is not. He completely misses the rationality of discursive processes of the legitimation and criticism of values and norms. Positive science cannot answer questions of right and wrong; however, this does not mean that there can be no rational approach to these questions at all. At least from Kant's practical philosophy on to the formulation of discourse ethics by Habermas we have clues to such a rational approach to questions of morality. How these questions can be answered and what the contribution of moral discourse is to the development of society cannot be approached from the point of view of Pareto's theory of derivations.

Though Pareto was a famous political economist he did not transmit the fruits of his economic writing to a sociological analysis of the development of modern capitalism that could be comparable to Marx's theory of capitalist development or even Durkheim's treatment of the development of the division of labor or Weber's theory of the rise and development of rational capitalism. His economic and sociological writing were both too formalistic in character to allow such a synthesis and application to historical development.

What Pareto most rigorously demonstrates is the dynamics of gaining and losing power. Here he is better than his colleagues. This contribution is indispensable for a close understanding and explanation of the dynamics of power systems. His theory of the rise and fall of elites provides interesting insights not available from the other classic authors. And he formulates the theory in a much more systematic way and with much more precision than the comparable theory provided by his colleague Gaetano Mosca. Here is also the place where he makes best use of his theory of residues and where his conceptualization of the residues reveals their specific nature of being closely linked with the struggle for power. They are instruments for gaining and maintaining power. The same is true of his conceptualization of ideas as ideologies. Ideas become ideologies inasmuch as they are used as instruments in the power struggle.

Pareto's theory of the dynamics of power systems can be applied to long-term transformations of power systems and also to short-term replacements of political elites in democratic systems on the level of society, parties, trade unions, and other power systems. History is full of examples that correspond to Pareto's theory. One may, for example, look at the fate of the Russian Revolution of 1917. The Bolshevik revolutionaries were "lions," men of strong faith oriented to the future establishment of the communist society. But the longer the Communist party was in power, the more it was captured by the "foxes," men addicted to short-term appetites and interests, the functionaries, who perverted the system more and more into a self-service shop for privileges. At the same time the original faith had completely gone and was replaced by cynically playing with the rules of the system. This is the point at which Gorbachev began to overthrow the old elite by a new rising elite of men and women committed to the faith in *glasnost* and *perestroika*.

We can look at any victorious party in democratic systems. Beginning with strong commitment to a common cause, it is weakened more and more by the uncontrolled play of appetites and interests and by the fading away of the original faith so that it is ripe for replacement by the opposition.

However, what Pareto does not show is how the dynamics of the power system can be shaped by the influence of cultural legitimation, transformation of solidarity structures, and economic rationalization. Inasmuch as these processes are considered by him, they are part and parcel of the power dynamics themselves. This is why he can see only the continuous replacement of elites without any qualitative change with regard to approaching the realization of cultural values resulting from a strong influence of the logic of cultural discourse, with regard to the integration of society resulting from a strong influence of processes of inclusion, and with regard to economic, technological, and scientific advancement resulting from the strong influence of processes of economic, technological, and scientific rationalization. The more these processes exert their effects on the dynamics of the power system, the more historical development amounts to more than simply a cycle of rising and declining elites.

Further Developments

Vilfredo Pareto made a distinctive contribution to sociological theory. However, he did not create a school. Furthermore, later work on conflict theory was based much more on the Marxian model than on Pareto's. This is why his influence on further developments has remained minimal in extent. Nevertheless, Pareto has provided insights into the dynamics of power that are not available in any other classical or modern theory. These insights deserve their proper place in the wider network of sociological theory (see Powers, 1986).

SEVEN

THE DIALECTICS OF CONFLICT: GEORG SIMMEL

GEORG SIMMEL was born on March 1, 1858, in the center of Berlin, a truly metropolitan city where many social groups and intellectual movements intersected. It was a place of flourishing modernity, which shaped Simmel's outlook. He was not raised in a secure family context. His father, a Jewish businessman who converted to Christianity, died early in Simmel's life. His relationship to his mother apparently was not very intensive. Thus he found himself in a rather marginal position from the beginning of his life, and this remained characteristic throughout his life. He studied history and philosophy at the University of Berlin, and graduated with a dissertation on Kant in 1881. He became a *"Privatdozent,"* who was paid only by student fees, at the same university in 1885. In 1890 he married. His wife, Gertrud, was also a philosopher, and together they lived an intellectually sparkling bourgeois life.

After fifteen years of teaching as a *Privatdozent*, Simmel was granted the title of *ausserordentlicher Professor*, which still did not give him full academic privileges; these were reserved for *ordentliche Professoren* only. It was not until 1914 that he was finally appointed to the position of an *ordentlicher Professor* at the University of Strassbourg, right at the beginning of World War I. Four years later, on September 28, 1918, he died of liver cancer.

Simmel was a brilliant metropolitan intellectual, an extremely creative mind, a very popular lecturer with broad intellectual interests ranging from history to philosophy, psychology, and sociology, who participated extensively in the intellectual life of his time. However, in formal academic terms he remained an outsider throughout his life for two reasons: Because of his Jewish origin and because of the enormous diversity of his interests he did not conform to the dominating model of the German professor.

Of all European classics, Georg Simmel drew the sociologists' attention most vigorously to the multifaceted web of interactions that take place on the smallest scale. For him society was a finely graded network of interactions between individuals. And what Simmel's analysis of the forms and patterns of social interaction demonstrates again and again is the potential for conflict enmeshed in social interaction. Simmel shows that conflict is not an abnormal state of society but part and parcel of any social interaction. It coexists with harmony and consensus and is interlinked with them in paradoxical ways. Society and individuals live in conflict and consensus.

It is this everpresent and normal feature of conflict in social interaction that is the lasting insight presented by Simmel's sociology. This is why we can use most of his work if we read it as a theory of conflict. In doing so we have to interpret Simmel's work in a more consistent way than he formulated it himself, and we have to read it in a specifically selective way. This is all the more necessary as Simmel was a sparkling spirit full of ideas and associations that he was not able to manage in a systematically ordered way. His work is a collection of brilliant ideas illustrated with innumerable examples from everyday experience and history, but lacking any order. However, a reading of his work in terms of conflict is well confirmed by most interpreters of it (see especially Simmel, 1890, 1892, 1900, 1906/1912, 1908a, 1908b, 1911/1919, 1914/1926, 1917, 1918, 1971; for translations see Wolff, 1950, 1959; Oakes, 1984; Simmel, 1955, 1959, 1968, 1978).

Methodology

Simmel was concerned about establishing a specific object domain for sociology as a distinctive and legitimate scientific discipline. He struggled against the historical school of German idealism that drew a sharp distinction between the natural sciences (*Naturwissenschaften*) and the humanities (*Geisteswissenschaften*). According to this view the natural sciences search for general causal laws in nature, whereas human action is a realm of freedom and cannot be explained by general causal laws. Human action is open to reason and moral considerations. One has to understand human action interpretively rather than causally explain it, in terms of its reasons and moral orientation. Human action is part of culture, not part of nature. To understand why human action occurs in certain ways and has certain qualities, it is necessary to discover its particular meaning by way of pointing out its place in its particular cultural context. Any action takes place in a particular context. Therefore there is no place for generalizations in the cultural realm of human action. And because society is nothing but a name for a particular cultural context, society and social action have to be studied in their historical individuality. In this perspective, sociology is not a distinctive discipline but only a branch of historical science.

The denial of a distinctive place for sociology in the family of sciences is what Simmel attacked with his approach. This is no surprise when we take into account the influence of Darwin's and Spencer's evolutionism on Simmel's early work. Such influences are particularly apparent in his works *On Social Differentiation* (Simmel, 1890) and *Introduction to the Science of Ethics* (Simmel, 1892). Although Spencer's theory of differentiation is undoubtedly present in *On Social Differentiation*, Simmel never became an apologist for pure empiricist positivism. The more he matured, the more important Kant's critical philosophy became for his methodological perspective (Simmel, 1892, 1908a: 1–31). He took up Kant's idea of the *a priori* synthesizing function of the pure forms of intuition, like time and space, and the categories of understanding, like causality, for turning the wide variety of sense perceptions into ordered knowledge.

In correspondence to this Kantian idea, Simmel was in search of the formal categories that could perform a synthesizing function to bring order to the vast historical knowledge about society and social interaction. In his later phase Simmel (1908a) was particularly influenced by Bergson and Nietzsche and began to emphasize the vital energy that constantly renews life in an endless process and endless struggle against its constriction by formal structures. This vitalistic philosophy, however, only emphasized the other part of what constituted the fundamental dualistic perspective in Simmel's thought: the dualism between form and substance, which can be read as the basic conflict between order and vital life and as the Kantian relationship between formal categories and substantial sense perceptions as well. This is the deepest level at which one may understand Simmel's thought in terms of conflict.

Simmel's (1908a: 1–31) attempt at defining a specific object domain in order to establish sociology as a distinctive scientific discipline has to be understood from the point of view of his Kantian perspective. He first singled out a distinct aspect of reality as sociology's object domain in its own right. He called it "*Wechselwirkung*," which can be translated as "interaction." Sociology, he maintained, studies everything that makes up and results from the interaction of human individuals. *Wechselwirkung*, or interaction, means that what one individual does, sees, or expects has effects on what another individual does, sees, or expects, and vice versa. Simmel would study, for example, how the behavior of a person sitting in a room changes when another person enters the room, how their interaction changes when a third person becomes the object of their love, or how a conflict between them can be resolved by the third person functioning as mediator between the two.

Social interaction as demonstrated by the above examples is a specific aspect of total reality. Intermingled with such interactions are physical aspects of the environment, organic aspects of the individuals' bodies, psychic aspects of their personalities, the aspect of their intelligence, and cultural aspects of the values and norms prevailing in their society. These aspects all shape what goes on in that room. It surely makes a difference whether the third person is intelligent and strong enough and is even allowed by the prevailing cultural norms to serve as a mediator in the conflict between the first two persons. This is the intermingling of aspects that build up a concrete totality. However, in order to know the specific effects of one of these aspects on human action we have to single it out, separate it from the other aspects, and study it in its own right. This is Simmel's plea for an analytical procedure in sociological investigation: to differentiate social interaction from the other aspects of human life in order to study its features. The other aspects that are intermingled with social interaction in concrete reality have to be studied by other sciences: physics, biology, psychology, and cultural studies.

With his choice of social interaction as sociology's object domain, Simmel also argues for an understanding of the greater social phenomena: groups, organizations, and society as smaller or larger networks of social interaction.

Whenever social interaction occurs there emerges a new phenomenon: individuals who are otherwise separated from one another are drawn together, and they associate for a shorter or longer time. This is an emergent phenomenon that evolves from interaction and has its own qualities. People who interact also *associate* and *share* something: time, space, experiences, talk, physical contact, and so on. Such association and sharing can range from a short encounter on the street to a walk together, a cup of coffee, a dinner, a companionship, a club, a company, a lifelong friendship, or even marriage. In order to emphasize that all these different phenomena have this drawing together and sharing in common, whether they are brief encounters or established groups, organizations, and societies, Simmel introduces the term "*Vergesellschaftung*," which can be translated as "sociation."

Having singled out social interaction and sociation as sociology's specific object domain, Simmel's (1908a: 21–30) next question is one of how to study that object domain. Here he applies his Kantian perspective. He says that in a historical perspective social interaction and sociation occur in a multitude of different features. In empirically historical terms every single thing is different, and everything taken together is chaotic. He then asks a question similar to Kant's famous question, "How is natural science possible?" He turns Kant's question into one of "How is nature possible?" Kant's question addressed the problem that the experience of events and processes in nature by sense perceptions is chaotic, whereas scientific knowledge claims an order of natural laws. How can such an order emerge? For Kant (1781/1964a) it is the function of the pure forms of intuition, time and space, and of the categories of understanding, like causality, to synthesize the chaos of sense perceptions into a unified order, which can then be put to empirical test. While Simmel's question is "How is society possible?" he could also have asked in closer correspondence to Kant: "How is sociology possible?" The essence of this question is whether and how the chaos of historical facts about social life can be synthesized to build a unified order that can also be put to empirical test.

Simmel's answer to the question is that, in distinction to the natural sciences which have to rely on the synthesizing function of human intuition and understanding, synthesis in the object domain of sociology is not created by human intuition and understanding and imposed on that object domain but arises in the object domain itself, namely by the *a priori* conditions and forms of sociation (in short: social forms). The synthesizing function of sociation means that human activities that are scattered in time and place and that always have a particular meaning are set into a unified order by sociation. This means that actions are related to one another and separated from other actions, build up a network, and acquire meaning by being a part of a sociation. Sociation is the most elementary synthesis of otherwise scattered human actions. The letter one writes to a friend on his or her birthday, the work one does for one's company, the dinner one prepares for the family, and the smile one addresses to another person all have a place in a synthesized order of sociations and are understandable as parts of these sociations. Without knowing the order of these sociations we would not understand the actions: they would be no more than elements in a chaos of human actions.

Simmel, however, not only introduces sociation as the synthesizing force of social interaction and society but also continues to look for the *a priori* conditions and forms of synthesis in social interaction by investigating the various *forms* of sociation. In distinction to the limited and systematically ordered number of Kant's pure forms of intuition and of categories of understanding that are valid for the natural sciences, Simmel does not provide us with such an ordered set of forms in human sociation. He instead takes it as a task for sociology to discover and study such forms in the process of investigation itself. Imitation, competition, super- and subordination, division of labor, substitution, dyad, triad, small group, large group, leadership, party-group, internal solidarity, and external separation are examples of such forms of sociation. As Simmel emphasizes, these general *forms* of sociation occur in very different *historical, particular,* and *substantial* sociations like gangs, religious communities, economic associations, families, schools of art and relations between states. There are many different substances — for example, ideas, values, norms, interests, goals, members — underlying such sociations, but they are nevertheless expressed in the same forms. On the other hand, Simmel says, the same substance can appear in different forms. For example, family, religious groups, or parties may all be governed by one leader who directly relates to the other members; but religious communities can equally well be governed by one leader or by a number of leaders, or by one leader with a group mediating between leader and ordinary members of the community.

By assigning sociology the task of investigating the forms of sociation, Simmel succeeds in singling out an object domain for sociology that is different both from the natural sciences, with their search for causal laws, and from the humanities or cultural disciplines, with their search for an understanding of the particular meaning of historical individuals. The forms of sociation are not historical particulars but occur in the same or at least similar way in different historical, cultural, and social contexts with particular substances. They are universals like natural laws; however, they are not causal laws in the physical sense. They do not determine human action in a causal sense, but they define the opportunities, limitations, and boundaries of social interaction. They determine what can happen and what cannot happen in social interaction as long as it proceeds according to a specific form. In a dyad of two people, for example, nothing can happen without the cooperation of both of them, but both have maximum influence on what happens. In a large group many things can happen without the cooperation of a specific individual, but the latter has only a very small influence on what happens. With the introduction of money in economic exchange, there is maximum freedom for a plurality of consumers in their decisions on what to buy, but minimum influence of the individual consumer on any individual producer. Thus, the freedom of choice expands, but the freedom to exert specific influence on specific people diminishes. When competition between producers replaces the definite distribution of consumers between them, the competitors may stand to make higher profits, yet may also have to take lower profits; the consumers will be better served in general, but each will be served in the same way as everybody else, without any particular treatment. Groups acting out conflict between one another opens up chances for sharpening their division but also for renewing consensus. One person in a governing position has maximum responsibility but the governed have minimal access to that person; a plurality of persons in a governing position allows more access for particular interest groups of the governed to that position, but any one governing position has less responsibility for serving those interests.

These are some examples of the effects of certain forms of sociation on the opportunities and limitations inherent in social interaction. We can say that these are general laws pertaining to the forms of sociation that are effective in any particular historical, cultural, and social context with any particular substance. They are laws concerning the opportunities and limitations of social interaction that come about with certain forms of sociation. As we can see from the examples, their paramount feature is that they point out conflicting effects of such forms of sociation. Thus Simmel's socio-

logical theory is a theory of contradiction and conflict in social interaction
even at the very beginning when it defines its object domain. It is a dialectic
of interaction and sociation. The laws discovered by sociology in the forms
of sociation make it a distinctive discipline.

In distinction to the particular and individual facts studied by the historical disciplines, the forms of sociation entail general laws. However, in distinction to the causal laws studied by the natural sciences, the laws of the
forms of sociation are always laws of interaction, which have to take into
account the relationship of at least two parts to one another and the effects
of their interaction on each of them and on different aspects and subparts
of them. Because of this complicated web of interactions, there are no uniform effects, only contradictory and conflicting effects. For example, the
reign of one single person *increases responsibility for caring* about the concerns of the governed, but *decreases the capacity for noticing* what concerns the governed. This is a conflicting effect of one-person rule in
interaction with a plurality of governed people on two aspects of the ruler's
activities in favor of the governed people's concerns: *responsibility for* and
noticing of concerns. These conflicting effects of forms of sociation on different parts and aspects of social interaction are the object domain of Simmel's sociological theory. The laws discovered in this way are not
unidirectional but multidirectional and conflicting in character. They point
out opportunities and limitations of action coming about from the same
source.

Certainly, concrete events are multiply determined and not simply an
outcome of the working of forms of sociation on human action. Another
aspect, for example, is the effect of the personal attributes of the actors
involved in a situation. A personally irresponsible ruler may act in a less
responsible way than a plurality of personally very responsible ruling people in a governing committee. That is, the irresponsible ruler will refuse to
be made accountable for what goes on under his or her rule, whereas the
responsible plurality of rulers is well prepared to be made accountable for
everything that happens under their rule. Together with their power to resist
attempts to make them accountable, their different personal acceptance of
responsibility will influence the degree to which they indeed can be taken
as responsible for what happens. However, this effect of personal predispo-
sitions does not disclaim the validity of the law on the effects of the authority
structure on responsibility. That law in fact specializes in the degree to which
rulers can be made accountable by the governed simply on the basis of the
authority structure and nothing else. The law informs us about the effects
of the authority structure on the *opportunity* the governed have to make
their rulers accountable for what happens under their rule and not about
the extent to which they will achieve this in reality. What it says holds true
in concrete cases inasmuch as the effects of all other factors are held constant,

for example, the same personal acceptance of responsibility and the same amount of power vested in the one ruler or the plurality of rulers in a committee.

The study of forms of sociation is the task of Simmel's sociology. We can therefore call it formal sociology. This is the core of the discipline in Simmel's view. From this core, extensions are possible in two directions. The first of these involves the study of historical events by the application of knowledge about forms to particular instances. The second entails studying the preconditions for carrying out specialized social science, which is sociological epistemology, and the meaning of societal events and developments for human life in general, which is social philosophy. The main contribution of Simmel to sociology, though, is his study of forms of sociation. Let us now turn to this study.

Simmel makes apparent the conflicting effects of social forms on human action and interaction. He points them out with reference to numerous examples from everyday life and history. Because forms of sociation can be related to many different aspects of human action and social interaction, the conflicting effects of social forms are multiplied yet again. To add to that, there are also the effects of factors other than social forms, for example, personality traits, on these and other aspects of action. Finally, concrete human action and social interaction are a totality of all these aspects and an outcome of all the conflicting effects on them, so that we are faced with an incomprehensible complexity when we look at this web of conflicting effects, particularly when we choose concrete examples. Simmel's analysis of social forms and their illustration with examples becomes so multifaceted that it reaches a state of sheer incomprehensibility. His analysis then becomes a victim of his own methodology. It is therefore not only Simmel's sparkling but relatively unsystematic mind that is responsible for the complexity of his writing, but also his methodology. The two correspond to each other in the same way as form (his methodology) and substance (his mind). It is, however, impossible to reproduce this complexity. We can only select some of his ideas as exemplifications of his substantive work.

Group Size

A primary example of Simmel's studies in social forms is his analysis of the formal properties of social groups and their effects on social interaction. Of particular interest are the effects of group size (Simmel, 1908a: 32–100).

Group Size and Substance

It is a primary feature of a group's size that it sets limits on the substance manifested by the group (Simmel, 1908a: 32–36). For example, the working of the socialist idea of collectively producing and sharing goods and services is bound up with the need for relatively small groups, where everybody can be held responsible by everybody else and also feel responsible for everybody else. An elite can claim its exceptional character only as a relatively small group; the same is true of an aristocracy. With any new member outgrowing the limits of a relatively small group, the group's exceptional status diminishes along with its control over the exceptional character of its members.

Group Size and Radicalness

In the political arena a small group can be much more radical in its view than a large group, because it has to take into account only the views of a small circle of members and voters. The large group has to integrate the diverging views and interests of a great many members and voters. A group therefore loses programmatic consistency the more it grows in number (Simmel, 1908a: 37–38).

However, the radicalness of movements in politics increases the more the population is involved as a large mass that is emotionalized by demagogues. Thus, political debates become more radicalized up to a confrontation between simplified ideas the larger the public addressed by demagogic politicians trying to emotionalize the confrontation (Simmel, 1908a: 36–37).

Group Size and Regulation

Small, medium-sized, and large groups pose different problems for the regulation of interaction in order to make the actions of group members predictable. A small group can rely on trust in the personal morality of its members, because they know each other completely. A medium-sized group has outgrown that complete knowledge of each other and needs closer control of actions by the group and a binding definition of its group morality in mores and conventions. A large group cannot even rely on such informal standards embedded in group solidarity but needs much more formal establishment of control by positive law and a legal system. The large group will contain all three levels of regulation but with a growing importance attached to positive law (Simmel, 1908a: 38–45).

Group Size and Differentiation

A small group does not show much differentiation of functions and characters. Its members all tend to be the same and do the same. The more the group's size grows, the more it will be differentiated in terms of functions and characters. A first form of differentiation is the formation of divisions and subdivisions by number, for example, divisions of hundreds in the army (Simmel, 1908a: 45–53, 94–100).

Group Size and Character of Interaction

The small group involves a small number of people in close, comprehensive, and deep interaction; the larger group involves them only in selected, scattered, specialized, superficial, and impersonal interaction. For example, a conversation between six at dinner and the many conversations at a cocktail party differentiate in this way (Simmel, 1908a: 53–55).

The Dyad

The group of two — the dyad — depends in its existence and persistence on the contribution of each member. When one of the parties leaves, the group is dead. It also depends in its character completely on the individuality of its members. This implies that the individual can shape the group to the highest possible degree. The group has no "objective" existence independent of the individuality of its members. However, there are cases where the social environment controls the dyad so much that its existence and persistence can become independent of its members' will. A marriage partnership is the best example. Here a couple can be forced from outside to marry or to maintain an existing marriage just to conform to existing norms (Simmel, 1908a: 55–73).

The Triad

A group of three — a triad — differs very much from the group of two. Here the third person comes in and plays a crucial role. First, with this number the group exists and can persist independently of one member's decisions. In this sense, it takes on an objective character. A coalition of two is enough to define the group mind and group activities.

The third person can play different roles. The first of these is the role of the mediator. In this case the third person may initiate or strengthen the relationship between the other two in a direct or indirect way. For example, a couple's child may strengthen the bonds between them. Or the third person may mediate between the two others when they are in conflict, either as an impartial person or as someone who supports one in order to make him or her succeed in the conflict. The third person can also profit from the conflict of the two as a *tertius gaudens* (rejoicing third party). For example, the conflicting parties may be prepared to do anything for the third person to get his or her support. The consumer, for example, is the winner of the competition between producers. Finally, there is the chance for the third person to induce conflict between the two others in order to get him- or herself into a better position where they become dependent on his or her support. Or the third member may act similarly in order to weaken their opposition. He or she proceeds in these cases according to the principle of *divide et impera*, divide and rule (Simmel, 1908a: 73–94).

Group Persistence

The persistence of a group depends in general on the ongoing contributions of its members to group life and to the activities it engages in in order to attain its goals. How can a group secure these ongoing contributions to group life? Simmel (1908a: 375–459) singles out a number of devices for achieving this.

First, the group needs some form of local ties. It needs locality so that its members know where to meet each other and establish bonds to the common place, which then also serves as a symbol of the group's history. For example, a soccer club's ground serves as such a local bond with an eventful history.

Then, so that the group can survive beyond its actual members' lifetimes, there needs to be some interlocking of generations. The younger generation has to be included in group life and educated as early as possible so that the younger people have links with the existing membership and can continue the group's life.

Groups based on kinship depend on biological reproduction.

The more groups work on the basis of an authority structure, the more the succession of persons in positions of authority has to be secured.

Groups need symbolizations like a club meeting house, a flag, an emblem, and stories about group events in order to serve continuously as a common point of identification for generations of members.

The group needs to mobilize enough resources to organize group life. Financial resources from members and sponsors allow a most flexible organization of group activities.

The establishment of a position which is felt to be a special honor or that enhances one's esteem or reputation to be a member will continually attract new people to that group.

Inasmuch as the group has organs of representation, like an executive committee, it will have a greater capacity to concentrate its powers, to take quick decisions or unified action, and to uphold rational decision-making processes.

Group gatherings at regular intervals are the means to keep the group alive in its members' minds. They also allow the opportunity for feedback between the ordinary members and the group's representative organs. Together with other measures to maintain the interchange between leadership and "grass roots," this helps to ensure continuous contributions by group members to group life.

The group has to work not only to conserve its form in order to maintain its identity but also to vary that form in order to adapt to new challenges as long as this does not endanger its identity. The domination of an aristocracy will work in the direction of conservation, whereas pressure from the masses will result in change. A domination of the middle class will flexibly relate to both sides: to the aristocracy's conservatism and to the pressure for change by the lower ranks. An oligarchic party leadership, for example, will conserve the party program, while in-coming new members at the bottom will change the program because they have different experiences and views. The middle level of functionaries then has to mediate between these two extremes.

Superordination and Subordination

Simmel's emphasis in dealing with domination is that it is not a one-sided relationship of superordination but always one of super- and subordination (Simmel, 1908a: 101–85). There is no domination without at least the compliance of the dominated. But domination needs more than simply compliance. The dominated have to cooperate in carrying out the plans of the rulers. The ruler needs enough resources to get this cooperation by means of punishment and/or reward. However, specific forms of super- and subordination involve more than just the effective use of such resources. Authority is a relationship that relies very much on the belief of the subordinated people that it is rightfully exercised. Prestige is a form of superordination that is based on the subordinated's attribution of exceptional qualities to persons or groups. Special superordinated positions need even greater contributions by the subordinated in order to establish them: the positions of speakers before an audience, of teachers, and of political leaders. This interactive relationship between superordinated and subordinated also means that the superordinated's conduct is at least partly determined by the conduct of the subordinated. It is an interaction.

Simmel distinguishes three types of superordinations: one person, a plurality of persons, or an objective principle superordinated. He then looks at their interaction with the subordinated.

One Person Superordinated

The first effect of single-person rule is that it unifies the subordinated as one mass. All at least share the status of subordinated people; they also tend to be treated equally, which makes them a uniform mass. There is a further tendency for unification among the subordinated themselves when they unite in opposing the ruler's pressure. However, an intelligent ruler can also dissociate the subordinated in order to suppress opposition.

Unification of the subordinated can take place in two forms: by leveling or by gradation. The effect of leveling is that the subordinated become united in specific situations on the basis of very abstract principles, and these criteria only incorporate a smaller part of every individual in the group of the subordinated. The other part of the individual is not incorporated and remains free, which gives room for developing an individuality outside subordination. The individual can retreat from control in some parts of his or her life and has niches for developing an individuality separated from social control, because the common good is abstract and limited.

Gradation unifies the subordinated as subordinated, but in a differentiated form in a pyramid of different layers. Everybody below the top is subordinated, but between top and bottom each stratum—except the lowest one—has a double face: each is superordinated and subordinated at the same time. This has the effect that pressure does not apply to everybody in the same way and does not provoke uniform opposition. It moves downward, enabling the strata in between to hand down the pressure they receive to the next lower stratum. The lowest stratum, which cannot hand pressure down, is stripped of any chance to coalesce against domination, and the strata above the lowest lose interest in opposition, because they themselves profit from handing down pressure. Many conflicts do not occur between top and subordinated strata but between subordinated strata that are next to each other in the pyramid. This feature of the pyramid gives the top the opportunity to function as impartial mediator, to profit as *tertius gaudens*, or to rule by way of inducing divisions. On the other hand, the more the subordinated are divided, the more they will refuse to have anyone superordinated from their own group, but prefer to be ruled by a distanced stranger, who then seems to be an impartial mediator. A uniform group of subordinated, however, will prefer a ruler from among their own kind.

A Plurality Superordinated

A governing plurality of people can work in two ways: in a coordinated way and in an uncoordinated way. A coordinated plurality like an executive committee has more chance of being objective than a single-person rule and it also appears more objective to the governed, because particular standpoints have to be proved by a plurality of people. There are also more chances that the interests of the governed will be noticed and that a broader spectrum of information and points of view will be taken into account. This gives the governed better access to the governing. On the other hand, responsibility is divided among a number of people so that no one person can be made responsible for the actions of the governing body. This gives the governed less control over the governing.

If the governing plurality is uncoordinated, the governed are subject to diverging pressures that increase suppression to a maximum degree. However, if the governing people are in conflict with each other and the governed take an active role, they can profit from this conflict by playing the role of the *tertius gaudens*. Competition between parties in a democratic political system exerts pressures on them to please voters in order to get their support, at least during election campaigns.

Rule by an Objective Principle

Finally, we come to the form in which people are subordinated to an objective principle. What is called the rule of law originated in England from the first agreement between the barons and the king, the Magna Charta of 1215, up to the Bill of Rights of 1689. This is the most effective form of the superordination of an objective principle. It governs both rulers and ruled and is the form of domination that is most predictable for both governing and governed.

Freedom and Domination

Domination always involves the determination of freedoms to rule, freedoms to control rule, and freedoms to exercise self-government, including the self-responsibility of the individual in specified private spheres. Obtaining freedom always means two things: to be liberated from superordinated control in specified areas of life and to have the right to exercise authoritative control of one's own in these areas. The consequences for the individual is that he or she gets liberation from control by the top as part of his or her group but is subjected to control by the group, which is generally closer than the more distant control from the top. The result for the individual's freedom is therefore mixed. A liberating effect also comes from the separation of powers and from the separation of position and person. In this case, subordination covers only parts of a social relationship, whereas other parts remain free. Or the situation can even be the other way around, turning the person who is subordinated to another person in one dimension to the position of superordination in another dimension. This complex nature of different dimensions of superordination and subordination is increasingly a feature of the division of labor and separation of powers in modern societies.

Rule by the Best?

Taking up the question of whether rule by the best is possible, Simmel says that there are always more qualified people than governing positions and that selective procedures do not always guarantee an election of the best and most sensible people to the governing positions.

The Poor

It is within this context of superordination and subordination that we can locate Simmel's analysis of the poor. They make up an identifiable *social* group only inasmuch as society addresses the problem of poverty and applies special welfare measures to that group. The poor become constituted as a subordinated social group inasmuch as they become the object of special treatment by agencies of society: government agencies and private welfare agencies. In this way the poor become singled out as a disrespected group and closed out from participation in normal social life. In modern interactionist terms one could say that they become stigmatized with the consequence that their stigma very much decreases their chances of finding a way to a more reputable position.

Dispute and Conflict

Simmel gives special emphasis to the fact that disharmony, dispute, and conflict on the one hand and harmony, agreement, and consensus on the other are intermingled in complex ways, that they mostly occur together and are by no means mutually exclusive (Simmel, 1908a: 186–255). That means, depending on the special conditions in each case, that disharmony, dispute, and conflict grow from harmony, agreement, and consensus and the other way around. Simmel points out this complex nature of harmony and disharmony by showing the consequences of conflict for the relationship between parties in conflict and for society as a whole, and also with reference to the consequences of conflict for one of the parties.

Let us turn first to the aspects of conflict that contribute to the maintenance of a social relationship and of the whole of society.

1. If there are chances to act out conflict by articulating one's own opinion without being suppressed, there are better opportunities to settle latent disharmonies, to change the relationship to a more accepted state, and to adapt to new situations. The relationship and society as a whole are more flexible.
2. The acting out of conflict underscores the existing differentiation of society into castes, estates, classes, strata, and groups and contributes to their visibility and maintenance by renewing the specific group dissociations and solidarities.
3. The acting out of conflict by protest on the part of the subordinated makes it more acceptable to them to live in the subordinated position.
4. Expressing aversions makes it easier for us to live together with people with whom we do not empathize.

There are, however, also aspects of conflict that produce greater disharmony, harshness, intensity, and violence, namely when conflict combines with specific intensifying conditions.

5. The more the whole person is involved in a conflict and therefore the conflict is not limited to an objective matter of fact, for example, a conflict of interests, the more the conflict will be sharpened, intensified, and violent.
6. The more superindividual ideals merge with a conflict of interests, the more conflict will be sharpened, intensified, and violent.
7. The more a conflict is directed to a common basis, for example, a common faith, the more it will be sharpened, intensified, and violent. The conflict of religious and political groups over their own faith or ideology is especially sharp, intensive, and violent.
8. The more one has in common with another person or group, the more every conflict that breaks out will be experienced as directed against the relationship and will call forth reactions that again lead into conflict. Jealousy is an example of this.
9. The closer a social relationship is established, the more the outbreak of conflict will involve emotions, the whole relationship, and the whole of each person, and thus will be acted out with great intensity. Relationships of love in friendship, marriage, and the family also involve very intense conflicts. The latter is often the outcome of disappointed love. Indifference does not give rise to hate.

However, great sharpness and intensity of conflict do not necessarily increase disharmony and endanger the relationship:

10. The more the acting out of conflict is regulated by rules that control and/or close out violence and define the means of settling the conflict, the more intensely and sharply the conflict can be acted out without breaking the social relationship. This, for example, is the case with competition in sports, the economy, politics, or disputes in the courtroom. Competition also has the effect of increasing the achievement of competitors and the services businesses provide for consumers. However, this is not the case when scarcity of goods and services leaves too little for the loser in the competition to live on. In this case competition needs collective constriction by moral rules and positive law in order to eliminate these negative effects.
11. The more the personalities are separated from the object of conflict, the more conflict can be acted out without breaking the social relationship. Competition in sports, politics, and economic matters are examples.

12. The more opponents have something in common and understand each other, the more intensely and sharply they can engage in dispute without the danger of breaking the social relationship. This, for example, is the case with scientists engaged in debates. They understand that their common end is finding the truth.

Conflict between groups also has consequences for the internal relationship within each of the groups:

13. The more a group is in conflict with other groups, the more it will build up a stronger organization, control its conduct, and also become more predictable in the eyes of its opponents.
14. The more a group is in conflict with other groups, the more internal differences will level out and the members will bond together according to what they have in common.
15. The more a group is in conflict with other groups, the more intolerantly it will react to internal deviations and divisions, and thus will sharpen such divisions to internal conflict, aiming at the suppression of opposing elements.
16. The more a group is in conflict with another group, the more it is likely to build internal alliances and alliances with potential supporters in the conflict.

Finally, we have the question of how conflict is terminated. There are four major ways: disappearance of the object of conflict; victory of one party; compromise; and reconciliation. The disappearance of the object of conflict terminates a conflict completely, provided that it has been limited to that object. Victory holds only as long as the defeated party is not strong enough to fight back and is good for the victorious only as long as he or she does not need the cooperation of the defeated. Compromise needs equal determination of the outcome by the parties in conflict to be stable; otherwise it will eventually lead to the continuation of conflict. Reconciliation often terminates conflict on the surface without doing away with its deeper causes; thus, there is a danger of the causes of conflict becoming effective again.

Individuality

A considerable part of Simmel's work is devoted to the dialectical relationship between individuality and social constraint (Simmel, 1908a: 305–44, 527–73). The first example of this is his thesis that a person's freedom and individuality depend on the existence of the group, at least for the person's ability to separate him- or herself from it. The individual's freedom is a quality that exists not outside the social world but within that world as a specific relationship between the individual and the group. The first aspect of that relationship is one of liberation from group pressure; the second aspect of that relationship is that it may represent a negative measure for opposing one's individuality to the group; and the third aspect is the right to use one's freedom in relationship to others, which involves decisions that have to be taken into account by others. The exercise of freedom by one person limits the opportunities to act both of other persons and of the person him- or herself in his or her voluntary decision to join groups.

Freedom and building up one's individuality are always outcomes of a struggle for liberation and individual distinction against suppression and control by the group and by authorities. Even the voluntary decision to submit to an authority and to continue that submission, as is the case in any voluntary association, still represents such a permanent struggle:

> When set against this latter form of the relationships we hold, freedom proves to represent a perpetual process of liberation, a struggle not only for the independence of one's own self but also for the right — even in a state of *dependence* — to be steadfast in one's own *free will* at all times, and it proves to be a struggle which must be taken up anew after any victory. In reality, then, lack of restraint as negative social behavior is almost never a static property, but consists in incessantly shaking loose one's ties, which themselves never cease either truly constricting or ideally endeavoring to constrict the individual's fulfillment of the self; freedom is not a solipsistic entity but entails sociological activity, nor is it a state confined to the single subject, but a relationship, even if that relationship is considered from a subject's point of view. (Simmel, 1908a: 57, translated by Neil Johnson)

Simmel demonstrates that there is a specific relationship between the size of the group to which one belongs and individuality. The larger the size of the group grows, the more a differentiation of labor will take place and the more the individual will belong to the group only in an abstract sense, providing a greater opportunity to differentiate his or her personality from the group. Thus, there are two aspects of individuality here: individual specialization and liberation from group control. With the extension of the social circle to which an individual relates, his or her independence from specific groups also grows, and the determination of his or her character by the large group is limited to an abstract belongingness. The largest group is humanity. The more the individual relates to humanity, the more cosmopolitanism will be combined with growing individuality.

There is a further trend in modern society that sustains this process: the growing differentiation and number of social circles of which the individual is a member. In traditional societies, the individual's membership in his or her family includes membership in an estate and a nation.

In modern societies, group memberships become increasingly separated from each other and grow in number. The individual is the intersection of a great many social circles. He or she is member of a family, a professional organization, a company, a number of clubs, a local community, a state, a nation, a religious group, an ethnic group, a gender group, an age-group, and so on. With each group membership, the person's individuality is determined in a unique way. A person probably does not share all his or her memberships with any other person. The more the individual really chooses these memberships voluntarily, the more they truly will be a feature of his or her individuality when combined.

The more society is an organization of voluntary associations, the more it combines a growing individuality with a growing collectivity. There is ever more room for the individual's choice of group membership, but also an ever greater number of groups that regulate social interaction.

A special social type who is determined by his or her marginal position between groups is the stranger (Simmel, 1908a: 509–12). A stranger comes to a group but is not treated as an ordinary member. The fact that he or she is originally a member of another group determines his or her position. The person may be treated with suspicion if the new group is very uniform, but may be asked to act as an impartial mediator in cases of conflict or for advice by those not wanting to submit to their own companions.

A special effect on individualization of human life comes from the expansion of the money economy (Simmel, 1900). The obligation to pay for something in terms of money is the form of obligation compatible with the greatest degree of freedom. Money is also a carrier of impersonal relationships that cover only a part of a person and leave the other parts open for individuality. Money allows increasing differentiation of characters and functions, but it also increases the number of people on whom one depends. The latter effect of money is part of an ongoing process that produces what Simmel sees as a basic conflict in modern culture: the conflict between growing subjectivity and growing objectivity of culture that is alienated from the individual and exerts its pressure on him or her. The economy, the polity, the system of associations, science, and arts work on impersonal objective principles and produce objects that can be determined less and less by any single individual. They are objective cultural systems that limit the scope for individual spontaneity. However, it was the same process that has liberated the individual from concrete pressures of his or her smaller community. The individual has more scope for individuality by way of specialization but has less chance of making any difference to what is culturally produced in society and is dependent on ever more things that are beyond his or her control. This is the tragic dialectic of subjective and objective culture, freedom and constraint in modern society (Simmel, 1914/1926).

Summary

Methodology

1. Sociology is the study of interaction and sociation.
2. It studies the forms of sociation (social forms) and their dialectic, namely, the conflicting consequences of forms of sociation for human action.
3. The study of the forms of sociation differentiates the object domain of sociology analytically from that of idiographic humanities and nomothetic natural sciences.
4. Forms of sociation generally determine opportunities for and limitations upon action.
5. Forms of sociation provide an a priori synthesis of historically particular social interactions.
6. Social forms and substance are interrelated in a dialectical way.

Group Size

7. The smaller the group, the more each member's responsibility will count for group action.
8. The smaller the political group, the more radical it will be.
9. The larger the group addressed in political conflict, the more radicalized the conflict will be.
10. The more a group grows in size, the more its regulation will proceed from personal morality to mores, conventions, and positive law.
11. The larger the group grows, the more it will differentiate.
12. The smaller the group, the deeper and more comprehensive interaction will be; the larger the group, the more superficial and selective interaction will be.
13. The smaller the group, with the dyad the extreme case, the more its existence and character depends on each individual.
14. The larger the group, with the triad the first case, the more its existence and character becomes objective, that is, independent of single individuals.
15. In the triad, the third person has the opportunity to play the roles of mediator, *tertius gaudens*, and *divide et impera*.

Group Persistence

16. A group's persistence increases with its achievement in providing: locality, interlocking of generations, biological reproduction, succession in

authority positions, symbolizations of identity, mobilization of resources, honor of membership, organs of representation, group gatherings, interplay between leadership and grass roots, conservation, and variation of its structure.

Superordination and Subordination

17. Domination is a relationship of interaction.
18. One person rule produces a unification of the subordinated by leveling or gradation.
19. With the leveling of the subordinated, it becomes easier to submit them to the same central control, but there is a decreasing amount of control by any single person.
20. With the gradation of the subordinated, control over the subordinated is differentiated, closer in each case, but less unified.
21. The coordinated rule of a plurality becomes and appears more objective in character.
22. The uncoordinated rule of a plurality increases diverging pressures if there is no conflict between the governing and if the governed do not resist.
23. The uncoordinated rule of a plurality weakens the more there is conflict between the governing and the more the subordinated resist actively.

Dispute and Conflict

24. The more chances there are of acting out conflict, the more a relationship will be renewed, the more social stratification will be defined, the more a subordinated position will be accepted, and the more a person will be prepared to live with people he or she does not like.
25. The more a conflict on an object involves the whole person, concerns a common basis, breaks out between people who have much in common, or breaks out within close relationships, the more it will be intensive, sharp, and violent in character.
26. The more the acting out of conflict is regulated by norms, the more personalities are separated from the conflict, or the more opponents have something else in common in which they understand each other, the more intense and sharp a conflict can be without breaking the relationship.
27. The more a group is in conflict with other groups, the more it will level out internal differences, the less tolerant it will be against deviants, the more sharply it will conflict with them, and the more it will seek alliances.

28. Conflict can be terminated by the disappearance of the object of conflict, victory, compromise, or reconciliation.

Individuality

29. Individual freedom is determined by the interaction between individual and society.
30. Freedom means liberation from control, opposing oneself to groups, choosing one's group including the domination of that group over oneself, exercising one's freedom that involves that choice, and determining the choices of others.
31. The more one struggles for freedom within social groups, the more one will build up one's freedom and individuality.
32. The larger a group becomes, the smaller will be the part of the individual it controls and the greater will be the extent of individual differentiation.
33. The larger the group to which an individual orients him- or herself, with the whole of humanity as the extreme case, the more individuality and cosmopolitanism will converge.
34. The greater the number and differentiation of social circles one belongs to, the more one will be the unique intersection of these circles and the greater will be one's individuality.
35. The more money becomes the mediator of human association, the more obligations will allow freedom of choice, the more specialization of functions and character will occur, and the more individuality will be possible.
36. The more money mediates social association, the greater will be the number of people on which each member of society depends.
37. The more the circles of sociation expand, the more room there will be for individuality, but the less it will be possible for the single individual to influence social association and its products, and the more objective culture will be in conflict with subjective culture.

Critical Assessment

Simmel's most unique contribution to sociological theory is his emphasis on the omnipresence of conflict in social interaction, in the relationship between individual and society, and the degree to which it is interwoven as cause and effect with harmony, agreement, and consensus. In dealing with conflict, he particularly points out its dynamic character and multiple consequences with changing conditions. He gives us a lot of insights into this dynamic nature of conflict.

Simmel's sociological analysis is based on viewing individuals as strategic actors who are oriented to their specific goals and whose strategic actions interact with those of other individuals. This perspective and his sense of the dialectic nature of sociation led Simmel to point out the conflicting features of developments characteristic of the evolution of modern societies. The conflicts involved in the growing division of labor, in the changing structure of solidarity during the movement from smaller to larger groups and from convergent to multiple group membership, in the development of domination, and in the development of rationality are outlined by Simmel with a great appreciation of their complexity. Hence, Simmel informs us more about the complex nature of modernity than other classic sociologists do. But he does so in a more abstract way and with less information on the internal forces of these phenomena insofar as they are independent of their interrelationship with conflict. The economic features of modernization are more explicitly pointed out by Spencer, its features of solidarity more explicitly by Durkheim, its cultural features more explicitly by Weber, and the pure dynamic of power systems more explicitly by Pareto.

With regard to the development of individuality, we learn from Simmel about the development of the distinct individuality of the person in his or her permanent struggle with society much more than from Durkheim, Mead, or Piaget, but less about the development of moral conscience than from Durkheim, less about moral autonomy than from Piaget, and less about moral experimentation than from Mead.

Simmel does not open up paths to dealing with moral development in society and the individual at all because of his view of the individual as a strategic actor. He gives no access to communication in its true sense and its contribution to the development of individual and society and their interrelationship. His sociological perspective is very much like that of the Italian Renaissance political theorist Niccolo Machiavelli: the study of the effects which strategically acting individuals and groups exert on each other and on their relationships and the study of the effects of such relationships.

Further Developments

The lack of systematic order meant that Simmel did not create a paradigm that could serve as a crystallizing point of reference for any particular sociological school. Therefore, Simmel's influence remained scattered throughout the field of sociology. You can see the influence of some of his ideas at various places but not in a systematically established form. In Germany, Leopold von Wiese (1924–1929/1966), who taught at the University of Cologne, was the only one who carried on some of Simmel's ideas in what he called the theory of relationships (*Beziehungslehre*). But when von Wiese retired after World War II, there was no one who went on in this tradition. Very recently interest in Simmel's work has grown. This is indicated in the publication of his complete work, edited by Otthein Rammstedt. In the

United States (see Levine, Carter, and Miller Gorman, 1976a, 1976b), Albion Small and Robert E. Park, who taught at the University of Chicago, were influenced by Simmel's work. Simmel's concentration on social interaction was particularly useful for microsociological theory, which particularly flourished and still flourishes in the United States. Symbolic interactionism is the microsociological approach in which traces of Simmel's thought are most visible, however, mostly without being cited.

Lewis Coser (1956, 1967), Kurt H. Wolff (1959), and Donald N. Levine (1980) are the scholars who have contributed most after World War II to preserving and continuing Simmel's work as part of sociological theory. In recent years Simmel's work has attracted new interest in the process of theorizing about postmodernity. Simmel pointed out features of modernity that became particularly apparent in recent years and were discussed as features of postmodernity. Michel Maffesoli (1988a, 1988b) has contributed to this revitalization of Simmel's work. In the Anglo-Saxon context, David Frisby (1981, 1984) has provoked new interest in the work of Simmel.

PART FOUR

The Structure of Social Action

EIGHT

THE INSTITUTIONAL ORDER OF SOCIAL LIFE AND ITS TRANSFORMATION: EMILE DURKHEIM

EMILE DURKHEIM was born in Epinal in the eastern French province of Lorraine on April 15, 1858. He was the son of a Jewish rabbi and brought up in firm respect for his parents. He attended the Collège d'Epinal, the famous Lycée Louis-le-Grand in Paris, and the prestigious Ecole Normale Supérieure, where he graduated in philosophy in 1882. From 1882 to 1887 he taught at a number of provincial lycées. In 1887 he was appointed to a position at the University of Bordeaux to teach courses in sociology and pedagogy. It was then that he married Louise Dreyfus, with whom he had two children. In 1893 he defended his French doctoral thesis, *The Division of Labor*, and his Latin thesis on Montesquieu. After nine years of teaching at the University of Bordeaux he was promoted to a position of full professor in social science. While teaching at Bordeaux University he founded *L'Année Sociologique* in 1898, which became a very influential publication in the years to come. In 1902 he was called to a chair in the Science of Education at the Sorbonne, Paris. His chair was extended to the Science of Education and Sociology in 1913.

Durkheim took part in the public life of the Third Republic and was a scholar of great repute. He was devoted to making sociology a central scientific discipline that could even play the role of providing the foundation for a secular morality, taught at every school of the Third Republic. He died on November 15, 1917, after receiving the message that his son André had died from his war injuries in a Bulgarian hospital.

The French Tradition of Rationalism and Positivism

The work of Emile Durkheim is deeply rooted in French rationalist-positivist thought but also influenced by his familiarity with Anglo-Saxon economic thought, utilitarianism and evolutionism, and with German idealism, particularly as initiated by the critical philosophy of Immanuel Kant. In combining these different sources in his work, Durkheim went much beyond the original boundaries of French rationalist positivism. Nevertheless, compared to the works of his contemporaries who shaped the emergence of sociological theory at the turn of the century, the methodological and substantive ideas of French thought remained most apparent in Durkheim's work.

The French tradition of rationalistic positivism, the rationalist-positivist approach and organicist structuralism, viewing society as a reality *sui generis* distinct from the individual, bringing out the contrast between societal structure and individual action, and the search for the new social order that holds society together as an organic whole — these are the predominating ideas that Durkheim inherited from the intellectual tradition of his country. The most important source in the beginnings of that tradition is the rationalism of René Descartes (1596–1650), which shaped French thought in its predilection for starting from first principles in order to deduce every individual statement, observation, and fact from such principles. Stated in his *Discours de la méthode* in 1637, Descartes' rationalism became the leading paradigm of French thought. It influenced the Enlightenment philosophers of the eighteenth century as much as the positivist philosophers of the nineteenth century. From Montesquieu to Condorcet to Saint-Simon to Comte, we see the triumph of a rationalist science that aims at discovering the universal laws that govern nature, society, and the human being. With growing devotion to progress from Condorcet on, philosophers searched for the universal laws that guide the development of human society with a growing belief that there is one universe encompassing physical nature, human society, and culture that is determined throughout by the same universal laws. Durkheim continues that search on a new level on which he incorporates the achievements of Spencer's economic utilitarianism and evolutionism and of Kant's moral philosophy.

Montesquieu (1689–1755) looked for the universal societal laws and went on to the varying empirical conditions under which they are set in motion (Montesquieu, 1748). The Marquis de Condorcet (1743–1794) was not satisfied with that. He wanted nothing less than to discover the laws of progress in human history. He claimed that human society progresses in ten stages based on the evolution of knowledge from primitive belief to the emergence of positive science (Condorcet, 1795/1982).

Claude-Henri de Saint-Simon (1760–1825) saw human society progressing in three stages, from polytheism to theism to the positive epoch of physicism (Saint-Simon, 1865–1878). Auguste Comte (1798–1857) gave the new science of society its name: sociology (Comte, 1830–1842/1969a, 1851–1854/1969b, 1968). He systematized Saint-Simon's thought. According to Comte (1830–1842/1969a), human society progresses in three stages, from the theological to the metaphysical to the stage of positive science.

Next to the belief in the rationalism of science, the appraisal of the methods of positive science and the idea of a unified positive science that covers the whole world and its development, from nature to society and culture, there follows a special sense for society as a reality *sui generis*, for the establishment of social order and for understanding society as an organic whole. There is a clear primacy of society over the individual. In this perspective the organization and development of society is not an outcome of the spontaneous activities of individuals or of the self-realization of reason, and it is not an outcome of power struggles between historical actors. Inasmuch as these are features of historical development they play a secondary supporting role for the progress of society as an organic whole.

When the Physiocrats argued that society should be governed according to the laws of nature, they understood this as the function of the collective organization of society by an absolutist government (Quesnay, 1888/1965; Turgot, 1972).

For the Enlightenment philosopher Jean-Jacques Rousseau (1712–1778), the individual's freedom can only be re-established by collective association and regulation by collective government and collectively established laws once it has been lost in the struggle between egoistic individuals (Rousseau, 1762/1964). The establishment of a civil religion of each member of society's civic rights and duties is important for guaranteeing the order in this new society constituted by the social contract between all individuals.

Saint-Simon (1865–1878) proclaims the new society based on positive science as an organic whole hierarchically differentiated into classes, which all contribute their part to the functioning of the whole system and to which the individuals are allocated according to their natural talents. The industrialists are at the top of this hierarchy above the scientists and the artists. Approaching its final state, such an organic society will no longer need power to be exercised but will be governed on purely objective grounds of scientific knowledge, which are valid for everybody.

Auguste Comte (1830–1842/1969a) also conceives of the emerging society of the Positivist Age as a hierarchically ordered organic whole that does not work by the exercise of power but by the application of scientific knowledge and — as he elaborates in his later work — is based on the religion of humanity. The hierarchy begins on top with the spiritual classes, within which the subclass of scientists is ranked above the further subclass of artists. Below the spiritual classes are located the active classes in hierarchical order beginning with bankers, followed by merchants, manufacturers, agriculturalists, and laborers.

Comte paralleled stages of social formation, social instincts, and social association with the three stages of knowledge in the development of human society. The theological stage is based on military conquest and slavery, civic instinct, and a predominance of the family in antiquity. The metaphysical stage relies on military defense and feudalism, collective instinct, and a predominance of the state in the Middle Ages. The positive stage is grounded in industrialism, universal moral instinct, and humanity as social association.

The religion of humanity and of moral universalism would, he said, be the basis of the coming society. In taking this view Comte laid special emphasis on the integrative features of the new society. This is a particular example of conceptualizing society and its development in terms of transformations of an organic whole, of institutional structures, and of solidarity relationships. In this perspective positive science merges with a new religion of humanity.

It is this particular approach to studying society that most vigorously shaped the thought of Emile Durkheim. However, Durkheim went beyond the boundaries of the thought that prevailed in his society. From the Englishman Herbert Spencer, he incorporated the economic and evolutionary explanation of the division of labor (Spencer, 1851/1970) but liberated this approach from blunt utilitarianism and bound it back to the French claim to the *sui generis* character and function of society and its normative structure. From the German Immanuel Kant (1788/1964d) he included the notion of moral universalism but liberated this notion from idealist one-sidedness and bound it back to its roots in social solidarity moving from family to the state and to humanity as a whole. The strength of Durkheim lies in his ability to interrelate these realms. Nevertheless, his emphasis is on the predominance of the normative structure of society. This preoccupation limited his ability to come to a full appraisal of the internal features of economic transactions, politics, and moral discourse.

The Social Fact

Social life is not just a collection of accidental events. It proceeds, at least to a minimal degree, in regular patterns. Though much of human behavior varies from situation to situation and social life undergoes change, there are recurrent elements in human behavior and social life. To that extent, society has a social order. The major concern of Emile Durkheim's classical contribution to sociology as a discipline in its own right is to study the nature, preconditions, changing character, effects, and deficiencies of that social order.

Durkheim's central concept is that of the social fact, as he outlines in his methodological study on *The Rules of Sociological Method*, published in 1895. The social fact denotes the object domain of sociology and functions as a conceptual means for differentiating sociology from other disciplines, particularly from psychology (Durkheim, 1895/1973b: 3–46).

The social fact is an object of its own and needs a specific science in order to investigate it appropriately: sociology is that science. Social facts are things like the law, a currency system, language, institutions and institutionalized practices, and the collective consciousness. When we buy new clothes in a sportswear shop we follow rules that have existed before and will continue to exist after the act of purchase is completed. We do not just take the clothes away; we pay for them in the currency of our country. We did not create the rules of purchase and the currency by ourselves, and we cannot change them at will; they also exist independently of our personal act of purchase. When a sociology professor teaches Durkheim's notion of the social fact in an undergraduate class, he or she does something that has been done by many long before and which will be done by others in the future. What the person teaches has not been created by him- or herself, not even the fact that it is Durkheim's concept of the social fact that he or she teaches, because the social fact is a regular element of introductions to sociology that exists independently of a particular professor's teaching.

When we communicate with another person we make use of a vocabulary and of grammatical rules that have been used by others long before and will be used for a long time after our act of communication. We did not invent the vocabulary and the rules and cannot change them at will. When people go to worship on Sunday morning they do something that has been done long before and will be done for long thereafter, independently of a particular individual's action. When high-school graduates celebrate their graduation they do something that has been done before and will be done thereafter, independently of the individual graduate's wishes. These are all examples of social facts; our social life is full of them. Their first property is their *externality* to the individual, in Durkheim's terms. They exist externally to and independently of the particular individual, before and after his or her individual action, and they cannot be changed at will. What would happen if we took the clothes without paying for them, if the professor left out Durkheim's notion of the social fact in an introductory theory course, if we used the wrong vocabulary and violated grammatical rules, if a church member did not go to Sunday worship, and if the high-school did not celebrate graduation? Others will react in such a way that they exert pressures on the individual to conform to the established pattern: punishments, degradation, correction of mistakes, reminders, condemnation. The individual cannot disregard the established patterns without running into these negative sanctions. A constraint is exerted on the individual to conform to the established pattern. This is the second feature of the social fact: its *constraining character.*

Social facts extend far in space and time. Rules of purchase, sociology teaching, communication, worship, and graduation ceremonies are valid not only for particular cases but also for every single corresponding case. This is the third feature of social facts: their *universality.* It is a feature that is not peculiar to the social fact. Other things have a universal character, for example, the laws of physics. What makes social facts universal in character is that the corresponding rules are conceived as binding throughout a collective. It is not the universality of a fact that makes it collectively binding but rather the other way around; the collective's conception of them as binding makes them universal in character.

The social fact is thus a reality *sui generis*, which can be distinguished from other phenomena by the three features of externality, constraint, and universality, rooted in its collectively binding character. It has to be investigated as a "thing" that has an objective character in Durkheim's terms.

The center of the social fact is the institutional character of social life. Much of our daily action is determined by established patterns. Norms and rules prescribe ways of acting. Institutions are sets of norms and rules that guide social action in certain areas of life like marriage, family, work, buying and selling, traffic, the neighborhood, education, school, college, university, friendship, sports, literature, the arts, and so on. Most of our daily activities reproduce these regularities. Thus, social life is full of social facts that are external to the individual, exert constraints on him or her, and are universal in character. The source of these social facts is the collective. It is the bearer of norms and rules. The constraint exerted on the individual is the constraint of the collective and not just a constraint exerted on him or her by certain other people.

There has been a long debate on this collective explanation of social order. It has been opposed by individualistic explanations. Undoubtedly, it is the individual's expectation of sanctions by certain other people that motivates the person to conform to the institutional order. Inasmuch as it is more useful for the individual to conform than to deviate, he or she will conform. This is an individualistic and utilitarian explanation of an individual's conformity to norms and is often proposed as an explanation of social order. However, what happens if different people react differently to a single individual and to different individuals? There would then be no regular pattern of behavior, that is, no institutional order. This is Durkheim's point, which individualistic explanations of social order have completely missed as long as the debate on individualistic versus collectivistic explanations of social order has gone on. According to Durkheim, the origin of social order is the constraint exerted by the collective. What is at stake here is whether the societal collective reacts uniformly or differently to individual actions. Only with a uniform reaction will a regular pattern of individual behavior become established. Such a uniform reaction occurs only if the collective's members share common beliefs and norms about right behavior and if they feel a mutual solidarity so that there is mutual support in reacting to deviations from the commonly shared norms.

Thus, what calls for a collectivistic explanation is not the individual's motivation to conform to norms but the collective's reaction to individual behavior, which must be carried out uniformly, and this presupposes commonly shared beliefs and norms and solidarity. To the extent that these preconditions are met, the collective has a collective consciousness that can be distinguished from the individual members' consciousness. The collective consciousness is the members' awareness of belonging to the collective and sharing solidarity, beliefs, and norms. Their sharing of common moral views can be called "collective conscience." Such a shared collective conscience guides their uniform evaluation of individual behavior, and that is the basis of a collective moral order.

Certainly, individuals do weigh up the costs and benefits of their own behavior, and the collective's reaction with sanctions to undesired behavior means the application of power. Yet, neither the individual's utility calculation nor the collective's power is a sufficient explanation of the existence of social order in the sense of established patterns of regular behavior. What such utilitarian and/or power-based explanations miss is the uniform reaction to behavior that presupposes collective conscience and collective consciousness, that is, commonly shared beliefs and norms, and the solidarity of the collective's members. Without commonly shared beliefs and solidarity, reactions to individuals' behavior would be contradictory and would always involve debate and conflict; that is, no uniformity in evaluating and sanctioning behavior would come about. Inasmuch as the preconditions of social order are met, the average individual members, to begin with, normally follow a regular pattern in their behavior. In addition to that, if deviations occur, they present a uniform reaction to provide for correction. Deviations occur because the collective consciousness and the individual consciousness are not coincidental. The individual may share beliefs and norms with others but nevertheless also have his or her individual interests, which give rise to deviations from the commonly shared norms and beliefs.

The source of a social fact's constraining character is thus first the power of sanctions applied to deviating individual behavior. However, it is not just physical force that eventually guarantees the uniformly constraining character of a social fact, for this is also characterized by the criterion of universality within a collective. The combination of constraint and universality needs commonly shared beliefs, norms, and solidarity. Constraint, then, resides not only in the power of the collective but also in its moral authority, because the collective is perceived as a bearer of common moral norms. Therefore, constraint is not just physical in character in this case but also is moral.

Thus it is collective solidarity and the collective consciousness that is the center of social order. Inasmuch as they expand over society, the individual spheres of society are regulated by institutional orders, economic action by economic order, political action by political order, and communication by communicative order. Social order of this type is the source of the order of action, of the human personality's order, the behavioral order, and the symbolic order.

The Division of Labor in Society

The changing character of social solidarity as the center and source of social order is the question Durkheim seeks to answer in his first study on the *Division of Labor in Society*, published in 1893.

From Mechanical to Organic Solidarity

What characterizes the historical development of human society as distinct from the most primitive types to the modern type is the growing division of labor (Durkheim, 1893/1973a). According to Durkheim, the cause of this process is the growth of population, which increases the volume of society and its *material density*; that is, more and more people live within a certain territory, so their interactions and the interdependencies between their actions grow in number. With the growing material density, the *dynamic* or *moral density* also grows; that is, more and more people come closer to one another and exert influence on each other.

As volume and density grow, competition between people to make a living increases. The more people live within the same territory, the less they can all live from the same things. The only way to survive under these circumstances is to differentiate from other people and to specialize in living from specific things. We can add to this argument of Durkheim's that opportunities to exchange products also increase with the growth of the population. Thus, people's specialization in specific products and services gives them a chance to escape the competition of too many other people. The result of this growing individual specialization is a growing division of labor in society.

With this growing division of labor, a fundamental transformation of social solidarity as the institutional core of society takes place. Solidarity moves from a predominance of the mechanical type to a predominance of the organic type. *Mechanical solidarity* is the type of solidarity that predominantly holds people together in primitive societies. *Organic solidarity* becomes increasingly important with the advancement of society's division of labor and is predominant in modern society. Primitive clan-societies are differentiated into small segments of families that live together within a certain territory. The families are relatively self-sufficient units that perform many functions for their members: economic production, political decision making, religious salvation, and support of weak or sick people. The solidarity between the families is maintained by common ventures in hunting and agriculture, bonds of marriage, common decision making, and common religious rites.

The people of such clan-societies are very similar to each other, because they do all the same things. There is little individual differentiation. Their lives are predominantly determined by the group. They are first of all members of a family, a tribe, or a clan, and they think and act as members of these groups. Thus, there is a strong consciousness and feeling of mutual belonging; what is right and wrong, what is appropriate behavior is largely defined by the group as a whole and not left to individual choice. This is what Durkheim calls a strong, concrete, and definite collective consciousness. Members experience the strong authority of the group; the norms of the group are concrete and prescribe appropriate behavior very definitely. Because little behavior is left to individual choice and most behavior is definitely prescribed, conflicts rarely occur between individuals, but do occur between individuals and the group, or particular groups and the whole clan. Therefore, such conflicts can occur only in the form of individual deviation from group norms. Such deviations are not just deviations from individual expectations but violations of the group's binding norms and moral convictions. The group reacts by applying repression and punishment. The ceremony of punishing the violator of the group's collective order gives expression to the group's moral convictions and confirms its solidarity and collective order. An indication of the predominance of this type of solidarity is the predominance of penal law in the less-developed societies and little elaboration of civil, administrative, and constitutional law. Durkheim calls this type of solidarity mechanical, because there is an unreflected uniform and mechanical coordination of people's actions by the societal norms.

With advancing population growth, increased societal volume, and density and the resulting division of labor, mechanical solidarity loses ground and organic solidarity becomes predominant. First, people become different to each other by way of specialization in the process of dividing labor. Thus, whenever there is solidarity, it does not draw together similar people, but different people. People see themselves as different from each other and also as different from society. The awareness of being a member of a society weakens. There is a weak collective consciousness, and its content becomes abstract and indeterminate; only a very general sense of societal membership exists, and the members share only very general ideas. Correspondingly, the individual tends much more to build up a consciousness of his or her own than in societies that are less advanced in terms of division of labor. Individuals have their own interests and their own ideas according to their different positions in society. This is what Durkheim calls the process of individualization. One becomes an autonomous subject; one's individual consciousness increasingly occupies a greater part of one's life than one's participation in the collective consciousness.

Interaction between people also changes its character. Whereas in primitive societies with little specialization people cooperate in doing the same things under the uniform, mechanical guidance of the group's norms, in advanced societies with much specialization people do different things and interact in the process of exchanging specialized products and services. Their relationships are no longer determined by primordial ties but by complementary interests. What brings them together is the occasional convergence of such complementary interests. One party may have too much of what another party needs, and vice versa. The exchange of products and services on the basis of complementary interests becomes the most common social relationship.

The more this exchange takes place not as an immediate handing out of material things but as dealings involving commitments to delivering goods or services at some future time, which binds the individual to the provision of such goods and services, the more exchange involves concluding and fulfilling contracts. The more the division of labor advances, the more the contract becomes the predominant relationship between people. The English philosopher and sociologist Herbert Spencer (1851/1970, 1897–1906/1975) took this development as the factual basis for his thesis that the contract becomes the bond of solidarity in modern society, which has increasingly developed its division of labor. The whole of society is held together by an innumerable mass of small contracts between individual people, says Spencer. Neither primordial ties nor a single societal contract — as the Enlightenment contract theories of society proclaimed — hold modern society together. It is held together by an immense number of individual contracts.

Contractual Solidarity

Durkheim agrees with Spencer in the observation that the contract becomes the most common relationship in modern societies, and he also says that we cannot assume — as the Enlightenment philosophers did — that autonomous individuals could come together to conclude an overall societal contract in order to secure social order. Such an assumption presupposes that the individuals give up what makes them individuals: their autonomy. They have to think as members of a whole and to forget their individuality. The consequence is that they are then incapable of acting as individuals. Yet, the assumption of the Enlightenment philosophers was precisely that people are autonomous individuals. The problem is that, as autonomous individuals, they cannot see what is best for society as a whole, because they think in terms of individual utility. However, what is useful for one individual is less useful for another individual. The same is true of a social contract; it is not more beneficial for everybody and at all times than alternative ways of making profit. Convergence of individual interests comes about only occasionally and does not endure. Therefore, theories of social contract are built on unrealistic assumptions.

If no social contract is likely to be concluded between autonomous individuals, are the individual contracts between individual actors the only social bond in modern societies? This is what Spencer proclaimed; however, Durkheim rejects Spencer's thesis. According to Durkheim, contracts are concluded on the basis of occasional complementarity of interests. However, this occasional complementarity can fade away as quickly as it came about. Thus, it does not explain the regularity of social behavior nevertheless occurring in the fulfillment of contracts.

Individual utility calculation would move actors much more toward retreating from contractual commitments than is the case in reality. Abiding by a contract frequently imposes costs that are much higher than the profit expected from the contract. Whenever contracts are not broken as often as could be expected on the basis of this assumption, there must be other forces at work that contribute to maintaining people's commitment to contracts than their expected profit from the contract alone. This is what Durkheim calls the noncontractual foundations of the contract. People conclude contracts on the basis of individual choice, but whether they fulfill their contracts or not is not left to their individual choice but is in fact a matter for society as a whole, a matter of contract law and contract morals. The latter are not individual phenomena but collective ones. What is right and wrong in contractual relationships is not left to individual preferences but is determined collectively for everybody who enters contractual relationships in the same way. Whether a contract has been fulfilled sufficiently is not a matter for the contracting parties alone, but a matter for society. A party will be able to enforce its claims only if they can be justified in terms of contract law in formal legal procedures. And the organizer of these procedures is the societal collective represented by the judge.

It is true that the individual parties can nevertheless be guided by the calculation of their individual cost and profit regarding contractual fidelity and can take into account legal sanctions as a cost. However, this is not Durkheim's point and not a sufficient basis for an individualistic utilitarian explanation of social order resulting from individual contracts. If the reactions to the carrying out of contracts were left to individual choice, very different reactions would occur, and therefore no regular contractual behavior could emerge. Only a society-wide, uniform reaction to the honoring of contracts can bring about regular contractual behavior.

What needs explanation is this society-wide uniform reaction to contractual behavior. A central power may perform this function, but if neither this power nor the rule it applies is widely accepted by the members of society, there will be permanent conflict and power struggle that results in complete insecurity about the validity of rules. Thus, no uniform reaction to contract behavior will occur.

There must be more than just a centralization of power in order to back up the sanctioning of contract behavior. This is where the collective consciousness and solidarity come into play. Only insofar as there are collectively shared norms about right contractual behavior and only if there is solidarity between the members of a collective who support one another in cases of deviation from contract norms will there be an undebated uniform reaction to contractual behavior, therefore making it regularly predictable. This is true even if there is a centralized body responsible for enforcing the contract norms. Hence, in Durkheim's view, we need a collective explanation of contractual fidelity.

The fact that the division of labor and the expansion of contractual relationships is accompanied by an expansion of civil law—namely, contract law, but also administrative law and constitutional law—proves basically the collective nature of society's cohesion in Durkheim's eyes. The expansion of these types of law and their relative predominance compared to penal law in modern society is first an expression of the changing character of solidarity. Whereas penal law defines violations of the collective body and applies repressive punishment, civil law, contract law, administrative law, and constitutional law all define rights of individuals and their accommodation with one another and with the rulings of the state. Violations of these rights call for restitution and not for repressive punishment. As these types of law expand in society, they give expression to the growing individualization of society; nevertheless, they are collective in character, because they consist in collectively shared norms.

Contractual Solidarity and Individualization

Thus, there is by no means a retreat of the collective in parallel with the expansion of individualization. It is, rather, the other way around. Individualization grows with the expansion of collective regulation provided by the legal system. Without the growth of the legal system in this direction there would be no growing individualization. Society would fall back upon collective repression or disintegrate in an egoistic power struggle. Growing individualization presupposes a growth of the regulation of individual rights. Speaking of individual rights means speaking of collectively bringing about the autonomy of the individual. This is what Durkheim calls the cult of the individual; it is a collective sacralization of the individual personality that defines the rights of the individual and safeguards the individual against violations of his or her rights by other individuals, by administrations, or by the state. We can thus say that the expansion of the division of labor does not just transform society from a predominance of the collective to a predominance of the individual. It is much more a transformation of the form of collective solidarity, which is a precondition for establishing and securing the autonomy of the individual. There is growth of this type of collective solidarity together with growth of individual autonomy in the advancing process of the division of labor. Durkheim calls this type of solidarity organic solidarity. It has a negative and a positive element. The negative element means that individuals respect each other's rights and do not interfere in areas that count as others' personal possessions. The positive element means that they establish relationships in exchanging products and services and in concluding contracts.

The Growth of Organic Solidarity

Organic solidarity is a form of solidarity that does not hold together similar parts, as does mechanical solidarity, but holds together dissimilar parts, namely specialized autonomous individuals. The questions then are whether and how organic solidarity grows with the division of labor. Durkheim makes several attempts at answering these questions. The first answer is that the expansion of labor division brings about organic solidarity in itself. Why is that? Because the societal parts and the individuals become dependent on each other. In primitive society, which is composed of similar segments, such dependence does not arise. Therefore, it is not unusual that some families leave a community and go to another one. Because the other parts of the community do not depend on that family they do not react by attempting to keep that family within the community. It is different in functionally differentiated societies. Here the parts fulfill a very specific function that cannot easily be replaced by other parts. Ties of mutual dependence hold them together. However, is this mutual dependence a sufficient foundation for solidarity? Here Durkheim has doubts about his explanation, because it would not be very different from Spencer's complementarity of interests. This complementarity, though, is too short-lived to provide a stable basis for a stable solidarity, as Durkheim points out. A consciousness of mutual dependence that has grown during a history of exchange may contribute to establishing organic solidarity but is by no means a sufficient ground for its stabilization.

Therefore, there must be other forces at work. As Durkheim emphasizes, the expansion of labor division brings people into contact with each other who would otherwise live separate lives in small groups. With the expansion of labor division a network of social relationships covering ever more areas and corners of society to include them all in a whole system of interrelated parts becomes established. These are social relationships that are not only economic exchange-relationships but also relationships of association and cooperation. In expanding association and cooperation, people share a common life, acquire common views and norms, and establish feelings of belonging and trust. With economic exchange, ties of solidarity also will be established between people the more the corresponding relationships continue to bring people together on a regular basis.

People carry out contracts and share norms about proper contractual behavior not because their interests are complementary in character but because they live in a commonly shared world. This is what Durkheim meant when he argued that the expansion of labor division brings about organic solidarity in itself. This is an argument that has largely been missed by subsequent criticism, which has concentrated too much on the mutual dependence of functionally differentiated parts. This is indeed close to Spencer's complementarity of interests and does not provide sufficient grounds for establishing bonds of solidarity. Because people's association in links of exchange establishes a commonly shared world, there are elements in organic solidarity that are similar to mechanical solidarity. The fact that civil, administrative, and constitutional law expand together with the division of labor and the fact that the legal system is a collective phenomenon and is anchored in common norms and solidarity whenever it is stable and not just based on actually superior power point to this collective dimension of organic solidarity.

Abnormal Forms of Labor Division

Durkheim does not claim that the division of labor will necessarily bring about organic solidarity. In the final part of his book he deals with abnormal forms of labor division. One of these is the anomic division of labor that is characterized by the absence of rules or the lack of authority exerted by rules for regulating economic life. The result is confusion about what is right or wrong, or permanent deviation from norms and universal mistrust. Another is the imposed division of labor; this imposes exchange relationships on individuals, groups, or whole classes, like the working class, that are unequal. One part of society draws more from the exchange than it has invested, the other part less than it has invested. Permanent conflict and class struggle result from imposed division of labor. A third form of abnormal division of labor emerges when specialization involves establishing useless functions and a lack of exchange. In this case individuals have no joy in their work and do not relate to one another regularly, so cannot establish relationships of solidarity.

Organic Solidarity and Professional Groups

In the preface to the second edition of *The Division of Labor in Society* (1893/1973a) Durkheim concedes that he wrote the book with too optimistic a view of the division of labor's ability to bring about organic solidarity by itself. According to his argumentation in the preface to the second edition, there must be additional forces that bind individuals to common norms. Only the integration of individuals into groups can perform this function. But where do we find such groups? The family is too small to provide for society-wide solidarity. The same is true for any local community.

The state is too remote from the individual to bind him or her to common norms. There must be groups of some kind that are close enough to the individual but which are society-wide in their compass. The groups that can fulfill this function are the professional groups.

The greater part of an individual's life is occupied by work. Therefore, professional groups can regulate much of an individual's behavior. On the other hand, the professions reach throughout society so that they can draw an individual's attention to society. However, in order to fulfill this function, the professional groups must not regard themselves purely as interest groups. They have to take up a moral function, that is, the function of establishing a professional ethics that rules professional work and the professional's relationship to others and to society. Professional groups can occupy an intermediate position between the individual and particularistic groups on the one hand and state and society on the other. To fulfill this function, professional organizations should be represented in parliaments. Whereas parliaments would be the place of decision making, committees that include representatives of all professional groups of an industrial branch would have to apply these decisions, which again become even more specific in the individual professional organizations. In this way society becomes a system of closely interrelated professional groups. This is what would provide for organic solidarity. However, because the medieval professional groups went into decline after the rise of industrialism, there is no corresponding system of professional organization in modern societies that would perform this function. Therefore, Durkheim argues for the development of such organizations in order to work against modern society's development toward anomic forms of labor division.

Suicide

Durkheim saw modern society in a state of moral crisis, that is, lacking social order, when he wrote the introduction to the second edition of *The Division of Labor in Society* (1893/1973a). In his study on *Suicide*, published in 1897, he addressed this state of moral crisis explicitly (Durkheim, 1897/1973c). It is not the occurrence of suicide that indicates such a moral crisis, just as the mere occurrence of criminality and other forms of deviant behavior do not necessarily express disorder. If they are kept within certain limits, they are normal concomitants of the fact that social life is not regulated by instincts but by norms to which individuals orient their behavior and with regard to which they decide more or less voluntarily whether to conform or not to conform. As long as norms and behavior are not identical phenomena, deviation of behavior from norms is a common feature. Otherwise, norms would either demand too little from behavior, or behavior would be completely repressed and lose its freedom. In addition, the normal treatment of deviation in procedures of sanctioning contributes to keeping alive the collective consciousness about the validity of norms. On the other hand, deviation is a necessary precondition for innovation, which is a most important feature of modern societies.

It is not the mere occurrence of suicides, crime, and other forms of deviant behavior that indicates a state of moral crisis but a disproportionate growth of these phenomena. This is undoubtedly the case when we look at the development of modern societies. Durkheim observed this fact in studying the statistics of suicide from the 1840s to the 1880s. We can add that this trend has persisted in the twentieth century up to the present day. What are the reasons for this state of moral crisis in modern society? In dealing with this phenomenon Durkheim conceives of suicide as any case of "death resulting directly or indirectly from a positive or negative act of the victim himself, which he knows will produce this result" (Durkheim, 1897/1973c; for this translation see 1952: 44).

Durkheim is not concerned with individual cases of suicide and their individual reasons but with suicide as a social phenomenon that he wants to explain by social causes. Therefore, he studies rates of suicide. In doing so he distinguishes his sociologism from the psychologism of Gabriel Tarde, against which Durkheim had to fight during his time. He used social statistics in order to deal with suicide as a hard social fact that can be studied like a thing in an objectivistic sense, according to his definition of the social fact and according to his idea of studying social phenomena with positivistic methods of empirical and quantitative investigation.

In the first part of his book Durkheim points out the deficiencies of attempts at explaining suicide that take recourse to nonsocial causes like mental alienation, race, heredity, climate, temperature, and imitation, the latter being a favorite psychological mechanism of his opponent Tarde. After this criticism of attempts at explaining suicide in terms of nonsocial causes he turns his attention to three different social causes according to which he also distinguishes three types of suicide: altruistic, egoistic, and anomic suicide.

Altruistic Suicide

Durkheim (1897/1973c: book 2, ch. 4) shows that suicide is not a phenomenon of modern societies alone; he notes that it also occurs in primitive and traditional societies but has causes that are very different from those in modern societies. In primitive and traditional societies it is common that men on the threshold of old age or men stricken with illness commit suicide; women also do so after their husband's death, and followers or servants do so after their master's death. Because there is no longer a place for them in society, they are expected to leave. Thus it is society that imposes pressure on individuals to put an end to their lives when there is no longer a place for them. People have an obligation to commit suicide in these cases; thus, Durkheim calls this type of suicide obligatory altruistic suicide. It is altruistic because it comes from the individual's subordination to society's expectations. Society is everything; the individual is nothing. It is obligatory because it is prescribed for certain situations.

A second type of altruistic suicide is common in Asian societies, particularly in Japan. Here the life of the individual has no value. Therefore one does not gain a reputation by clinging to life but, quite the reverse, giving up life for the slightest reason is most praiseworthy. Durkheim calls this type of suicide optional altruistic suicide. It is altruistic because it follows from a collective devaluation of individual life, and it is optional because there are no prescriptions as to when the individual has to commit suicide. The individual is left the choice of committing suicide in a wide area of situations.

A third type of altruistic suicide is acute altruistic suicide, which is also very common in Asian societies, particularly those under the influence of Hinduism and Buddhism. Here the worldly life of the individual is completely devalued compared to the salvation one attains in retreating from life, finally entering Nirvana in the Buddhist view. This type of suicide is altruistic because it is caused by the collective devaluation of worldly life; it is acute because it is inspired by the religious desire for salvation. We can see that what Durkheim means by altruism in this type of suicide is the individual's submission to the collective devaluation of individual worldly life. A person commits suicide because he or she shares the collective devaluation of individual worldly life.

Studying the social statistics of suicide in European countries of his time, Durkheim made a striking observation: there was a persistently higher rate of suicide in the army compared to that in the civilian population. How could this feature be explained?

As Durkheim points out, it is not disgust with the service that explains this phenomenon, because suicide is more likely the longer the soldier has served, and it is highest in the group of volunteers and in the corps of officers. His explanation is that suicide in the army is a remnant of traditional society and corresponds to the altruistic type of suicide. It is a survival of traditionalism's devaluation of individual life:

Influenced by this predisposition, the soldier kills himself at the least disappointment, for the most futile reasons, for a refusal of leave, a reprimand, an unjust punishment, a delay in promotion, a question of honor, a flush of momentary jealousy or simply because other suicides have occurred before his eyes or to his knowledge. (Durkheim, 1897/1973c; for this translation, see 1952: 238–39)

The soldier commits suicide because of his subordination to a collective that devalues individual life. The fact that the difference between the suicide rate of the army and the suicide rate of the civilian population has gone down proves its traditional causation. Because the army has increasingly come under the influence of secular individualistic morality, altruistic suicide has become less common. The types of suicide that are typical of modern society are the egoistic and the anomic type to which we now turn our attention.

Egoistic Suicide

Durkheim (1897/1973c: book 2, chs. 2, 3) revealed what he called egoistic suicide by examining the statistics of suicides with reference to religious denomination and marital status. The statistics of several European countries showed a strikingly higher rate of suicide among Protestants than Catholics, and the lowest rate among Jews, with the Jewish rate always lower than the Protestant rate. How can this phenomenon be explained? As Durkheim pointed out, both Protestantism and Catholicism condemn suicide, whereas Judaism does not condemn it explicitly, though it does not explicitly allow suicide. Therefore, a different attitude toward suicide does not explain the difference in the statistics from one faith to another. What could be an explanatory factor is the status of a minority or a majority, as shown by the example of the Jews who had always lived in a minority situation and had very low suicide rates. However, Protestants in a minority position commit many more suicides than their surrounding Catholic majority. Thus minority or majority position also fails to give a sufficient explanation.

Durkheim therefore looked more closely at the character of the religious communities as social systems. A first hint toward such an explanation is the fact that the suicide rate increases with the level of education. Protestants' level of education in Durkheim's day was on the average higher than that of Catholics, both in terms of people going to elementary school and of people graduating from secondary school or even university. Durkheim sees this difference as a feature that accompanies another difference between the two denominations: the degree of integration and social control. The Catholic church is closely integrated, hierarchically organized, and controls the interpretation of religious dogmas centrally; it administers the religious life of its members. The Protestant church is less integrated, exerts less social control, and administers religious life to a lesser extent; the Protestants' relation to God is much more of an individual matter. Thus, it is the individual's task to interpret God's word. As Durkheim puts it, he or she has much more freedom of investigation. The Protestant is left alone in questions of finding meaning, and he or she is used to living alone much more than is the Catholic. Therefore the Protestant is much less controlled by the religious community and more easily detaches him- or herself from others, which includes the ultimate detachment of committing suicide. It is the much more advanced individualism, the isolation of the individual, and the weaker integration of the religious group that causes higher rates of suicide in the Protestant than in the Catholic faith. It is not higher education as such that is responsible for higher suicide rates but too little integration of the religious group and too much individualism that explains the higher suicide rates specific to Protestantism. The case of Jews is a good proof of this interpretation, because they combine a high level of education with a low rate of suicide. The individual's weak commitment to the group is the cause of suicide; this is Durkheim's reason for calling it egoistic suicide.

A second area where Durkheim observed egoistic suicide was the area of family life. He discovered from studying social statistics that there was a higher rate of suicide among unmarried and widowed persons compared to married persons. The rate of suicide also went down with the number of children. The effect on the different sexes in this regard was different in different countries. These observations offered Durkheim further proof of his explanation of egoistic suicide. The single person lacks commitment to and control by a group and lives a life on his or her own, an isolated individual life, so that there are no forces that hold him or her in society in situations of personal crisis. The member of a family has ties to a group that controls the person's life and prevents him or her from leaving society.

A third area of egoistic suicide is the area of political society. Durkheim observed that in times of political conflict, external and internal warfare, the rate of suicide went down. His explanation was that in these times the groups and society as a whole absorb the attention of the individual, so that there is little room for separating from groups and society as a whole and therefore little room for committing egoistic suicide. Political society or the political groups of society are more integrated in times of conflict.

Summarizing his analysis, Durkheim formulated the following three propositions:

> Suicide varies inversely with the degree of integration of religious society. Suicide varies inversely with the degree of integration of domestic society. Suicide varies inversely with the degree of integration of political society. (Durkheim, 1897/1973c; for this translation, see 1952: 208)

Anomic Suicide

The third type investigated by Durkheim (1897/1973c: book 2, ch. 5) is anomic suicide. This type of suicide is related to the dynamic changes that take place when society's social order undergoes transformations and social control at least partly breaks down. This is particularly true of economic change. The facts in this area are the following: Suicide rates increase in times of economic crisis; however, the same is true for times of abrupt increases in prosperity and for steadily growing prosperity. The strata mostly involved in economic achievement, the strata of commerce and industry, have the highest rates of suicide. How can these facts be explained?

Durkheim starts his explanation of these facts with the following assumption:

> No living being can be happy or even exist unless his needs are sufficiently proportioned to his means. (Durkheim, 1897/1973c; for this translation, see 1952: 246)

Whereas the animal's instinctive apparatus provides for a balance between needs and means, the human being is much less held in balance by such an apparatus. There are no implanted limits to the human being's needs. Therefore, he or she always lives in danger of being frustrated by a gap between his or her unlimited needs and his or her limited means. A balance between them cannot come from the individual because of the lack of instinctive control. Only an order imposed from outside can establish such a balance within the individual. Here is the point where the individual needs guidance and control by society. Only the norms of society can provide such a regulation of needs and means. Without such a balance brought forth by society, the individual is permanently plagued with frustration. His or her will to live weakens. Suicide becomes more likely.

How can society fulfill the function of regulating the relationship between an individual's needs and means? The individual has to have rules that define an appropriate level of aspirations and a corresponding level of satisfaction of those aspirations. Such definitions of appropriate levels of aspiration and reward have to be established collectively in society, because the individual is not disposed to do that on his or her own. But how can society define such levels of appropriate aspiration and reward? Traditional societies have an established order that determines a certain standard of living for each estate in a hierarchical system. In such a system nobody strives for more than can be attained. This traditional hierarchical order breaks down with the emergence of modern society, which allows everyone to strive for achievement. However, because not everybody can succeed, frustration abounds, particularly in times of economic breakdown when established levels of aspiration can no longer be satisfied, and in times of economic prosperity, when the level of aspiration rises faster than the means of satisfying them. Durkheim knew that there was no way back to the traditional hierarchy in modern society. A new collective order was needed, one that defined appropriate levels of aspiration and gave economic activity an institutional control.

Because the individual cannot establish such an order he or she needs guidance by society. And society will bring about this guidance only under two conditions: it has to be accepted as a moral authority by the individual, and the order that defines levels of aspiration has to be accepted as just by the individual. The individual has to be integrated into groups that regulate economic life and has to be involved in the process of discourse, which justifies the attribution of rewards to achievements. Here, again, Durkheim expected the development of a system of interrelated professional organizations to provide a solution to this problem.

A second area of anomic suicide is the area of marital status. Durkheim observed a growing rate of suicide with the growth of divorce; this held true much more for men than for women. Durkheim's explanation of this fact was the lack of sexual regulation in the state of divorce, particularly for men. They live in a state of sexual anomy.

Particularly the area of marital status brings egoistic and anomic suicide close to one another. However, they have to be distinguished: Egoistic suicide occurs when society or the social group is remote from the individual; it is a continuing state. Anomic suicide occurs when a society that is present in the individual's mind undergoes dynamic change resulting in disorder and in society's inability to control the individual.

Morality

With the publication of his study on *Suicide*, Durkheim believed that the moral order of modern societies was no longer a fact that had to be explained appropriately — as he had tried to do in the first edition of his *Division of Labor in Society* — but rather a problem which had to be solved. He then devoted his work to investigating the social foundations of a moral order appropriately designed for modern society. Because religion no longer was able to fulfill its original moral function in a modern rationalized society, Durkheim felt this moral basis had to be a secular rational morality. However, rationality is not enough, because rationality does not tell people why they should be rational. Some authority must back up rational morality. There is something in religion that has established its original authority; the task of a sociology of morality is to abstract these authority-lending elements from religion and to link them to rationality. In doing so, Durkheim (1914/1970, 1924/1974a, 1925/1974b; for translation see 1961, 1965, 1973d) argued that morality is composed of three interrelated elements: (1) the spirit of discipline, (2) the attachment to groups, and (3) the autonomy of self-determination of the individual.

The Spirit of Discipline

The first element, the spirit of discipline, points to the fact that moral action always involves acting in a regular way. It is predictable, recurrent behavior on which we can base our expectations. However, it is not just customary action performed purely out of habit. There is something more: the submission to the authority of a rule that has an absolutely binding character. The moral act cannot result from situationally varying interests and expected utility, because this would not bring about a constant pattern of action, which is a central feature of moral action. It is something much more like a duty that binds the actor to a rule independently of its utility for the actor. This is what Durkheim (1924/1974a) takes up from Kant's (1788/1964d) moral philosophy. Kant clearly states that a moral rule that is valid independently of any situation cannot be observed because of some expected utility but has to be adhered to because it is demanded from everybody as a duty. However, Durkheim criticizes Kant to the effect that he does not see personal commitment and motivation as a major element of moral action. Without this personal commitment and motivation, moral action would be a bloodless, disinterested process of following prescriptions, not a passionate commitment to doing something that is good. Thus, there is another side to moral action: the individual's desire to do good. Duty and individual commitment to do good have to be linked to each other in the moral act. Education has to not only impose duties but also attract positively the individual's passion for doing good. In the moral act, societal external duty and individual passion penetrate each other. According to these two components of the moral act, we can distinguish two moral characters: the self-controlled, disciplined character who carries out his or her duties with absolute reliability, and the passionate, earnest character who is fully devoted to doing good and to living for an ideal.

Durkheim conceives of the human individual as a dual being: mind and body, reason and senses, the sacred and the profane, the social and the individual, and duty and desire determine the human being's conduct. The one component stands for order, and the other for dynamics. The more the human being grows toward a moral personality, the more the two components mutually penetrate each other. Reducing this moral development of the human personality to the utilitarians' unfolding of self-interest is as wrong as its reduction by Kantian rationalism to reason and duty. In moral conduct duty and desire have to penetrate each other.

Everyday moral action cannot come about by derivation from abstract moral norms like Kant's categorical imperative. Such abstract norms cannot bring about concrete rules for everyday action. They can only serve as a rational measure for them. Everyday morality that is binding in concrete situations consists much more of many particular rules that define concretely what is right and wrong in specific situations. The origin of these concrete moral norms is not philosophy but the traditional life of a concrete society.

Morality imposes discipline on the individual, insofar as it is an external constraint exerted upon him or her by society. However, this does not mean that there is a contradiction between moral constraint and individual freedom. Without self-control provided by morality, the individual would be a prisoner of his or her organic drives and individual desires, which the individual could never bring into balance without the guidance of a moral order. Furthermore, the very principle of individual autonomy in our modern society is a moral principle established collectively and is responsible for liberating the individual from arbitrary domination. The cult of the individual, the enlightenment of the individual are collective undertakings with a moral message aiming at emancipating that individual. In this light, moral discipline is the originator of individual autonomy.

Attachment to Groups

Yet where does this moral discipline come from? According to Durkheim, neither one individual nor a plurality of individuals can be the originator or the object of a moral act. Such a determination of the moral act would bring about not a uniform pattern of moral action throughout society but a multitude of contradictory actions. However, a crucial aspect of moral acts is that we consider them to be binding for everybody. How can such a binding character and uniformity of actions occur? Durkheim's answer is that this must be something above and beyond the individual. In a religious setting, God fulfills this function. However, such a solution is no longer feasible in a secularized society. What is it, then, that occupies a place above single individuals and reaches beyond them? It is society that fulfills this criterion. Only society has the authority to bring about rules that are binding beyond specific individuals and situations. Durkheim's answer to the question of the origin of a moral rule's binding quality for everybody and every situation has been interpreted as an outcome of his inclination toward authoritative solutions to the problem of social order. There is certainly some truth in this interpretation. However, there is also a more abstract element in Durkheim's argument that has mostly been missed. "Society" stands for the argument that there will be no regularly patterned moral conduct without society-wide uniform reaction to individual behavior. Thus, the universal validity of moral rules can never be established on the level of the individual's unavoidably particularistic interests but only on the level of society.

In order to perform this role, society needs commonly shared moral rules, a moral consensus, and solidarity in backing up these rules by uniformly applied sanctions. As regards the relationship between the individual and society, the individual will not respect the moral rules if they are just imposed by external power. Only if the individual feels respect for society will he or she also feel respect for its moral rules. Punishment of immoral conduct has to be carried out in a way that it is never felt to be arbitrary, an outburst of rage, or the cool application of superior force. Rather, punishment must reinstate respect for society's moral authority and for its moral rules. Society has to be perceived as a moral authority by the individual. This moral authority, however, will never be established if the individual does not feel a commitment to society and if he or she does not feel society's efforts to establish and apply rules are generally accepted as just.

Forming a moral consensus shared by the members of society becomes the major device for establishing a moral authority. Agencies responsible for establishing and applying rules, like legislative bodies, courts, and administrations, will not be accepted as moral authorities if they do not manage to establish and maintain a moral consensus throughout society. This is what Durkheim means when he says that morality begins with the attachment of the individual to social groups, which is the second element of morality. This attachment to social groups begins with the individual's attachment to his or her family, which is the first moral authority for the individual. However, the family's moral authority is restricted to the small circle of domestic life. It cannot regulate social life throughout all society and even beyond the boundaries of national societies. In order to surpass these limitations the individual has to be attached to ever wider social groups in the process of his or her socialization: to a national society via school and professional groups and to humanity via the national society. In this process the individual breaks through the moral particularism of particularized groups and becomes committed to a truly moral universalism.

The same process has to turn the individual's commitment away from society as it factually exists in its institutions and toward the moral ideals that are praised by society. The individual has to learn to respect these moral ideals as sacred and to differentiate them from everything that is profane. The sacred thing is untouchable and unchangeable, with an external, absolute validity, everywhere and for everybody. Profane things are those that can be changed and used instrumentally according to varying interests. The moral ideal of modern society has established the individual personally as the sacred thing backed up by basic human and civil rights. This sacralization of the human personality is far from preaching egotism. It is much more a collective concern for the rights of the individual personality and for the mutual compatibility of different individuals' rights.

Autonomy

The third element of morality is individual autonomy. An act that is not conducted voluntarily does not have the quality of a moral act, according to our modern understanding. An action conducted because one is forced by external sanctions to do so is not praiseworthy in moral terms. Only the individual's voluntary commitment to do so gives him or her moral esteem. In this regard, Durkheim again follows Kant's moral philosophy. However, he says, the freedom moral sociology is concerned with cannot be a metaphysical freedom of the reasonable human being as such. According to Kant, the human individual is free as soon as he or she leaves behind any involvement in organic drives, physical causation, and particularistic desires and manages to attain the position of a being guided by nothing but universal reason. As such a being, the human individual is free from external causation. At the same time this freedom allows him or her to see what is right and what is wrong. The individual will make the categorical imperative a guiding principle: "So act that the maxim of your will could always hold at the same time as a principle establishing universal law" (Kant, 1788/1964d; for this translation, see 1952b: 302).

Durkheim does not attribute the individual's moral conduct completely to this freedom as a reasonable being. Whereas Kant sees freedom and commitment to the moral law as one and the same thing, Durkheim still locates the individual's commitment to moral conduct in an attachment to society's moral authority. With the freedom of the reasonable human being, there will be knowledge about moral reasons for action but no concrete commitment to disciplined moral conduct. The latter can only be an outcome of the individual's attachment to the social group. Durkheim cuts back Kant's moral freedom to its specific function: the enlightenment of the individual that opens his or her eyes to see and understand the reasons for the validity of moral rules. Enlightening the individual is the task of moral science. Durkheim himself wants to establish this moral science with his own sociology of education, which he wants to have institutionalized in education at school. After the breakdown of religion the school has to teach this secular morality. The outcome of this teaching of moral science should be the autonomous personality that is committed to moral conduct by an attachment to social groups but nevertheless enlightened about the reasons for moral conduct by moral science.

State, Civil Morality, and Democracy

The quest for a moral order of modern society is also a major concern of Durkheim's theory of the state, civil morality, and democracy (Durkheim, 1950/1969; see Prager, 1981; Müller 1983). Durkheim's concern here is how political decision making can proceed in such a way that it is open for the pluralism of interests on the one hand but guided by moral ideas on the other. He first rejects purely individualistic and purely collectivistic theories of the state. Individualistic theories like John Locke's contract theory derive the establishment of the state and its decision making from the occasional convergence or complementarity of individual interests. The collectivistic theories like Jean-Jacques Rousseau's (1762/1964) contract theory conceive of the state as a collective organization that imposes its power on the individual without leaving room for individual choice. The individualistic theories are unable to explain the state as a reality *sui generis*. The collectivistic theories are unable to explain the participation of the individual as a true individual in political decision making. Durkheim's theory combines collectivism and individualism. The state is a collective organization *sui generis* that secures the uniform establishment and application of laws but needs the participation of the individual's motivation in order to set its laws in motion. The human individual is a being motivated by his or her desires who needs the order provided by the laws of the state in order to keep these desires in balance and in order to unfold his or her individual personality.

The state emerges as a specific center of collective decision making in the process of dividing labor (or functions) in society. In this process the state is differentiated from political society. The latter is composed of a plurality of particular groups with particularistic interests. The former becomes the center of social deliberation. In that central role, the state has to organize political decision making in such a way that political decisions on lawmaking become abstracted from the diffuse feelings, particularistic interests, and prejudices of particular groups and oriented toward the common good. Lawmaking thus becomes a matter of finding out what is right for society as a whole. In order to perform this function of an organ of central social deliberation the state has to be free from any domination of particular groups, but it must not be cut off from society. Without some degree of distance from society the state cannot raise decision making above the struggle of interests to the level of finding out what is right for society as a whole. If, however, the state is completely separated from society, it receives neither the information about society's problems nor the motivation of individuals and groups in making and carrying out collective decisions. Democracy is the form of political authority in which state and society are differentiated but at the same time are mutually linked in close communication. Democracy at least allows such a combination of differentiation and interpretation that has to be expanded in modern society. Here Durkheim assigns a central function to secondary groups, particularly the professional organizations, to mediate between the state and the mass of individuals and to organize their communication.

The state plays a central role in binding the individual to the nation and also in leading the individual toward a concern for global humanity. In doing so the modern state combines internal patriotism with external universal humanism. The state is also the liberator of the individual inasmuch as its lawmaking is guided by a civil morality that defines the rights and duties of the individual with regard to the state and the rights and duties of the state with regard to the individual. The more collective decision making is organized as social deliberation, the more it will be oriented toward finding out and applying moral ideas that are binding for everybody. The civil and human rights of the individual are the basic credo of modern society, and the state, particularly its courts, becomes the major agency for securing these individual rights. In this way the state is the organizer of the cult of the individual. State and individual become intimately linked. Without the guardianship of the state's courts there would be no sacred individual autonomy; without the individual's motivated participation, the state would be a bloodless, bureaucratic organization.

Religion

In his final major work, *The Elementary Forms of the Religious Life*, published in 1912, Durkheim engaged in an investigation in the most elementary forms of social order (Durkheim, 1912/1968; for a translation, see 1976). He expected to find out these elementary forms by studying the religion of the primitive tribal societies of the Australian Aborigines. In doing so he studied the original ethnographic reports of anthropologists of his time. His study provides a theory of Australian totemism, of religion in general, and of knowledge in general. His primary concern, though, is the roots of social order.

In his approach to the phenomenon of religion, Durkheim rejects every attempt at conceiving of religion in purely intellectual terms. Religion is not only a system of beliefs, a cultural system, but also an ordered practice organized by society, that is, a social system. Religion is on the one hand a practice of a group integrated by mutual solidarity, a practice of a moral community, for example, a church, and on the other hand it is a system of beliefs. But practice and beliefs are directed to things that are conceived of as sacred. What is conceived of as sacred calls upon the respect, the admiration, but also the fear of the individual; it is seen as untouchable and unchangeable. In distinction to the sacred, the profane things of life are open for manipulation and change according to situational interests. The sacred can be a totem, for example, a tree, an animal, a certain place, a building, a book like the Holy Bible, a text like a constitutional agreement, or a moral ideal. The profane are the superficial and instrumentally used things of everyday life. The function of a religion is to separate out the untouchable sacred things from the profane spheres of life, which is nothing other than to secure the maintenance of certain moral ideas as stable roots of social order. Without such a maintenance of sacred ideals society would lose its identity and would be unable to continue life as one and the same society.

How does society manage to maintain such an identity by separating the sacred from the profane? The central precondition for this achievement uncovered by Durkheim's study of primitive religion is a vital religious practice that is anchored in social solidarity and confirms that social solidarity.

There must first be a social solidarity in society that is represented by a tradition of common action, confirmed by a stable membership, and specified by the recurrent arrival at a social consensus. Then there must be symbols (e.g., emblems, banners) that give the group's identity a visible and continuing expression. Religious rites, as regular gatherings, reconfirm the group's solidarity. Cults direct the group toward its unique sacred objects (totems, ideas). Symbols, rites, and cults contribute to maintaining the group's solidarity and are themselves anchored in this solidarity. Furthermore, religious symbols mediate the group's solidarity with religious beliefs, particularly moral ideas; religious rites mediate the group's solidarity with the individual's situational religious experience; the cult mediates the group's solidarity with the religious organization directed by religious leaders like medicine men and priests.

This is Durkheim's picture of a society that is capable of maintaining its social order in religious practice and beliefs directed toward upholding the sacred against the profane, derived from his analyses of primitive religion. Inasmuch as society has an order it is rooted in such a system of religious practice and belief. Hence, Durkheim points out that religious belief is not irrational in character but the very origin of social knowledge. The production of social knowledge proceeds in the very way in which religious belief is produced in an immense collective cooperation. As Durkheim puts it, the collective representations of modern science are the outcome of an immense collective cooperation. Without such cooperation there would be no collectively binding knowledge. And it is this dimension of knowledge that is Durkheim's concern: its universal validity and collectively binding character. Without being rooted in this cooperative process of society, no scientific knowledge would be taken as valid and collectively binding. This dimension of the universal (that is, society-wide, approaching worldwide) validity and binding character of knowledge is Durkheim's concern when he speaks of the social origin of science and of its evolution from religion.

Although Durkheim points out the collective production of religious beliefs, moral ideas, and knowledge in primitive societies, he nevertheless claims to have uncovered the vital collective processes that lie in religious terms at the very origin of human social order and human thought from which social order and human thought evolve; furthermore, he claims that the same collective processes are needed in secular terms in order to produce social order and human thought in modern society.

Summary

Social Fact

1. Society is a system of social facts.
2. Social facts are external to the individual, exert constraint, are universal in character, and have to be studied like an objective thing.

3. Social facts and society are a reality *sui generis*.
4. Social facts are institutional patterns of social life, that is, recurrent patterns of behavior.
5. The more patterns of behavior are the outcome of a society-wide uniform reaction to them that is backed up by commonly shared norms, consensus, and solidarity, the more firmly these patterns will be institutionalized.

The Division of Labor in Society

6. The more the population grows, the greater the volume of society and its material, dynamic, and moral density.
7. The greater the volume and density of society, the greater the pressure toward specialization and the greater the growth of the division of labor.
8. The more people live in close intimate contact, live in the same world, and are therefore similar to each other, have a concrete collective consciousness of commonly shared norms, and control conduct by repressive law, the greater will be their mechanical solidarity.
9. The more people are dissimilar to each other but interact closely in exchanging products of specialized labor, have an abstract collective consciousness with commonly shared abstract ideas, share norms of contract and control conduct by restitutive law, the greater will be their organic solidarity.
10. The more the division of labor progresses, the smaller will be the part played by mechanical solidarity and the greater will be the part played by organic solidarity in society.
11. The more professional groups link the individual to society and interrelate in common consultative bodies, the greater will be organic solidarity.

Suicide

12. The more closely integrated a society and the more it devalues individual life, the greater the rate of suicide.
13. The weaker the integration of social groups and the greater the individual isolation, the greater the rate of suicide.
14. The more aspirations outgrow the means of satisfying these aspirations, the greater the rate of suicide in a society.

Morality

15. The more an individual respects the moral authority of the group, the more he or she is attached to the group, the more he or she becomes included in ever larger groups from family to society to humanity, and

the more he or she is enlightened by moral science, the more the individual's conduct will have the quality of disciplined self-control backed up by individual passion, moral universalism, and personal autonomy.

State, Civil Morality, and Democracy

16. The more the state mediates between universal moral ideas and particular interests, diffuse feelings, and prejudices of particular individuals and groups, thus acting as a center of social deliberation, the more political decision making will establish a moral order in society.
17. The more democracy encourages the social communication between the particular groups and the state via organized secondary groups, the more democracy will establish a moral order.
18. The more the state organizes the cult of the individual, the more intimately it links society and the individual.

Religion

19. The more a society is rooted in the solidarity of its members who share a tradition, a stable membership, and a consensus and who commonly practice a cult that singles out the sacred moral idea from the profane world and mediates group solidarity with group organization toward specific ends, and the more they renew this in regular ties, which mediate group solidarity with individual experience, and generalize this in religious symbols, which mediate group solidarity with religious beliefs, the more this society will establish a moral order.

Critical Assessment

Durkheim's major contribution to sociology is his establishment of the social fact as a unique dimension of reality that gives sociology its unique object domain and differentiates sociology from other disciplines, particularly from psychology. Furthermore, we owe to him the most central insights into the production, reproduction, and breakdown of social order as the center of social life. His concern was the institutional and ordered side of social life and its counterpart: the breakdown of that order. However, his preoccupation with social order biased his view of social life in this direction. We therefore learn much about the roots of any ordered aspect of social life in collective solidarity, consensus, cooperation, rites, cults, common symbols, commonly shared beliefs, experiences, and undertakings. But we learn less about the other dimensions of social life. Durkheim's bias toward collective order begins with his definition of the social fact, which fully concentrates on the institutional regulation of social life. However, social life is much more multifaceted: Max Weber's concept of social action is more general in character. It singles out the mutual orientation of actors toward each other in their action as the specific social dimension. This more general definition of sociology's object domain uncovers mutual understanding and misunderstanding, conflict, exchange, and deviation from expectations as dimensions of social life that have to be analyzed independently of institutional regulation and cooperation. The same holds true for power, money, and arguments in distinction to cooperative influence as media of social interaction. They have no independent place in Durkheim's system.

What is true for Durkheim's definition of the social fact also holds true for his various studies. In his study on *The Division of Labor in Society* we learn how the process of labor division proceeds as a transformation of systems of solidarity, from mechanical to organic solidarity. However, we do not learn much about the economic, political, and cultural transformations that accompany this process of the evolution of modern society; they have their own sources and laws and are interdependent with the associational evolution. The economic transformation turns a traditional economy into modern capitalism and gives rise to the political conflict between capital and labor. The political transformation replaces traditional authority with rational-legal authority and gives rise to the bureaucratic domination of social life, including the administration of the economy, and of the differentiation of society. Cultural transformation replaces traditional belief in an established order with a rationalism of mastering the world that consciously intervenes in the process of economic life and social differentiation. The phenomenon of labor division itself has to be conceived of in associational, economic, political, and cultural terms relating to the rise of capitalism, bureaucracy, and instrumental rationalism. Without taking into account these interdependencies we do not arrive at a sufficient explanation of the process of dividing labor in society. We also cannot address the problem of solidarity in modern society without consideration of the interrelationship of the collective cooperation of professional groups with the dynamic functions of voluntary association, the generalizing functions of moral discourse and the formalizing functions of lawmaking and law application in political and judicial decision making. We cannot understand and explain modern forms of solidarity without the liberalizing contribution of voluntary association related to the economic calculation of individual utility, the contribution of formal legality by way of political and judicial decision making, and the contribution of universal rights via rational moral discourse.

In his study on *Suicide*, Durkheim gives insightful explanations of the various types of suicide, but he expects too much from the integration of the individual in professional groups and from the rebuilding of collective order. We live in a *culture* that expects of the individual that he or she will develop a personal self as much as possible, to actively realize his or her idea of him- or herself. This always implies failure and falling short of one's idea of oneself. Thus, our culture is resistant to subordinating the individual to a group and to some collective constriction of levels of aspiration. Individualization and levels of aspiration will rise and expand throughout society, and they have done so since Durkheim published his study. Therefore, it is not surprising that rates of suicide have steadily increased since that time and have included groups that were once much more immune to suicide, particularly women and young people. This is an effect of our culture, which has made individual achievement its central value.

Durkheim's sociology of morality and education is biased toward an authoritative imposition of rules on the individual. He does not see moral advancement in terms of the universalization of moral rules, which takes place when the individual no longer subordinates to a superior authority like parents and teachers as representatives of society but to a group of equals of which he or she is a member. Durkheim makes some steps in this direction, but does not approach a position such as those developed by George Herbert Mead and by Jean Piaget.

According to Mead (1934), moral universalization takes place inasmuch as the child does not simply engage in the *play* of taking the role of a significant other, like mother or father, but takes the role of everybody in a team as is the case in *games* like football, basketball, or baseball. Taking everyone's role in this way, which allows the child to understand the complete network of interrelated roles, is taking the role of the generalized other. Even more generalization will be attained if the child also takes up the role of the opposing team and gets an idea of the whole game, as represented by the umpire. Mead and Durkheim are very close to each other when they expect moral universalization from the individual's inclusion into ever larger groups, leading up to humanity in its entirety. However, Mead is clearer about the fact that the relationship of the individual to the group changes in this process from one of subordination to one of participation. Durkheim and Mead are very close in conceiving of the individual self as a double being: social and individual. However, Durkheim conceives of their interrelationship in terms of a hierarchy in which the individual is obliged to contribute his or her motivation to morally prescribed conduct, whereas Mead conceives of their relationship as an exchange and mutual support between "me" and "I" on equal terms. Thus, the spontaneity of individual experimentation is the moving force of moral advancement against the conservatism of society for Mead, whereas for Durkheim moral advancement is the work of society, which imposes itself on the individual. Moral learning is a collective process of consensus formation for Durkheim. For Mead it is an interplay between individual experimentation and social regulation. We should not exaggerate the difference between Durkheim and Mead, because both have a dual notion of the human individual; however, the sources of creative moral advancement and the sources of moral universalization have been more clearly demonstrated by Mead than by Durkheim. What is deficient in Durkheim's sociology of morality is his insufficient conception of moral universalization and of moral learning, and his bias toward the authoritative imposition of morality on individuals.

These deficiencies also become apparent when we compare Durkheim with Piaget (1932/1973). According to Piaget, a decisive transformation of morality takes place when the child no longer is exclusively oriented toward the superior authority of his or her parents but toward the authority of a peer group of which he or she is a member with equal status and equal rights. In the first phase, a child conforms to norms because he or she fears the sanctions resulting from deviation. This is moral realism and a morality based on external constraint. In the second phase, which Piaget studied with children playing marbles, the child conforms more and more to norms because all the children hold them for valid. In this phase the child attains moral autonomy, and morality is universalistic. Because Piaget turns our attention to the transformation from subordination to the equality of the group he specifies much more precisely than Durkheim the social conditions of moral universalization.

An extension of Piaget's sociology of moral development has been worked out by Lawrence Kohlberg (1969, 1975, 1981, 1984, 1987). He distinguishes three levels of moral development: the pre-conventional, the conventional and the post-conventional. On the pre-conventional level, the individual subordinates him- or herself to some external force or expects profit from conformity to norms; on the conventional level, the individual conforms to norms because of a commitment to formal legality; on the post-conventional level, the individual conforms to norms only insofar as they can be justified by abstract moral principles. In making this distinction Kohlberg has stripped moral development of any social conditions and conceives of this process in purely cognitive terms, as a self-determined process moving toward a logical end. This would reduce moral conduct to Durkheim's third principle only. Piaget's cognitive psychology certainly gives rise to such an extension of his theory. And Piaget himself explained the transformation from moral realism to moral autonomy as an outcome of the improving cognitive capacity of the individual. Nevertheless, his study on playing children demonstrates that this process involves a major transformation of social organization from the domination of authorities to the equality of peers. We can conceive of this transformation as the social foundation of moral universalization. The two processes, cognitive generalization and social universalization, cannot be reduced to one or the other and contribute their different effects to the individual's moral development. We can improve Durkheim's sociology of moral development by both features of Piaget's study.

To get a complete understanding of moral development we therefore should combine Durkheim with Mead and Piaget. Moral development proceeds with the help of the following occurrences: the individual's attainment of moral discipline by respecting the moral authority of the group; moral learning, which flows from individual experimentation; moral universalization, which takes place by rooting morality in the consensus of peers; and cognitive generalization, which proceeds through the individual's growing cognitive capacity and the development he or she undergoes as a result of enlightenment by the progress of moral science.

Durkheim's theory of the state, civil morality, and democracy tends to draw different functions too closely together in one moral function of the state. Inasmuch as the state is the center of collective decision making, it cannot itself perform a major function in society. We have to differentiate what Durkheim conceives of as a moral function of the state into different functions attributed to different institutions that interpenetrate. We may conceive of legislation as a center of this interpenetration. In legislation the following institutions interpenetrate: (1) interest groups and parties, which gather information and interests in society and transmit them as dynamic forces to the process of legislative decision making; (2) the administration, which plans and implements legislation from the point of view of the rational organization of society; (3) legal institutions, which exert control over legislation in terms of the existing legal tradition; and (4) constitutional courts, which transmit moral discourse to the process of legislation, thus setting general standards that it must meet. These are very different contributions by very different institutions to the process of political decision making. We have to keep them apart in order to understand their functions better than Durkheim did by drawing them together into one moral function of the state. We can also assume that a society that differentiates and interpenetrates these functions fulfills them at higher levels than a society that draws them together in a single moral function of the state.

Durkheim's sociology of religion is a major contribution to our understanding of the production and reproduction of social order insofar as we look at the continuation of that order in social cooperation. However, the cultural dimension of religion is much less highlighted by Durkheim. We learn much about the laws of social reproduction, but less about the laws of cultural reproduction, not to mention political and economic reproduction. In modern society we have even more to conceive of social reproduction in terms of its interpenetration with cultural, political, and economic reproduction. Thus, we would have to extend Durkheim's processes of social reproduction to add their interpenetration with rational cultural discourse moving toward the generalization of ideas, with economic production moving toward the accumulation of economic wealth and with the political power struggle moving toward the establishment of hierarchies. We can conceive of this interpenetration as a process in which the social order undergoes a development toward secularization in the sense of cultural rationalization, economic pluralization, and political legalization, and social order extends into these spheres in a process of the sacralization of reason, labor, and legality. In expanding Durkheim's sociology in this way by contributions of theories of culture, economics, and politics we move toward a more comprehensive sociological theory. Durkheim himself has contributed a major part to this undertaking by starting from a theory of the institutional order of society and moving toward embracing the whole of social and individual life. However, we have to move his approach much more in this direction than he did because of his primary concern with the institutional order of society.

Further Developments

Emile Durkheim was most successful in establishing his school of thought in the French academic context of his time. *L'Année sociologique* became the central publication organ of his group. Nevertheless, his direct influence faded after his death, but his indirect influence is still very evident in the school of structuralism, created by Claude Lévi-Strauss (1947, 1962, 1964, 1967, 1968, 1971a, 1971b, 1976; for translation see 1966, 1969a, 1969b, 1973, 1978, 1981). In Germany, Ferdinand Tönnies's work *Community and Society* (1887/1963) became influential. Published some years before Durkheim's *Division of Labor* (1893/1973a) this work dealt with similar problems. The book was reviewed by Durkheim (1889/1975) himself. After World War II, René König (1962, 1978) has contributed to preserving Durkheim's thought, though he has not been successful in establishing a Durkheimian type of sociology. Durkheim's influence was much more effective in British anthropology (Lukes, 1985) and particularly in American sociological functionalism of Parsons's (1937/1968, 1940/1954a, 1951, 1954b, 1954c, 1959, 1961a, 1961b, 1964, 1966, 1967, 1969, 1971, 1977a, 1977b, 1978) analytical and Merton's (1949/1968a, 1968b) empirical kind. The phenomenological part of Durkheim's sociology has been revitalized by Edward A. Tiryakian (1962, 1977). For interpretations, see Nisbet (1974), Pope (1976), Strasser (1976), Lukes (1985), and Gephart (1990a). For renewal, see Besnard (1983).

PART FIVE

The Symbolics of Social Action

NINE

THE DIALECTICS OF FORMAL AND
SUBSTANTIAL RATIONALITY: MAX WEBER

MAX WEBER was born in Erfurt, Germany, on April 21, 1864. The eldest
of seven children, he grew up in Berlin. His father had studied law and made
a career in political government, to the point of becoming a member of
the German Reichstag. He lived a self-contented, hedonistic life. Weber's
mother was the opposite type, a person with a strong religious commitment
to Calvinist Protestantism. The tension between the two shaped their children's lives, particularly that of their eldest son.

After graduating from the *Gymnasium* at the age of eighteen Weber
began studying law at the University of Heidelberg. After three terms he
left Heidelberg to do his military service in Strassburg, where he spent a
lot of time in the house of his uncle, the historian Hermann Baumgarten,
and his aunt Ida, his mother's sister, who was also committed to Calvinist
Protestantism. Weber's intellectual development was shaped by both of them
at that time. He also fell in love with their daughter Emmy, but the complicated relationship broke up after six years. In 1884, Weber returned to Berlin to continue studying law. After graduating in 1889, with a dissertation
on the history of commercial societies in the Middle Ages, he was first a
junior barrister in the Berlin courts and then a lecturer (*Dozent*) at the
University of Berlin. In 1891 he finished his *Habilitationsschrift* on Roman
agrarian history. This type of second dissertation entitled him to be appointed
to the position of professor. Weber lived in his parents' home at this time.

In 1893 Max Weber married; his wife, Marianne, was a well-educated,
emancipated woman who took part in the intellectual and public life of her
time. Their relationship was shaped by deep mutual respect, though it
suffered from a lack of fulfillment in sexual terms. In 1895 Weber was
appointed to the position of an *ordentlicher Professor* in economics at the

University of Freiburg, where he gave an inaugural address on *The Nation-state and Economic Policy*. The next year he was called to the University of Heidelberg to take a chair in economics. Max and Marianne Weber's home in Heidelberg became a center of intellectual life. However, Max Weber never taught regularly at the University of Heidelberg. In 1897 his mother was supposed to spend some time at his home without her husband; however, Weber's father insisted on accompanying her. The young Weber clashed with the old man and told him to leave his house. Weber's father died about a month later. After that, young Max Weber had a complete breakdown, which lasted for the next five years.

In 1903 Weber again began working, first on methodological problems, then on his famous *Protestant Ethic and the Spirit of Capitalism*. A visit to the United States was part of his recovery. Years of productive work followed, but he did not return to teaching at the University of Heidelberg. In 1918 he lectured for the first time in many years for a full semester at the University of Vienna. The next year he accepted a call to the University of Munich, but only a year later, on June 14, 1920, he died of pneumonia.

Max Weber was a scholar who left lasting impressions on his contemporaries; after recovering from his illness he was much involved in establishing sociology as a profession, and later in his life he was also much involved in political debates.

Max Weber is one of the great founders of sociology as a distinct scientific discipline. His work is still of major importance today, not only as a classical source of contemporary sociological thought but also as a contribution to sociology that is still of current relevance for studying major problems of social organization in general and of contemporary society in particular (see Käsler, 1988).

The German Tradition of Idealism and Historicism

Any attempt at understanding the special contribution of Max Weber to sociology has to pay attention to German idealism and historicism that made up the intellectual life-world of Germany during Weber's lifetime. Their roots go back to Kant's critical philosophy, and they are still of major importance for contemporary German thought.

Since Immanuel Kant (1781/1964a, 1784a/1964b, 1784b/1964c, 1788/1964d, 1790/1964e, 1793/1964f, 1795/1964g, 1964h) radically drew the distinction between nature and culture that includes the division of the human being into body and mind as realms of causal necessity on the one hand and of freedom on the other, German thought has continued to claim a special character for the cultural dimension in human existence, which demands the application of special methodological means to cultural studies in distinction to the natural sciences. The scholars who followed Kant and created the philosophy of German idealism, with Georg Wilhelm Friedrich Hegel (1964–71) as the leading figure, even tried to superimpose cultural studies above the natural sciences. Hegel saw the knowledge of the natural sciences as being ultimately subsumed under the overarching synthesis brought about by the absolute knowledge of dialectical philosophy. He also claimed in his philosophy of history a teleological movement of human society toward the reconciliation of reason and reality, which would bridge the Kantian gap between the realms of culture and nature, mind and body, freedom and necessity. Karl Marx (1843/1956, 1844/1968, 1845/1969, 1852/1960, 1859/1961, 1867/1962, 1885/1963b, 1894/1964; Marx and Engels, 1846/1969, 1848/1959a) turned Hegel's philosophy of history upside down, but also claimed a reconciliation of these realms as the final state of human history.

Academic thought, however, turned away from such claims but maintained the distinction between the natural sciences' approach to nature and the humanities' approach to culture. Idealism underwent a historical turn. The major idea was now that human action has meaning and that this meaning has to be *understood* rather than causally *explained* by interpreting it as part of a particular historical cultural pattern. Older historical economists like Wilhelm Roscher (1854–1892) and Karl Knies (1853), and younger historical economists like Gustav Schmoller (1900–1904, 1904, 1918) and Lujo Brentano (1901, 1908a, 1908b, 1916, 1920), rejected the natural science approach of classical economics, which aimed at stating general laws of economic behavior. They emphasized that economic life has to be understood in its meaning by interpreting it as part of a particular historical cultural pattern of a society.

Wilhelm Dilthey (1883/1968, 1924/1964) was the philosopher who drew the distinction between the natural sciences and cultural studies most vigorously. He tried to establish the cultural studies as sciences in their own right, namely as sciences of the mind (*Geisteswissenschaften*). Their method is hermeneutics, the method of discovering the objective meaning of cultural phenomena like texts and works of art by interpretation. Dilthey carried on the hermeneutics of Friedrich Schleiermacher (1911), on whom he published a biography. The text, in the hermeneutic approach, has an objective meaning in itself that has to be separated from the subjective motives and intentions of its author, though hermeneutics has to engage in reconstructing the cultural context from which a text emerged in order to understand its meaning. In this contextual sense, the production of a text by an author who lives in a certain historical situation and has certain intentions is of interest for discovering its meaning. However, the interpreter might arrive at a better understanding of a text's objective meaning than it's author did, as Schleiermacher emphasized.

Nowhere else was this claim to be a science in the most rigorous sense made as vigorously as in Germany at that time. The Anglo-Saxon "arts" and the French "lettres" never made such a claim and therefore always remained part of their object: artistic in character. They never made any major attempts at establishing a distinctive scientific methodology. The German sciences of the mind, however, did do so.

According to Dilthey (1883/1968, 1924/1964), the natural sciences try to discover universally valid causal laws and *explain* particular phenomena causally by such universal laws. However, because there is always a gap between nature and the human mind, the knowledge of the natural sciences that is a product of the human mind always remains external to its object. This is not so for knowledge of the sciences of the mind (*Geisteswissenschaften*). Here, both the subject and object of knowledge are of the same kind and parts of the same realm: culture. Cultural phenomena like human action, literary texts, and works of art have meaning, and it is the *understanding* (*Verstehen*) of this meaning that is the aim of any cultural study, rather than *explaining* (*Erklärung*) its occurrence in causal terms. In taking this approach the student of culture has to place him- or herself emphatically in the particular historical and cultural context of a phenomenon and to understand it by interpreting it as part of that historically particular pattern. For example, in order to understand the German Reformation one has to derive the action of Luther and the actions of his followers from their interpretation of Christian belief. In order to understand a question raised by a member of the audience to a lecturer, one has to derive it from the meaning of the speech as interpreted by this particular member of the audience. One has to re-experience (*Nacherleben*) the meaning given to the speech by that particular person in that particular situation. In this way Dilthey contrasted the particularizing cultural studies to the generalizing natural sciences.

The distinction between generalizing and particularizing sciences was carried on by later generations, but it was liberated from the distinction between the natural sciences and the humanities. Wilhelm Windelband (1873, 1878–80, 1909) and Heinrich Rickert (1896–1902, 1910, 1921, 1924), who shaped what was termed Southwestern German Neo-Kantianism at the turn of the century, drew the distinction between *nomothetic* and *idiographic* sciences independently of the distinction between natural sciences and humanities. This boiled down to assigning a legitimate status to the search for general laws in human behavior. At that time economics and psychology apparently successfully established such a generalizing approach outside the realm of the natural sciences. This had to be taken as a matter of fact. Nevertheless, Windelband and Rickert continued to claim for what then was called cultural science (*Kulturwissenschaft*) a special object domain that was not accessible to the methods of the nomothetic sciences. Inasmuch as their object domain is a historically particular phenomenon it has to be understood by ideographic methods, rather than explained by nomothetic methods.

There is, however, one generalizing aspect in cultural studies introduced by Rickert, namely the methodological device of value-relevance. What a historian studies is always selected from a great many singular events and individuals. However, inasmuch as he or she singles out those events and individuals that are of special relevance for the realization of universally valid values, in the negative or positive sense, his or her study is not arbitrary in character but has general value-relevance, as have the events and individuals studied. These are then historical events and individuals with special historical importance for the realization of generally valid values. Rickert was convinced that there is a limited set of such universally valid values with regard to which historical events and individuals can be studied and measured. As such he tried to renew Kant's critical philosophy of history. Rickert's attempt to formulate a set of universally valid values was much debated, but his notion of value-relevance also remained important for those who didn't follow him completely in his project. Emil Lask (1923), for example, interpreted this notion in a historically relative sense, which means that the historian studies phenomena in relation to values that dominate in a certain historical epoch.

Max Weber's thought was very much shaped by the outlined tradition of idealism and historicism and also by his attempt to overcome its one-sidedness and limitations. A first counterpart to this tradition that is important for understanding Weber's approach is the economic materialism of Karl Marx and its concentration on the impact of capitalism on the development of the modern world. A second counterpart to idealism that shaped Weber's thought is Friedrich Nietzsche's vitalistic philosophy, which abandoned the idealist belief in the realization of universally valid values in the process of historical development and attributed the dynamic force for historical development to the exemplary acts of exemplary individuals. For Nietzsche the idealist heaven of universally valid values has broken down forever. What moves history forward are not universally valid values but the exemplary and powerful acts of exemplary and powerful individuals. With these three roots the interrelated realms of values, interests, and power, of religion, the economy, and politics build up the basic matrix of Weber's thought.

Social Action

If we seek to establish Max Weber's major contribution to sociology, the best answer is that it is the insight that culture makes a difference to the organization and development of society and the insight into the linkage between culture, social structure, and social action. Though Weber's major contribution is on culture and its impact on society, he does not fail to recognize the interdependence between culture, social structure, and social action.

As he puts it, cultural ideas and social interests relate to one another like the tracks and the locomotive in a railway system; that is, cultural ideas mark out the possible path of societal development, whereas the interests of groups impute dynamic motivation. The interrelationship between ideas and interests is of major importance for understanding Weber's contribution to sociology.

Weber's sociology is as much concerned with the dynamics of social action as with the meaning of cultural ideas; it interrelates both of these as the two major aspects of social action. Social action itself has this double face of orientation to meaning on the one hand and motivation by interests on the other. And it is the very concept of social action that Weber introduced as sociology's fundamental concept of the most elementary social phenomenon (Weber, 1922a/1972c: 1–30, for translation see 1968; 1922b/1973: 427–74, for a translation, see 1949, 1968, 1974, 1978; see Stephen P. Turner, 1983). What for Durkheim (1895/1973b) is the concept of the social fact is for Weber the concept of social action: sociology's most elementary concept serving as starting point for any construction of a sociological frame of reference. Durkheim's concept of the social fact locates sociology's most elementary subject matter in the collectively organized and institutionalized dimension of social life. Max Weber's concept of social action does so by referring to the interrelationship between individual actors. Durkheim sees the social in the subordination of the members of a collective to collective constraint and in their control by the collective conscience. Weber sees it in the interdependence between the actions of individuals who are related to each other in a process of carrying out interests and interpreting the meaning of actions and intentions. What for Durkheim is the subordination to collective constraint is for Weber the orientation of an individual's action to the actions of other individuals; what for Durkheim is the control of the individual by the collective conscience is for Weber the individual's interpretation of the meaning of actions. What for Durkheim is the collective conscience is for Weber culture. Thus Weber's basic sociological concept, the concept of social action, covers a much broader area of phenomena, reaching from the dynamic articulation of interests via social action to the interpretation of meaning:

> Action is "social" insofar as its subjective meaning takes account of the behavior of others and is thereby oriented in its course. (Weber, 1922a/1972c: 1; for translation, see 1968: 4)

This is Weber's definition of *social action*. It is a much broader concept of social phenomena than Durkheim's concept of the social fact. It covers not only the collectively organized, constraining, and institutionally controlled part of social action but also the uninstitutionalized accommodation or clash of interests and the mutual interpretation of meaning in social action. Durkheim's social fact is one dimension of social action's several dimensions. In this view the social fact is institutionalized social action and thus a subtype of the general concept of social action.

It is also possible to see Durkheim's and Weber's approaches to the social as divergent if we concentrate on the element of meaning in Weber's concept of social action. In this view Durkheim specializes in studying the collective origins of institutionally regulated social action, whereas Weber specializes in the cultural origins of social institutions and social action. According to Durkheim social order resides in collective solidarity, rites, cults, and collective symbols, and there is nothing that reaches beyond the boundaries of society. God is nothing but the expression of society's authority. According to Weber the maintenance or change of social order depends largely on the meaning actors attribute to that order; this attribution of meaning to social order takes place in procedures of legitimation in which social order is related to cultural ideas of meaningful order that transcend the boundaries of society. God does not just stand for society in Weber's view but also stands for the much more basic human quest for meaning that cannot completely be kept within the boundaries of any existing society. In Durkheim's terms, culture is reduced to the collective conscience; in Weber's terms, culture transcends society. Their interaction is a major force in human history, constituting the dynamics of cultural and societal development. Durkheim studies social action from the perspective of its collective organization; Weber studies social action from the perspective of its cultural determination — however, he does so by acknowledging the interaction between culture, social structure, and social action, of ideas and interests.

The importance of the cultural determination of action for Weber is apparent in the very concept of social action. According to Weber, action is meaningful behavior and social action is meaningful social behavior, that is, mutually oriented action that basically involves the mutual interpretation of an action's meaning. Actors attribute meaning to their own action and to the actions of others, and this is a major determining force of social action. What one does and how one reacts to the action of others depends largely on the meaning one attributes to an action. The Puritan who works hard and reliably in his profession does so because he attributes religious meaning to his profession. His work is part of an overall construction of meaning in his life. He reacts to unreliable behavior from others with moral condemnation because he interprets this behavior not only in economic terms of advantage and disadvantage but also in moral terms of right and wrong. Meaning thus makes a difference to social action. It takes on a different form or substance according to different attributions of meaning. This is the basic message we receive from Weber's view of social action as meaningful social behavior. It is the starting point for an approach to studying social action that takes the determination of social action by culture and its development seriously. Weber's studies of the religious foundations not only of modern capitalism but also of the modern world as such and the different consequences of the world religions for societal order and change and of the legitimatory foundations of domination and authority have their background in this basic understanding of social action as meaningful behavior. In order to understand and explain social action and social development we have to study their determination by the quest for meaning and by systems of meaning and their development.

Starting from the concept of social action Weber constructs a conceptual frame of reference that differentiates types of social action, types of regularities in social action, types of social order and of beliefs in the legitimacy of social order, and types of social relationships and of social associations. Like any other action, social action can be differentiated into four types: means-end (instrumentally) rational, value rational, affectual, and traditional action.

Means-end rational action is oriented toward specific ends and calculates the effectiveness of means for attaining the ends. It also calculates the consequences of using specific means and of attaining specific ends with regard to attaining other ends. The merchant who calculates the success of an investment with regard to the goal of increasing his or her profit and the costs involved that put limits on the money available for consumption acts in a means-end rational way. Yet this is no less the case when a shopper calculates the success of buying a new sweatshirt to help his or her image as a good-looking person and also takes into consideration the costs, which involve having no more money to buy the newest record by George Michael or someone else. The same holds true for the couple who invite guests to a party and calculate which combination of guests would be most entertaining and whether certain people would be disappointed if they were not invited.

Value rational action is guided by the conscious belief in the value of a certain action in itself without any consideration of its success and consequences. The religious believer who devotes his or her whole life to worship, hard work, helping the weak, and the search for meaning and truth does so because of a belief in the value of this action in itself and not because he or she expects any instrumental value for reaching other goals. The democrat who is committed to the rules of democracy maintains that commitment because he or she believes in the value of democracy and not because the rules are instrumentally effective for attaining other goals. The ecologist who fights for ecological balance does so because he or she is convinced of its absolute value in itself and not because this belief will be effective for reaching other goals.

Affectual action is determined by spur-of-the-moment affects and emotional feelings. Everybody who acts spontaneously because of outbreaks of feelings of happiness, sadness, or rage acts affectually.

Traditional action results from firmly established habits; it is carried out because it has always been carried out in the same way. Many of our actions are traditionally determined because we repeat certain routines in everyday life from day to day. Much of our schedule for the day, the week, the month, the year is the same every day, week, month, and year: working hours, breaks, meals, division of labor, invitations, celebrations, visits, forms of communication, and use of words.

Concrete action is mostly a mixture of the analytically pure types of action that we can call ideal-types in Weber's terms. The member of parliament who gives expression to his or her anger about the speech of an opponent in parliamentary debate acts as a socialist who believes in socialism, follows parliamentary rules by taking his or her turn, and looks at public opinion in an instrumental way by accommodating his or her speech to public opinion in order to get public support.

Social action displays *patterns of regularity*, of recurrent behavior. Such patterns can result from the *interplay of stable interests and external conditions*. The regularity that the inner cities in Germany are overcrowded every first Saturday of a month is brought about by the stable interests of many people in going shopping when they have enough time to do so and the external condition that shops are only open much beyond working hours on that first Saturday every month. Highways are overcrowded at the beginning of the vacation period every year. These patterns in social action are founded in the convergence of means-end rational calculations. The stability of these patterns depends on the stability of interests and external conditions.

Other types of regularities are more independent of interests and means-end rational calculation, such as customs, mores, conventions, and law. *Customs* are practices of social action we can expect from every member of a society who acts in a certain situation. They are followed just because of habit, without being obligatory. Deviations from customs do not call for severe sanctions; nevertheless, they are considered as unusual. Examples of this are accepted ways of doing things like having a break between two hours of discussion in a seminar, having coffee after lunch, drinking wine with dinner, and eating popcorn while watching a movie. *Mores* are more firmly established than customs and have deeper roots in history. Deviating from mores provokes more serious irritations and questions about why—that is, sanctions are slightly more serious. Mores are practices of eating, dating, approaching someone, talking to another person, controlling one's behavioral conduct and organic processes, sexual behavior, and so on. Still more binding in character are *conventions*. Violating conventions provokes disapproval by others within a certain circle of people who share the conventions. Coming on time to a meeting means conforming to a convention. Turn-taking in conversation and in negotiations is regulated by conventions. The most firmly established regularity of behavior is founded in the *law*, which is backed up by sanctions applied by the judiciary, an authorized agency holding a monopoly on the means of physical force.

Social action can be oriented toward assuming the existence of a *legitimate order*. Insofar as this is the case we speak of the socially binding validity of that order. An order gains stability inasmuch as it is not just composed of regularities based on the convergence of interests or of customs and mores but resides in assuming its legitimacy, its binding and exemplary character, by as many people as possible. It then has collectively binding validity. In this case every actor, even the deviant, has to take into account the collective assumption of the collectively binding validity of an order and then has to expect collective sanctions as the reaction to deviation. Therefore, the actor will conceal his or her deviance or will try to escape the sanctions. The collectively binding character of an order does not presuppose the conformity of everybody but much more generally the orientation of everybody's action toward assuming that collectively binding validity, including the deviant actor. Deviation does not dissolve an order as long as it is collectively treated as deviation, but if it is not we may have different orders existing within one society. People can attribute legitimacy to an order according to the type of action involved on the basis of *tradition, affectual attachment, value rational belief* in the order, or *legality*; the latter — legality — refers to orders that come about either by agreement or imposition and compliance.

Repeated social action between actors establishes a *social relationship* between them. Social relationships can take on different forms:

Struggle is a social relationship within which the actors want to enforce their will against the resistance of their counterparts. A peaceful type of struggle, regulated by common rules, is called competition. The unconscious struggle for survival is called selection.

Communal association (community) is a social relationship within which the actors are bound together by a common feeling of mutual belonging. *Societal association* is a social relationship that is based on balancing interests or on linking interests.

A social relationship can be *open* or *closed* to varying degrees. At one extreme, everybody can enter the relationship, while at the other, nobody can enter a relationship from outside. Within closed social relationships monopolized rights are attributed to individuals or groups. The right to possess something is property; inasmuch as one can have access to or treat property according to one's will it is free property. The closure of a social relationship may result from traditional, affectual, value rational, or means-end rational reasons.

Actions of participants in social relationships can be *attributed* to other participants, either such that an action by any one participant is attributed to any other participant (a solidary responsible community) or such that the action of representatives (trustees) is attributed to any other participant in the relationship.

A social relationship that has limited or closed participation is called an *association* inasmuch as its order and its action are guaranteed by leadership and possibly by an administrative staff. An association is *autonomous* if it decides its order on its own; it is *heteronomous* if its order is imposed from outside; it is *autocephalous* if it selects its leader by itself; and it is *heterocephalous* if its leader is imposed from outside.

The statute orders of an association can result from *voluntary agreement* of its members or from *imposition* by its leaders. The rules that regulate leadership make up the *constitution* of an association.

A continuously organized action oriented toward specific ends is an *operation*. A societal association that acts in this way is an *operating association*. An association based on agreement and voluntary membership with an order that is binding for its members is a *voluntary association*. An association that imposes its order on everybody according to specific involuntary qualities is a *compulsory association*.

The enforcement of action within a social relationship requires *power*, which is the chance of enforcing one's will within a social relationship even against resistance. The chance of receiving compliance for a command is called *authority*. Schematic compliance is called *discipline*. Power depends on having the chance to interfere in the need-satisfaction of persons. Insofar as I can prevent the satisfaction of another person's needs I can force that person to do something which he or she would not do otherwise; thus I can overcome his or her resistance. The most general means of overcoming such resistance is physical force. Authority depends on the belief in its legitimacy. Power and authority are linked when the incumbents of authority positions have a legitimate right to apply power if there is resistance to their commands.

An association that subordinates its members to authority relationships is an *authority association*. Such an authority association that imposes its order successfully on people within a certain geographical area by threatening or applying physical force through a specific administrative staff is called a *political association*. An operating compulsory association that has monopolized the legitimate use of physical force for carrying out its orders is a *state*. An association that guarantees its orders through the application of psychic constraint by granting or refusing salvation is a *hierocratic association*. An association that has monopolized the legitimate exercise of this hierocratic constraint is called a *church*.

Methodology

Max Weber's methodology is based on three principles: (1) the adequacy of meaning and the adequacy of cause, (2) the ideal-type, and (3) the abstinence from value-judgments (Weber, 1922b/1973; partly translated in 1949, 1968, 1974, 1978; see Runciman, 1972; Burger, 1976; Weiss, 1975).

Adequacy of Cause and Adequacy of Meaning

The principle of adequacy of meaning and adequacy of cause is an expression of Weber's attempt at integrating his idealist background with positivist conceptions of causal explanation. According to Weber, sociology is a science that attempts to understand the meaning of an action and seeks to explain it causally, both in the course it takes and in its effects. He combines hermeneutic understanding and causal explanation; however, the leading role rests with hermeneutic understanding, because it gives the information for causal explanation. Weber introduces two different criteria of proof for the two methods: adequacy of meaning and adequacy of cause.

Whenever we want to explain a certain phenomenon as an effect of the causal determination by another phenomenon, the cause, we have to prove the causal adequacy of this statement, which means proving a statistically significant relationship between the two phenomena. We also have to monitor systematically the sequence of the two and control for the influence of other possible causes. Adequacy of meaning is fulfilled if we can prove that a certain phenomenon can be interpreted as a meaningful derivation from another phenomenon under certain conditions, or that a certain phenomenon is part of another broader phenomenon. As Weber puts it, the proof of such an adequacy of meaning tells us something about the causal relationship between the two phenomena.

Let us look at an example. In his study on the relationship between ascetic Protestantism and the *spirit* of capitalism, Weber begins by proving a significant statistical relationship. He points to the fact that regions with a broad influence of ascetic Protestantism developed industrial capitalism earlier and to a wider extent than other regions. A particular proof is that Protestant regions like Pennsylvania, which were very underdeveloped, began to flourish economically quite early. Another proof is the much greater number of Protestants in the class of industrialists and highly educated professional people than one would expect from their number in the total population. Still further proof is that highly developed economies and technologies like those of ancient China and India did not establish any kind of capitalism comparable to modern Western capitalism. This is Weber's proof of the causal adequacy of his explanation. A much greater part of his study is devoted to proving its adequacy of meaning. Here Weber points out that the capitalist work ethic is a derivation from Protestant this-worldly asceticism; that is, the former can be meaningfully understood as a form of this-worldly asceticism. The other world religions did not develop such a this-worldly asceticism. In proving the adequacy of meaning of his statement, Weber explicitly notes that he is concerned with the meaning-relationship between two cultural phenomena: the *spirit* of the Protestant ethic and the *spirit* of capitalism, though the latter is indeed a major part of the whole phenomenon of modern rational capitalism. As Weber demonstrates, culture has enormous effects on long-term societal development, which makes cultural studies and the proving of the meaning adequacy of their explanations of first importance.

The Ideal-Type

The ideal-type is a construction of a phenomenon in favor of its distinction from other phenomena. In constructing an ideal-type we analytically separate certain aspects of a concrete phenomenon in order to understand their distinctive nature and to be able to single out their production by specific causes. When Weber studies the relationship between ascetic Protestantism and the spirit of capitalism he separates a specific form of the capitalist spirit, namely, the devotion to hard work without enjoying the pleasure of consumption, reliability, and legality in economic transactions, from other expressions of capitalism, particularly from adventurous and speculative elements. In doing so he does not describe the historical phenomenon of capitalism in its multifaceted concreteness; he explicitly singles out a specific aspect from historical concreteness in order to investigate the causation of *this* specific aspect and nothing else. He does the same when he singles out those forms of the Protestant ethic that provide the most extreme examples of this-worldly asceticism, thus leaving aside other forms of Protestantism. His "spirit of capitalism" and his "Protestant ethic" are both conceptual ideal-types; the statement of the meaning and causal relationship between them is an ideal-type formulating a relationship between aspects of reality that have been analytically singled out.

Weber's studies work by constructing such ideal-types. We have no problems with this method when we are aware of its orientation to understanding and explaining specific aspects of reality and not the multifaceted concreteness of historical reality in its entirety; this is simply not the task of a sociology that aims at *generalizable* knowledge of that reality. Weber's selection of specific aspects was not motivated in an arbitrary way. He tried to single out those aspects that were of major importance for the whole historical reality because of their lasting influence. In describing the capitalist spirit he claimed that it is precisely its specific work ethic that distinguishes it from any earlier type of economic activity and that has lasting effects on the development of capitalism and the whole of modern society. The same holds true for his singling out of ascetic Protestantism as a major cultural root of modern Western rationalism.

The Abstinence of the Social Sciences from Value Judgment

Weber's plea for the abstinence of the social sciences from value judgment is grounded in his insight that modern science can answer questions of what is, why that is so, what is possible, and what is not possible, but not questions of what should be. Answers to questions of what should be always presuppose that questions and criticism will have to be halted at some point in order to come to a binding commitment to what should be. Science, however, cannot stop at any point in its radical questioning of any claim to truth. Whenever we place such inalienable truths on a pedestal we do what religion has done since time began and we sacrifice the intellect. However, there is no longer a binding religion in modern society, because the very effect of the triumph of science has been the possible questioning of any enthronement of an untouchable truth. A claim to an untouchable truth results in nothing more than claiming universal truth for a very particular standpoint. Any scientific enterprise that participates in such attempts to answer questions of what should be produces nothing but a very particularistic ideology.

Because there are many particular standpoints the struggle between particular values is common to modern society. It is a struggle like that between God and the devil. The commitment to values is a matter of personal decisions that cannot be generalized to be universally valid under these conditions. What science can do here is help us to know what is, why that is so, what is possible, and what is not possible. It can inform us about the logical structure and consistency of our ends, about effective means, and about the primary and secondary effects of applying certain means in order to realize certain ends. Science enhances our knowledge and enlightens us, but it cannot free us from the responsibility for our decisions.

Weber's plea for social science's abstinence from value judgment is accompanied by a plea for orienting science to values and of demonstrating the cultural relevance of scientific investigations. Science is an enterprise that takes place within our culture; thus it is unavoidable and also desirable that it takes up urgent questions of our culture and orients itself to values of that culture. In doing so it has cultural relevance. There is no better example than Weber's comprehensive investigations into the contradiction between formal and substantial rationality for demonstrating the cultural relevance of a social science committed to abstaining from value judgments. Weber's sociology informs us a lot about the origin, structure, and consequences of our modern societies, and we get information about its basic problems and about possible solutions. However, we have to make our own choices. We cannot be freed from this responsibility by a science that can tell us what to do with absolute bindingness. This is not a question of science but of individual moral responsibility.

Formal and Substantial Rationality

Weber's substantial sociology is devoted to the question of what specific kind of rationalism has emerged in Western culture and what consequences it has for the development of modern Western society (Weber, 1920–1921a/1972a, for translation see 1964 and 1976; 1920–1921b/1972b, for translation, see 1967; 1920–1921c/1971a, for translation, see 1952; 1921/1971b, partly translated 1968 and 1974; 1922a/1972c, for translation, see 1968; 1922b/1973, partly translated 1949, 1968, 1974 and 1978; 1924, for translation, see 1927/1981; see Münch, 1986). He examines these questions by comparing the Western type of rationalism with Oriental types. In contradistinction to Marx (1867/1962), he locates the major forces that determine modern society's fate not in its economic structure or in any other material structure, but in its unique culture, in its specific type of rationalism. Modern rational capitalism, bureaucracy, law, science, and technology are specific institutional variants of one culture: Western rationalism. Whereas Marx's attribution of the determining forces of modern society's rational and irrational features to its economic structure implies the hope that the transformation of that structure from capitalism to socialism and communism will also bring about the dissolution of that contradiction, Weber's position is much more radical. In Weber's terms such a hope is nothing but wishful thinking that does not take notice of the much deeper cultural roots of modern society's rationalities and irrationalities.

In Marx's terms capitalist society suffers from the contradiction of collective production and private appropriation of products, which means a well-planned, rational, and collective organization of production in large companies, but an archaic determination of investment by uncontrolled market forces on the level of the societal (national, world) economy. For Weber the fundamental contradiction of modern society is located in its culture and is thus much more deeply rooted and reaches much farther; it is the contradiction between formal and substantial rationality. Whereas Marx believes in overcoming the contradictions of capitalism by establishing socialism and then communism, Weber sees Marx's socialism, then communism as just another variant of modern Western rationalism that will never escape the much more fundamental contradiction between formal and substantial rationality.

What then is the nature of this contradiction between formal and substantial rationality? It is a contradiction that appears in specific form in every modern institution: capitalism, rational-legal authority, the legal system, bureaucracy, science, and technology. In its most general sense it is a feature of modern Western rationalism itself (Weber, 1920–1921a/1972a: 1–16, 237–275). This specific type of rationalism sees the actual world full of irrationalities, evils, suffering, and injustices requiring intervention in order to approach a less irrational world. This is a rationalism that aims at mastering an irrational world according to principles of rationality and at mastering an evil and unjust world according to principles of ethics and justice. It is a rationalism that actively intervenes in the world. However, the more such intervention takes place, the more man creates an artificial world of technology, law, and regulations that is full of new irrationalities, evils, and injustices. Nearly every intervention in the world, even with the best intentions, has consequences that create new problems. Thus the more man intervenes actively in the world, the more new problems are created, which again call for new interventions in an endless process.

Let us look at an example. It is a common intention of modern politics to increase economic equality of opportunity. This indeed increases the chances of many disadvantaged people to improve their lot. The same political measures also increase the level of aspirations and of competition, so that the level of frustration increases too. This increased level of frustration results in higher rates of crime, physical and mental illness, and suicide. Because there are consequences that contradict substantial values – that people should be saved from criminality (both victim and delinquent), illness, and suicide – we evaluate them as evils.

Our understanding of rationality as a process of actively solving problems by intervening in the world creates new evils, that is, problems that again call for intervention. Measures for increasing equality of opportunity are formally rational inasmuch as they contribute to increasing equality of opportunity. What is formally rational is our application of the right knowledge about the relationship between a political measure and the growth of equal opportunity. Whether this formally rational measure has only valued consequences is, however, a very different matter. A multiplicity of consequences touch very different substantial values, so that the realization of one substantial value (equality of opportunity) brings about phenomena that are evils from the point of view of other substantial values (avoidance of frustration, crime, illness, suicide). Because it is part of our understanding of rationality that we want to create a world that reduces evils and increases the realization of substantial values, we evaluate the evil consequences of enhanced equality of opportunity as substantially irrational. The measure that aims at increasing equality of opportunity is formally rational insofar as it corresponds to the best knowledge about the most effective means for attaining that goal, it is formally rational in the sense that it instrumentally intervenes in an evil world in order to create a better world, but it is substantially irrational because it not only does away with an evil but also creates a lot of new evils. It does something that is contrary to a rational conception of a world without frustrations, evils, and injustices.

Formal rationality is limited to specific causal knowledge about specific means-end relationships and to the realization of a specific end and one substantial value. Substantial rationality has to include many substantial values; it has to look at the whole world as something that should be made better. The many evil consequences of actions (e.g., political measures) that are good for one thing make it unavoidable that formal rationality is always accompanied by substantial irrationalities. This is the basic contradiction between formal and substantial rationality that is part and parcel of our Western understanding of rationality as instrumental intervention in an evil world in order to create a better one (Weber, 1920–1921a/1972a: 44–45, 57–60, 78–79, 166, 396, 493, 503–5).

Oriental cultures have developed a very different understanding of rationality (Weber, 1920–1921a/1972a, 1920–1921b/1972b). According to their understanding the world is good insofar as it is kept in balance. Mankind's intervention in the world always endangers the maintenance of this balance; everything people do has to be adjusted to this balance. A person's actions have to be considered as part of a whole that always has effects on that whole. In order to maintain a balance, a person has to accommodate his or her actions to the whole. Or if that balance has been disturbed, a person has to keep a distance from worldly activities or to retreat from the world in order to restore equilibrium or to find access to the concealed eternal balance of the cosmos outside worldly activities.

This is a very different type of rationality; it starts with an idea of the world as a whole that has to be kept in balance. No intervention in the world is called for here, only accommodation to its balance, distance, or retreat. A much more holistic concept of rationality prevails in these cultures. And it is also much more conservative in character: the existing world has to be kept in balance; any change would destroy that balance. Or, if it is out of balance, that balance has to be restored by a better accommodation of mankind's action to the world, which usually means restoring an old order and rejecting transformations that have taken place.

This is a type of rationality that does not fall into the traps of the contradiction between formal rationality and substantial irrationality. If you do not change anything, you do not create new evils. However, this is a culture devoted to traditionalism: change is evil, because it disturbs an order that already exists or that had existed at an earlier time before man changed the world. There can be no movement toward the future realization of a better world if any movement is only a movement back to an original state of balance, because there is no tension between good utopian ideas and a bad world. This type of rationality avoids the Western contradiction between formal and substantial rationality by dispensing with any formulation of ideas and values that reach beyond an actually or formerly existing society.

However, linking rationalism to the active mastery of the world is not the only unique feature of modern Western culture. This culture has also replaced the dignity of the collective by the dignity of the individual, and the particularism of groups (family, clan, caste, estate) by the universalism of citizens. These are features of Western culture that have no comparable place in Oriental culture.

Religion and Society

Max Weber locates the roots of the difference between Western ideas of instrumental rationalism, mastery of the world, individualism, and universalism and Oriental holistic rationalism, maintenance of the world's balance, collectivism, and particularism in religion and its interrelation with its formulators and carrier strata. Every religion is concerned with man's quest for meaning (Weber, 1922a/1972c: 245–381; 1920–1921a/1972a: 237–75). Yet a fundamental experience of the human individual is lack of meaning. Things happen that do not make sense: evils, disasters, suffering, and injustices occur contrary to the human individual's expectations, desires, and values. There is also the basic human experience of illness and death. The human individual asks why and wants an answer. Giving such explanations is constructing meaning. This is the task of religion.

Magic

The most primitive form of dealing with these questions is magic that differentiates the world into two parts: the perceivable and the unperceivable. The latter is full of demons that have influence on the course of the perceivable world. In order to guard against disasters, evils, and suffering, magical procedures try to influence the demons. Meaning construction by magical instruments is immediately intertwined with practical interests in a good harvest, health, peace, and so on. The medicine man or woman who carries out magical procedures is a practician in helping people with their everyday problems. Therefore, magic remains adjusted to practical interests.

Archaic Religion

The emergence of archaic forms of religion introduces a hierarchical order into the relationship between the perceivable and the unperceivable world.

Confucianism

Such an archaic religion is Confucianism (Weber, 1920–1921a/1972a: 276–536), which conceives of the world as hierarchically differentiated into a worldly order and a superimposed heavenly order. The worldly order replicates the perfect heavenly order and is thus the best of all possible worlds. The human individual has to accommodate to that order so that its balance will not be disturbed. One has to do what is appropriate in a given situation according to customs and mores, and a man has to save face in order to maintain his reputation within society. There is no tension between an ideal order and the worldly order. Rationality means maintaining and recognizing the balance of the world; instead of active mastery of the world, the human being has to accommodate to the existing order.

Religion remains tightly connected to the cult of deference to ancestors within the family and to the administration of society by the *literati* civil servants. The cult of deference to ancestors contributed to maintaining group particularism and to maintaining the group's rule over its members, who never became free individuals. As economic trade expanded, it was not backed up by rules that transcended the boundaries of clans and families. Clan particularism didn't allow any morality of business dealings to develop. A sharp differentiation between in-group morality and out-group immorality of crude utilitarianism prevailed. The principles of appropriate behavior and of saving one's face made universal mistrust a common feature of economic trade under these conditions. Thus we have: a rationality of maintaining balance, accommodation to the existing order, clan particularism and clan domination, and crude utilitarianism as major features of Confucian culture. It can be explained by the close connection of the idea of a balanced world with the authority of the clan over the individual and of the *literati* civil servants over society.

Ethical Religion I: Hinduism and Buddhism

The ethical religions have developed a fundamental tension between a divine order and the worldly order, between God and the world. The articulation of this tension is the work of intellectuals who see their quest for meaning confronted with a seemingly meaningless world. Religion looks for meaning though the world seems to be meaningless. The first step toward a solution of that problem is imagining a perfect divine order or divine being that is not perceivable but nevertheless exists. Two questions arise from such a conception of meaning: The first question asks why the world is imperfect, bad, and irrational even though it is subordinated to a perfect divine order or it has been created by a perfect divine being. This is the question of theodicy. The second question asks how the human being can escape the damnation of living forever in a bad world, implying suffering, illness, and death. This is the question of the right path to salvation. There are two solutions to the problem of theodicy: the world-immanent and the world-transcendent.

The world-immanent theodicy assumes an eternal order without injustice and suffering. It is only the human being who intervenes in this order with his or her worldly aspirations and is therefore exposed to illness, suffering, injustice, and death. Insofar as the individual dispenses with his or her worldly aspirations the eternal order will be kept in balance. The path to salvation, for average people, is one of dispensing with worldly aspirations and complying with ritual duties; for distinguished people, it is one of finding a way to eternal peace, either by keeping a mystical indifference to one's action that just follows conventional rules or by mystical contemplation or ascetic techniques of bringing one's body to a complete lack of feelings and aspirations: this-worldly mysticism, other-worldly mysticism, and other-worldly asceticism.

According to the world-transcendent theodicy, the tension between a perfect divine being and the bad world of human life on earth will be dissolved only if the bad world is ultimately destroyed and a new world is created. The whole world will be transformed someday and only one perfect order will exist. The path to salvation in this case is to belong to those elected people who will live in the newly created paradise. In order to belong to the Elect, the individual has to prove his or her character in his or her everyday actions. This is this-worldly asceticism.

Hinduism

An exemplification of world-immanent theodicy has been developed by Hinduism (Weber, 1920–1921b/1972b). According to its teachings, there is an eternal cycle of retribution and reincarnation in the world. The conduct of the individual will be retributed in his or her next life in a lower or higher caste or even in animal life or divine life. The person's obligation is to comply with the ritual duties of his or her caste and to observe the boundaries between castes. This teaching is a perfect religious legitimation of the Indian caste system. It assumes a perfect order of the world in eternal terms. All suffering, evil, and injustice occurring here and now can be brushed aside by the teaching that everything will be retributed in a later life. Three different ways to salvation are connected with this teaching. The way to salvation for average people is to obey the rules of their caste; the way for the *virtuoso* is to maintain indifference to his or her action, so that he or she will not be involved in generating evils that will be retributed in a later life. The individual's conduct obeys externally given rules but is not motivated by will. The individual is concerned with keeping an inner peace while participating in this-worldly life. This is what Weber calls inner-worldly mysticism. A more radical form of this path to salvation is to attain inner peace by way of retreating from worldly life so that one cannot be involved in causing evils at all. This is other-worldly mysticism. An ascetic form of this retreat from the world is to close out bodily involvement in actual life by specific body-techniques like Yoga. This is other-worldly asceticism.

Hinduism teaches a rationalism of finding meaning in unity with the divine order attained in retreated contemplation. It negates active intervention in the world, leaves the particularism of the ethics of the different castes as it is, and teaches retreat from individual responsibility for one's actions by maintaining indifference to one's externally determined, this-worldly conduct. Hinduism is the religion created by the caste of *Brahmins*, a noble and privileged educated elite that, however, mostly had to leave the exercise of political power to the soldier-caste of *Kshatryas*. The position of being well-educated and privileged but separated from the exercise of power explains the teaching of Hinduism: Theodicy explains the world as perfect in eternal terms. The path to salvation is conformity to caste-rules for average people, indifference and retreat for the well-educated.

Buddhism

A more radical path to salvation occurs in Buddhist thought (Weber, 1920–1921b/1972b). According to Buddha's teaching the causes of suffering in this world are the this-worldly aspirations of the individual—his or her thirst for life, for pleasure, and enjoyment—the struggle for life. This is called individuation.

Buddha teaches four truths:

1. This-worldly life is transient and entails suffering.
2. The reason for suffering is the individual's thirst and struggle for life.
3. The end of suffering comes with the end of the individual's thirst for life.
4. The path toward the end of suffering is the noble eightfold path to salvation:
   (a) proper recognition of suffering's origin in the thirst for life;
   (b) proper willingness to dispense with individual aspirations;
   (c) speaking properly by controlling one's passions;
   (d) proper conduct by avoiding any aspirations for this-worldly success;
   (e) the sacralization of life;
   (f) proper power of concentration on the path to salvation;
   (g) attainment of sacred thought and feeling;
   (h) admission to the eternal peace of Nirvana by perfect concentration.

This is a path to salvation that Weber calls other-worldly mysticism. It draws the individual's attention away from this world but does not change this world. Therefore, it is still part of a world-immanent theodicy. There is a perfect eternal order; the individual has only to find his or her path to that order. This world is full of evils only because of the misguided involvement of the individual in the thirst and struggle for life. Buddhist teaching does not give rise to this-worldly motivation to prove oneself in this world and to change it by way of active intervention, because that very intervention is caused by the thirst and struggle for life and is thus the origin of suffering and evils. Not intervention but retreat is the path to salvation.

Buddhism teaches a rationalism of finding meaning (truth) in unity with the eternal peace of Nirvana by retreating from the world. It negates active intervention in the world and individual active involvement in the world, and it leaves the existing world as it is, differentiated into particularistic groups. It does not teach a universalistic ethic for this world. The carriers of Buddhism, the Buddhist monks, shaped the religion according to their societal position, a position apart from the exercise of power, withdrawn from the world. Salvation was open only to them.

Ethical Religion II: Judeo-Christian Religion

A world-transcendent theodicy in combination with this-worldly asceticism as the path to salvation is the work of Judeo-Christian religion (Weber, 1920–1921c/1971a, 1920–1921a/1972a: 17–236, 1922a/1972c: 245–381, 1924; Troeltsch, 1912/1922, for translation, see 1931). This makes the most lasting difference between Western and Eastern culture.

Ancient Judaism

Yahweh, the God of the Jews and the God of the Old Testament of Christian religion, is a powerful God who dominates the world with ethical commands; He is the one and only God whose authority holds over all the world, a God of warfare who guards the Jewish people against its enemies. Moses is the founder of this religion; he led his people from their enslavement in Egypt to the land of Palestine; he received the tablets with the Ten Commandments from God on Mount Sinai.

The theodicy here is the myth of the Fall of man. It is man's weakness and sinfulness that provokes God's rage and punishment. This is why the world is full of suffering and evils. The only way to escape God's rage and punishment is to obey His ethical commands. All of the Jewish people are responsible for each other in obeying God's commands. God has agreed on a covenant with them to lead them through the earthly valley of misery to the promised land. Thus all Jews are responsible for not breaking the covenant; nobody is allowed to deviate, otherwise God's rage will punish the whole people.

The pre-Exilic prophets, in particular, were powerful interpreters of God's will and commands who spoke to the Jewish people with their pronouncements in extraordinary situations. The Levites played a specific role in transforming God's commands into a set of specific rules for everyday life in teaching the Torah. The theodicy of this religion sees this world as bad because of man's sinful deviation from God's ethical commands. Suffering comes from God's punishment. Only man's obedience to God's commands can lead man to the promised land. At some future time this world will be destroyed, that is, sin, suffering, and evil will be done away with and a new world will be created. The precondition is man's work on his character and on the world to make them conform to God's ethical commands. The path to salvation here is man's obedience in shaping his conduct according to God's ethical commands. This is this-worldly asceticism. Neither retreat from this world nor mystical contemplation will lead the human being to an eternal peace; but proper ethical this-worldly conduct is a presupposition for escaping God's rage and punishment and for being led to the promised land with His people. Thus the human being has to intervene in this world in order to shape it according to God's ruling.

This is a religion that conceives of rationality in constructing meaning as an active intervention in this world according to ethical commands. That is, meaning is the outcome of active intervention in this world. Meaning has been destroyed by the sinful Fall of man. Lack of meaning is the contradiction between God's ethical commands and man's sinful conduct; meaning can be created only by working against sin in this world and by shaping it according to God's ethical commands. Intervention in this world and its transformation according to ethical commands is part and parcel of this religion. It is also a religion that has a potential to overcome ethical particularism because of God's universal rule. He tolerates no other God besides Himself. Monotheism provides the potential for ethical universalism. However, the exclusive covenant of the Jewish people with God and their religious separation from other groups has maintained ethical particularism, with a strong differentiation of in-group morality and out-group morality. The group covenant with God committed the individual to the group and furthered the group's control over the individual, but it left less room for the establishment of individual responsibility. It is certainly a conception of a warfaring and dominating God and the political situation of permanent conflict with enemies, along with the message of the ethical prophets who pronounced God's ethical commands that contributed to the creation of a theodicy with such a powerful effect on intervening in this world. This is the origin of the ethical rationalism and instrumental activism that are peculiar to our Western culture. Further developments elaborated on this potential for ethical rationalism and instrumental activism in different ways according to forces that shaped Judeo-Christian religion.

From Jesus Christ to Early Christianity to the Ancient Church

Jesus Christ complemented God's strong rule by his love for everybody. The Old Testament speaks of rage and punishment, Christ of forgiveness. The Old Testament teaches "An eye for an eye, a tooth for a tooth"; Christ teaches "Love your enemies." This is universal love, the key to the universal association of people. For Jesus, the world is full of evils because of man's sinfulness; however, because man is and remains a sinful being, meaning cannot be constructed by intervention in this world but only by the final destruction of this world by God when Christ comes again to save God's people. The only path to salvation here is the recognition of one's sinfulness and the awareness of God's grace mediated by Christ's love of His people. The gratefulness of the weak sinner is the path to salvation. Those people who have this gratefulness will be chosen at the end of this world and will be accepted into the new paradise. This is a teaching that broke away from Jewish ethical particularism, but replaced God's rage by grace. It opened paths of meaning construction by way of contemplative unification with God in participating in His universal love. Whereas the Yahweh of Judaism is an unapproachable ruler, the God of the New Testament is a universally loving God with whom one can unite by way of grateful devotion. Thus there is much less intervention in this world by Jesus but more expectation of paradise in another world and a recognition of this world as sinful as it is. However, individualism is strengthened, because each human being is called to God's love individually, not as one of a people or any other particular group. In order to take part in God's love, one even has to cut the ties with one's family.

The Christian religion as created by Jesus was disseminated by his followers. Apostle Paul's missionary work was most important, because he taught that everybody can be a member of the Christian community, independently of his or her ethnic or national group membership. This was a precondition for Christianity's expansion breaking through any particularistic group membership and for the establishment of a universal community of Christians. As such, Christianity played an important role in bridging the gap between in-group and out-group morality, because now everybody could be a member of one community devoted to one and the same set of ethical principles.

In its beginnings Christianity was a religion of simple people and maintained a distance from the Roman state where it was disseminated but also persecuted. However, its successful dissemination also reached well-established people and culminated in toleration by the Edict of Milan in 313, the baptizing of Emperor Constantine in 337, and finally its establishment as the state religion by Theodosius I in 391. Christianity expanded and moved from an alienated position to a state-supporting position because of its establishment as the state religion. Christianity was systematized by the teachers of the Church at that time, particularly by Origen (184–254) and Augustine (354–430). These teachers accommodated the Christian teaching with the Hellenistic theory of natural law and with the Roman state. In this way natural law became a mediator between divine order and this-worldly order; the original tension between God's ethical commands and the sinfulness of man became reconciled. An overall rightful order reaches from the divine order via natural law to the state order.

Christian teaching became similar to the Asian ideas of a balanced eternal order. The replacement of the idea of a powerful God commanding His sinful people by a divine order that was reconciled via natural law with state order was due to the Hellenistic idea of a balanced natural order and the alliance of the church with the state. No longer did a powerful God demand from His people that they intervene in this world. The path to salvation was conformity to the existing order accompanied by union with God in mystical contemplation.

The Medieval Church

After the breakdown of the Roman Empire, the Christian church became the treasury of culture until life in the Middle Ages began to blossom again. However, the Scholasticism of the Middle Ages continued to teach the reconciliation between the divine order and the lower orders of earthly life in an overall hierarchical order reaching from the divine down to the lowest levels of earthly life in economic trading and the utilitarian satisfaction of needs. This reconciliation of divine order with earthly order also brought Christian teaching much closer to Asian models of balance and organic order than to the ethical rigorism and instrumental activism of the Old Testament. The path to salvation was again conformity to the existing order and union with God in mystical contemplation.

Ethical Religion III: The Reformation and Protestantism

It was the Reformation that reestablished the ethical rigorism and instrumental activism of the Old Testament.

Lutheranism

Luther applied the monk's standards of religious life to the everyday life of every average Christian. He did away with reconciliation of religious ethics and this world by Scholasticism. This-worldly conduct became the field for proving one's religious qualifications. Man's calling to God was no longer left to the priests and monks but was expanded to every Christian. Luther's translation of the expression for working activity as "vocation" gave all such activity the sense of a calling to God. This made work the main field for proving one's religious calling. The world was again open for being shaped and transformed according to God's ethical commands. However, Luther interpreted this teaching in a traditionalistic sense. His teaching of the two kingdoms legitimated the worldly political authority as instituted by God. One had to conform to the requirements of the existing order within one's profession and as a subject to political authority and to preserve one's union with God in mystical contemplation: the *unio mystica*. This was the path to salvation. The major reason for this reconciliation of God and the world was Luther's accommodation to the worldly power of his sovereign (see Eiben, 1989).

Calvinism

A much more revolutionary teaching of Christianity was established by John Calvin in Geneva. His teaching reinstated the powerful emperor-God of the Old Testament. Calvin's teaching established the methodically rational and thoroughly organized conduct of the human individual, the systematically organized self-controlled personality who actively intervenes in this world in order to organize it to the glory of God. Restless professional work became the only right way of living, because it is work on oneself and on the world that is necessary in order to organize this world according to God's command and to His glory. Luther's Protestant proves his or her religious qualification in mystical union with God, in the state of feeling that accompanies everything that a person does, not in his or her works. The important point is what the person feels, not what he or she does. It is quite the other way around for Calvin's Protestant, who proves him- or herself as qualified in his or her works to the glory of a God-emperor.

At the core of the teaching of Calvinism is Calvin's idea of predestination. According to Weber, this is logically the most rigorous world-transcendent solution to the theodicy problem. The question is, Why is the world full of suffering, evils, and injustice when it was created by a perfect and absolutely ruling God? Calvin answers this question by saying that God's authority is absolutely valid and there is nothing that is not determined by Him; however, the human being is simply unable to know God's reasons for why the world is as it is, why things happen as they happen. Knowing that would elevate the human being to the status of God, which is impossible. The world is as it is because of God's absolutely hidden decree. And this also involves the individual human being's fate. God's decree determines whether one belongs to those who are elected to eternal life or to those who are condemned to eternal death. Why He did so is beyond the human capacity of knowing God's reasons. We could also ask why other living beings were born as animals, whereas we were born as human beings. To find an answer to that is not possible for human thought. God is perfect; the human individual is an imperfect creature. God knows why He created the world as it is. The human individual cannot know.

The idea of predestination had a tremendous effect on the Calvinist Protestant. How to know whether one had been elected to eternal life or condemned to death became the most urgent question. According to Calvin, nobody can know. However, he taught trust in God, because everything He does is right. The church is divided into the invisible group of the Elect and the group of those who are not elected. This question was much too pressing for the individual faithful, so Calvin's followers changed the interpretation of Calvin's teaching. According to this interpretation one can still not influence God in His decree, but one can know whether one belongs to the Elect. People can see their elected status in their conduct. Those who are elected are the people who are full of trust in God, who exemplify His ethical commands in their conduct, who contribute to His glory in their worldly activities. Hard work, honesty, reliability, and modesty are qualities that characterize the Elect.

The effect of this teaching was enormous internal ethical constraint, because each person wanted to see his or her elected status in his or her conduct. This pressure for ethical self-control was enhanced by the abolition of administration of God's grace by the church as it was organized by the Catholic church. Because God's decree was unchangeable there was no place for administration of God's grace by the church. The individual stood before God completely on his or her own. And because God did not negotiate about grace there was no chance of compensating with good deeds for bad ones. Only people whose conduct showed no deviation from ethical standards could have been elected to eternal life by God's decree. The result of this teaching was a complete methodical and rational organization of life according to God's ethical standards with no stone left unturned. This teaching produced systematically organized personalities. Human conduct was not a collection of good and bad deeds that would finally be balanced; it was the outcome of a systematically organized, completely self-controlled personality. The internalization of ethical control reached the highest possible level.

This highest level of self-control was complemented by the type of external social control exerted by Calvinism on its people. Calvinism was organized as a voluntary association of religious people in sects, reformed churches, and denominations, not like the Catholic and Lutheran church as a community into which one was born. Voluntary membership strengthened the commitment to the norms of the religious community. The more vital participation of the laity in the organization of worship than in the Catholic and Lutheran churches established the religious community as the religious authority instead of a clergy that was separated from the people. Social control was closely exerted by the religious community itself, unlike the relatively weak control exerted by the administrative body in the Catholic church. In this way membership in the religious community became a major precondition for being considered a trustworthy person in economic activities. Calvinism strengthened both internal self-control and external social control.

Calvin's idea of predestination solves the problem of theodicy by saying that whatever exists and happens in this world is determined by God. However, this is not a theodicy that leaves the world as it is, for it states that this world will be replaced some day when the Son of God returns, and the Elect will enter paradise. Compared to God everything on Earth is imperfect and cannot be loved in a similar way, otherwise one would commit the sin of elevating worldly creatures to a god-like status. Because this world is full of imperfect people, the Elect are called by God to work on that world and its imperfect people to His glory. Beyond this, everybody was called to work to the glory of God. The cool and impartial organization of poverty, unemployment, orphanhood, and criminality in asylums particularly designed for that purpose is part of that rational organization of this world. Thus, Calvin's theodicy implies an extraordinary intervention in this world to shape it according to God's ethical commands. There is no path to salvation in the sense that people can influence God's decree; however, there are hints of being on this path to salvation insofar as one's conduct is methodically and unfailingly organized according to God's ethical commands.

Restless professional work became the most prominent sign of an elected status. In contradistinction to the traditional Catholic understanding of work as penance for man's sin and something that was devalued, work now became the foremost domain of positive religious activity. The fruits of this work are signs of God's grace. However, because of God's strong ethical command there is no place for consuming these fruits of hard work in pleasurable activities. The only way open is to reinvest the fruits of hard work in further hard work. This is the complementary sacralization of work for its own sake and of reinvesting its fruits in upgraded levels of work to the capitalist principle of reinvesting the profits flowing from an enterprise in further enterprise instead of consuming that profit. Here is the point of convergence of the spirit of ascetic Protestantism and the spirit of capitalism.

Calvinism was the most extreme type of ascetic Protestantism because of its radical idea of predestination. It became most influential through its dissemination in the Dutch Reformed church and in the Puritan sects and denominations in England and America. Other types of ascetic Protestants that contributed to the sacralization of this-worldly work were Pietists, Methodists, Baptists, Mennonites, and Quakers.

Ascetic Protestantism established an unprecedented ethical rationalism that implies that meaning is achieved not by accommodating to a perfect order or by retreating from this world and attaining peace in an eternal order but by applying ethical standards commanded by the Lord to this-worldly conduct. The rationality of the ethical standards rests in their universal validity. Action itself is rational when it realizes the ethical standards in its conduct. This ethical rationalism is complemented by an unprecedented instrumental activism. The elected individual is called by God to intervene in this world and to shape it according to His ethical commands. There is also an extreme individualism in the sense that the individual personality stands completely on his or her own before God. The self-disciplined, individually responsible person becomes the dominant human type. Finally, there is a universalism in the sense that God's ethical commands are universally valid and have to be implemented by the Elect all over the world.

The features of ascetic Protestantism, particularly in its Calvinist version, resulted from the interpenetration of some basic features of its teachings with the natural life-world of the carriers of the doctrine. The teachings placed the signs of an elected status unmistakenly in work on that world to the glory of God. For Luther, the human being was a vessel of God's love; for Calvin, he or she was an instrument serving His domination over the world. The bourgeois strata became the main carriers of Calvinism and the other forms of ascetic Protestantism. The fact that they worked in order to make their living was the demarcation line between them and the aristocracy. The sacralization of work, honesty in economic relations, systematic organization of conduct, and individual responsibility were building blocks of the bourgeois life-world. And the bourgeoisie made its ethical standards universally valid for the whole society and worked toward breaking down the established hierarchical differentiation of society into estates. Status had to be attained according to achievement and should no longer be ascribed by birth. The teaching of ascetic Protestantism and the life-world of the bourgeoisie were related to each other by what Weber termed an "elected affinity."

Modern Secular Culture

The culture that emerged in the evolution of Judeo-Christian religion from Ancient Judaism to ascetic Protestantism did not disappear with the process of secularization that was set into motion by the Enlightenment in the eighteenth century. The Enlightenment replaced God by reason and is still devoted to an ethical rationalism that wants to command an imperfect world full of evils, suffering, and injustices according to ethical standards. It is devoted to the dignity of the human individual and his or her self-disciplined self-responsibility, to the universalistic idea of the equality of human rights and citizens' rights, and the instrumental mastery of nature and society. These are still the peculiar features of our modern Western culture. Indeed, the contradiction between formal and substantial rationality is becoming ever more apparent as a peculiar feature of our modern Western culture. In the process of mastering nature and society we have created technologies, legal systems, institutions, and orders that have a lot of consequences running contrary to basic values, so that we are more occupied with repairing the negative effects of our interventions in nature and society the more we intervene in them. However, leaving them as they are would also lead to a great many negative effects. Loss of freedom also results from this work on mastering the world by creating technologies, legal systems, and orders; we are more and more the prisoners of an "iron cage" that we have created in this process, as Max Weber puts it. Whereas the Puritan wanted to be a professional human being, we have no other choice. Modern capitalism, bureaucracy, the legal system, and technology make up systems that proceed according to their own inner laws; they are independent powers that exert an external constraint on the human individual. Created by human beings, they appear as independent powers, alienated from the human individual.

The human quest for knowledge about society, the human being, and nature implanted in the rationalism of modern Western culture pushes forward the progress of science to an unprecedented degree (Weber, 1922b/1973: 582–613). The expansion of knowledge leaves no place for magical belief, leading finally to the destruction of religion itself. Calvinism did away with all magical elements between God and human beings. No magical device can influence God. It is God's word alone that counts. Modern science has replaced all kinds of belief by knowledge, even the belief in God. And it is the Puritan quest for knowledge about God's Providence that very much contributed to the rise of modern science. However, knowledge can tell us what is and why that is so, but cannot tell us what we should do. Science cannot answer questions of meaning or questions of moral conduct. Thus there is also a loss of meaning and of moral guidance in modern culture resulting from the triumph of its specific type of rationality that has transformed the search for meaning and moral guidance into the search for scientific knowledge. It is now the individual who has to find meaning and who has to decide what is right and wrong. Every individual has to find his or her own "demon who holds the fibers of his very life" (Weber, 1922b/1973; translation 1974:156).

A progresive development of individualism in modern Western culture also originated in the individual responsibility before God. The Enlightenment generalized this individualism to the complete self-responsibility of the individual paired with the sacralization of the individual personality. This gives much responsibility to the human individual and has contradictory consequences. The highest forms of self-responsible and self-disciplined organization of individual conduct stand next to the crudest forms of egotism and narcissism. They are all children of the same cultural valuation of individualism.

Finally, the moral universalism of modern culture also has contradictory consequences. It is the basis for truly working on doing away with suppression and injustice. However, it is also the source of a cultural imperialism that both legitimates and goes much beyond economic, political, and ethnic imperialism. Missionaries, warlords, and merchants have often worked hand in hand. Amnesty International and the U.S. Army are both carriers of the same cultural universalism all over the world.

The Institutional Orders of Modern Rational Society

This is the legacy of modern Western rationalism, which is accompanied by an instrumental activism, a self-responsible individualism, and a moral universalism. It is the merit of Weber's approach to society from its inter-relationship with culture that sociology can understand the origins, peculiarity, and consequences of this modern culture for society and the individual. In Weber's perspective, an analysis of the major institutions of modern society—capitalism, bureaucracy, rational-legal authority, the legal system, science, and technology—has to understand them as specifications of the same cultural code.

Capitalism

Modern capitalism as a rationally controlled form of economic activity has to be distinguished from any form of traditional living from hand to mouth and from any form of speculative, adventurous, and politically determined capitalism. What characterizes modern Western capitalism is its rational organization and its control by the law and by self-disciplined persons. This rational capitalistic spirit correlates with Western cultural rationalism as it culminated in ascetic Protestantism.

According to Weber (1922a/1972c: 31–121; 1924), rational capitalism is an exemplification of rational economic activity that concentrates on the mobilization of scarce resources and their distribution to meet given needs. This can be done in households and in businesses.

Economic activity in the household is oriented to marginal utility; it distributes resources so that the least satisfied needs have most resources applied to them, and vice versa. The law of marginal utility says that with any item designed to satisfy a specific need, each further item loses utility because of the increased level of that specific need's satisfaction. If we eat ten apples, the tenth will have ten times less utility than the first one, because we are ten times more satisfied with eating apples by the time we arrive at the tenth apple.

Economic activity in business is oriented toward making profit. Any business will be economically rational only as long as it is profitable, that is, as long as it makes more money than has been invested in that business.

There are several preconditions for rational economic activity:

1. Mobilization of resources at lowest costs.
2. A system that informs people where to get resources at what costs. The market or a centrally administered plan are alternative systems for giving such information.
3. An efficient work organization, that is, one that is most productive at lowest costs, which is most effectively provided by the following devices:
   a. free wage labor,
   b. private ownership of means of production,
   c. free entrepreneurial decision making as regards
      (1) free selection of workers,

   (2) work discipline, and
   (3) work specialization.
4. Calculability of marginal utility and profit, which presupposes:
   a. market freedom,
   b. market competition,
   c. market exchange,
   d. monetary accounting, which allows
      (1) accounting for postponed services.
      (2) accounting for credit,
      (3) storing of value,
      (4) accounting for economic opportunities,
      (5) capital accounting,
      (6) *ex ante* and *ex post* calculation, and
      (7) individualization of need satisfaction.

If there is no market, a centrally administered plan will have to fulfill the functions of the market, but it can do so only to a limited degree and with severe difficulties. Instead of a flexible adaptation of a multitude of enterprises, we have centralized administrative decision making. Accounting in material products has to replace accounting in monetary terms. A comparison and accounting of products and services is possible only to a limited degree. The centrally administered economic system can be much better oriented to specific ends, but it is very inflexible and full of problems in allocating resources to needs.

Modern capitalism is the better solution to the problem of allocating scarce resources to given needs; however, it also has tendencies to undergo periodic crises, namely:

1. instability of prices (inflation, deflation),
2. crises of economic growth (recession),
3. unemployment, and
4. imbalances in external trade.

There are periodically changing causes of such crises: exaggerated demand causes inflation; declining demand causes deflation and recession; and tough competition causes technological rationalization, which leads to the shedding of labor that cannot immediately move into the new jobs created by technological progress. Periodic unemployment results.

External regulations can reduce the chances of making profit, such as state support for declining industries and growing costs of job security, workplace safety, health care, unemployment or retirement insurance, and participation of labor unions in economic decision making.

Capitalism is a formally rational economic system inasmuch as it solves the problem of allocating scarce resources to given needs in the most economic way so that ever higher levels of mobilization and distribution of resources can be attained. However, the same system is substantially irrational inasmuch as

- it satisfies only those needs that can be articulated by substantial purchasing power on the market,
- it is oriented to profit for its own sake;
- it creates needs that can be satisfied by its industry via an expanding system of advertising,
- it proceeds according to the principle of rewarding economic achievement and cannot proceed according to norms of social welfare ethics.

Working on these irrational consequences of capitalism's formal rationality calls for its control by counteracting institutions: cultural discourse, politics, and the legal system.

Modern capitalism of this type cannot exist on its own. It is dependent on the services of other institutions and of cultural foundations:

1. The inner core is the market: It necessitates orientation to marginal utility and profit.
2. Rational calculation, rational technology, and a methodically rational attitude toward work and rational qualification of the work force rest on cultural foundations: rational science, Protestant asceticism, and scientific-technological education.
3. Reliability, legality, and normative order come from communal and legal foundations: the universalism of modern Western culture and the rational legal system.
4. Entrepreneurial goal-setting and calculation of profit need political foundations: rational economic policy and rational bureaucracy.

Rational-Legal Authority

Modern political authority is characterized by its rational organization, which makes it an institutional specification of Western rationalism (Weber, 1922a/1972c: 122–176, 541–868; 1921/1971b).

Political authority always involves a specific relationship between ruler, administrative staff, and the people subjected to political authority. What gives political authority its collectively binding validity is the belief of the dominated people in its legitimacy.

Weber distinguishes three types of political authority according to their different roots of legitimacy: traditional authority, which corresponds to the traditional legitimacy of social order in general; charismatic authority, which orresponds to legitimacy of social order resulting from affectual attachment; and rational-legal authority, which corresponds to the legitimacy of social order based on its legality. He does not introduce a fourth type of political authority, which would correspond to what he calls value-rational legitimacy of social order in general.

Traditional authority is grounded in the everyday belief in the sacredness of traditions that have been binding forever and in the legitimacy of leaders who are called into authority by that tradition. Traditional authority involves a personal relationship between lord and an administrative staff whose members are personal servants of the lord. Traditional authority varies from patriarchalism, to patrimonialism, to feudalism. Patriarchalism is the unlimited power of the head of a family or clan. Patrimonialism extends that form of authority to a wider geographic area and includes a much more important role for the administration of that area by the administrative staff. Feudalism is a form of traditional authority in which the administrative staff has acquired its own rights to exercise power within a specific territory of the overall territory of domination. Traditional authority is unstable and not very predictable in its character, because there is no exact limitation of the political authority's rights and powers. Thus, though it replicates the patterns of the past, it leaves much arbitrary power to the ruler. Therefore it is not suitable for the emergence of a rationally organized economy.

Charismatic authority is grounded on the extraordinary devotion to the sacredness, heroic power, or exemplary quality of a person and to the orders revealed or created by that person. It is characterized by an affectual attachment of personal servants and followers to their leader. The greatest problem for charismatic authority is the provision for succession to leadership, because leadership normally breaks down with the death of the charismatic leader. Charismatic authority is unstable and unpredictable in character, because of the arbitrary nature of the leader's decision-making and because his or her charisma is in danger of being disproved if it lacks success. The nature of the affectual attachment involved is that it comes and goes spontaneously. This unstable and unpredictable character of charismatic authority is contradictory to the emergence of a rationally organized economy. Whenever charismatic authority tries to stabilize its position it has to create a tradition or legal procedures of decision making; that means the institutionalization of charismatic authority leads to the establishment of traditional or rational-legal authority.

The modern type of political authority that corresponds to the rationalism of modern Western culture is rational-legal authority. It is grounded on belief in the legality of statute orders and of the right to command of those persons who are called to exercise authority. The relationships between ruler, administrative staff, and those subject to political authority are regulated by binding rules: the constitution and statutes.

Rational-legal authority replaces the authority of persons by the impartial authority of the law. It is an ordered form of political authority. Legislation and judicial decision making are separated from one another and ordered by formal procedures. The legitimacy of a decision does not come from any substantial quality but from the fact that it has been produced in accordance with formal procedures that are determined by law set down in a constitution. Because it proceeds according to firmly established rules, rational-legal authority is stable and completely predictable in its process in terms of its formal qualities. Therefore, it is suitable for a rational organization of the economy.

Rational-legal authority displays the following qualities:

1. Any substantial law can be set down in legislation with the claim to compliance by members of the society insofar as it is produced according to the formal rules of legislation.
2. Political decision making determines statute law as a system of abstract and purposefully prescribed rules, which are set down in legislation, applied in judicial decision-making, and enacted by the administration.
3. A lord and those subject to authority abide by the same rules.
4. The law is not an arbitrary personal rule of a lord, but the common foundation for the lives of the fellow members of society.
5. Compliance is directed not toward a person but toward an office.

Rational-legal authority is organized as follows:

1. It is a continuous operation ordered by rules.
2. It has an order of competence to decide.
3. It has a hierarchy of offices.
4. It is based on technical and legal rules. Their application necessitates technical education.
5. The administrative staff does not own the means of administration.
6. The civil servant does not have a property right to his or her office.
7. Any process is recorded in a filing system so that its examination with regard to the established rules can be carried out at any time, even a long time after a decision was made.
8. The administration of rational-legal authority is organized in a bureaucracy.

Rational Law

Rational-legal authority involves rational law in its procedure of decision making. Rational law is another specification of modern Western rationalism (Weber, 1922a/1972c: 387–513). It is the outcome of an evolutionary process that started from the domination of the common law of closed communities that had a traditional legitimacy. This is the basis of the binding

character of the law and of the equality of the community's members before
the law. The evolution of modern rational law resulted from its shaping by
historical actors who drew it away from the common law tradition:

1. Theoreticians of the law, like law professors at universities, subordinated
   the law to a process of rationalization, which means systematization,
   generalization, and codification (abstraction, analytic differentiation,
   resolution of contradictions, formalism). The law was made into a system of general law statements with general validity.
2. Economically interested parties, namely capitalist entrepreneurs, tried
   to adapt the law to the change of economic requirements. They were
   supported by the practicians of the law, that is, by the lawyers. This
   had the effect of making the law a collection of practical regulations
   of economic transactions. The law became changeable, and property
   rights were institutionalized.
3. Politically interested parties, like political authorities, tried to subject
   their territory of domination to a unified control, and they wanted to
   direct the law toward the realization of specific political ends. Hence,
   the law became an instrument of the unified enactment of political
   authority.

Rational law is subjected to the same contradiction between formal and
substantial rationality as any other institutionalized specification of modern
Western rationalism. It is formally rational in the sense of the orderedness
of its decision making according to general laws, which makes its decision
making absolutely predictable. It is a major device for guaranteeing the rights
of individuals, including rights to freedom. Yet its formal rationality implies
a substantial irrationality, because the very process of guaranteeing the rights
of individuals covers more and more areas of everyday life with prescriptions of the law, so that individual rights are limited by the very process
of guaranteeing them by the law. This is what we call the juridification of
everyday life. Another effect is the inability of general law to take into account
the concrete circumstances of a case, which very often turns abstract justice
into concrete injustice.

Bureaucracy

Rational-legal authority is administered by a bureaucracy that is characterized by the following qualities (Weber, 1922a/1972c: 551–79): (1) An order
of competence to decide; (2) a hierarchy of offices; (3) recording of any decision making in a filing system; (4) technical education of administrative staff;
(5) full-time professional work of administrative staff, and (6) decision making according to general rules.

The position of the administrative staff has the following qualities:
(1) The office a person holds is a vocation; (2) the civil servant receives particular social approval; (3) the civil servant is appointed by a superordinated authority; (4) he or she has tenure (life-long appointment); (5) he or she is remunerated with a fixed salary; (6) he or she is oriented to a predetermined professional career with firmly established rules of promotion, mostly according to years in administrative service.

The expansion of bureaucracy in modern society originates from the following considerations:

1. The expansion of the money-economy allows remuneration in money so that the administrative staff cannot usurp the means of administration, as was the case when the administrative staff was forced to make its living from fees imposed on its clients.
2. The quantitative and qualitative expansion of the tasks of the administration call for its expansion and for its rational organization.
3. The concentration of the means of administration in the hands of the ruler allows for the establishment of an impartial administration that is oriented to applying rules and not to making a profit.
4. The leveling of social and economic differences allows an administration of a territory according to general rules without regard to any distinction of status.
5. The technical superiority of bureaucratic administration encourages its establishment. Its technical superiority resides in the following qualities:
   (a) its prompt reaction to external stimuli;
   (b) predictability of administrative decision-making;
   (c) technical education of its staff;
   (d) impartiality; and
   (e) formal orderedness.

The establishment and expansion of bureaucracy in modern society has consequences that culminate in the contradiction between formal and substantial rationality. It is formally rational in the sense of an exactly predictable and impartial process of decision making. However, this formal rationality is unavoidably accompanied by a set of features that are contrary to other values firmly established in modern society; thus modern bureaucracy is also substantially irrational in character:

1. The domination of bureaucracy wherever it has been established is unbreakable.
2. It has leveling effects, because it deals with everything according to the same rules. Its impartiality resides in the application of abstract rules to concrete cases, which cannot be honored in their concreteness; thus,

abstract impartiality often results in concrete substantial injustice, because the concrete circumstances cannot be taken into account.

3. The bureaucratic staff acquires a particular power position because of its technical knowledge, knowledge about the internal processes of administrative service, and knowledge about the secrecies of administrative service, which are not accessible to lay people, including politicians.

4. A domination of bureaucracy is therefore all the more likely to be established in modern society the less the countervailing power of parliament is institutionalized (with rights of investigation into administrative processes) and also that of public control (with the public right to be informed about administrative processes).

5. The domination of bureaucracy also implies a domination of the administrative spirit in politics inasmuch as there is no countervailing power exerted by politicians and political responsibility is much more located in bureaucracy than in parliament, or inasmuch as political positions are occupied by civil servants or by persons who have made their career in the civil service.

6. Bureaucracy proceeds according to its own laws and establishes an "iron cage" to which we are subjected.

7. Because of its procedure according to general rules, bureaucracy increasingly suppresses any residue of the individual's autonomy to act according to his or her own self-responsible will.

These are the substantially irrational effects of modern bureaucracy's formal rationality.

Politics

Because modern society is in danger of becoming petrified by bureaucracy, it needs a dynamic countervailing power that breaks up the petrifying effects of bureaucracy. This is the function that Weber (1921/1971b) assigns to politics (in addition to the economically dynamic function of the capitalist economy; both are necessary to keep society in motion).

Politics is the sphere of power struggle between the different groups of society. Value discussions unavoidably become politicized because values clash like God and the devil in the demagicalized world without a binding religion. Politics becomes the center of collective deliberation and decision making. The democratization of politics is a precondition for keeping society in motion, because it allows the spontaneous articulation of interests, claims, and problems that call for collective decisions. However, motion is not everything in politics. Without leadership, motion will occur in contradictory directions. Politics needs to be directed toward ends, needs, mobilization of resources and support, organization of movements, and the transformation of divergent interests into unified collective decisions. This is the function of leadership. Democracy is particularly in need of such leadership. A democracy without political leaders in movements, parties, and government articulates problems but does not solve them. The differentiation between leaders and those who are led by them is part and parcel of a democracy in a large territorial state. Parties and party leaders fulfill the function of mobilizing political support for political programs, of bundling up divergent interests, and of transforming them into collective decisions. The success of political leaders is due to their charismatic qualities, which introduce a charismatic element into modern politics. Politics becomes a vocation in this process.

The proper supervision of political leaders depends on the following preconditions: (1) An open competition between political leaders to gain votes; (2) a strong parliament with far-reaching rights to investigate and to control government and administration; (3) the socialization of political leaders in the everyday political work in parties and committees; and (4) the institutionalization of a specific ethic of responsibility for the politician emerging from the above-mentioned conditions. According to this ethic of responsibility, the politician works with a passion for values, a sense of proportion, willingness to compromise, and readiness to take responsibility. He or she is devoted to values but also keeps an eye on the consequences of means applied to realize these values with regard to other values and has a sense of conflict between values. The politician sees the need to compromise but also looks for far-reaching decisions that cannot compromise with everything. The ethic of responsibility distinguishes itself from a naked power politics or *"Realpolitik,"* which is oriented to nothing but the maintenance of power positions, and from an ethic of conviction, which is devoted to the realization of specific values without taking into account the consequences for other values and without a sense of the contradiction between values and of the unavoidability of compromise.

The process of political decision making is located in a force-field between the egotism and particularism of interest groups and parties and the requirement to make a collectively binding decision. Weber wanted to maintain and regulate this tension by the mutual control of a number of institutions. At the time of his political writing, when the breakdown of the German *"Kaiserreich"* and the foundation of the Weimar Republic was at stake at the end of World War I, Weber argued for a constitution that was designed to institutionalize the tension between divergent requirements:

1. A president elected by the people was intended to be responsible to the whole of society.
2. The parliament was intended to articulate the conflict between interests and to control government and administration.

3. The bureaucracy was intended to provide for a predictable administrative process.
4. The courts were intended to watch over the conformity to the rules of decision making.

Weber's recommendation for coping with the basic contradiction between formal and substantial rationality was the institutionalization of countervailing forces that allow on the one hand a high level of formal rationality but on the other hand help to break up its petrifying effects, to remedy its harmful consequences, and to keep society in motion.

Summary

Basic Categories of Sociology

1. Definition: Social action is any action that, according to its subjective meaning, is directed toward the behavior of others by an actor or several actors and is oriented to that behavior in its process.
2. The more social action is determined by cultural ideas, the more it will maintain a general meaning in different situations; the more it is guided by interests, the more it will be dynamically driven toward specific ends and will vary according to the change of situations.
3. The more social order can be traced back to cultural ideas, the more it will have meaning for actors and be respected.
4. Definition: Action can be traditional, affectual, value-rational, and means-end rational in character.
5. The more action is traditionally determined, the more it will reproduce the past; the more it is affectually determined, the more it will be spontaneously directed to specific ends; the more it is value-rationally determined, the more it will maintain a general meaning; the more it is means-end rationally determined, the more it will change according to the change of situations.
6. The more interests converge regularly, the more social action will display a regular pattern.
7. The more social action is determined by customs, mores, conventions, and law, the more it will display a regular pattern to an increasing degree in the sequence of these phenomena.
8. The more social order is considered as legitimate, the more stable it will be.
9. Legitimacy can be based on traditional, affectual, value-rational, and means-end rational grounds.
10. Definition: Repeated social action between the same actors establishes a social relationship that can take on the forms of communal association, societal association, and struggle.

11. A social relationship can be more or less open.
12. Definition: A social relationship with limitation of participants is an association when its orders are guaranteed by leadership and possibly an administrative staff.
13. An association can be autonomous, heteronomous, autocephalous, and heterocephalous.
14. Definition: Continuously organized action toward specific ends is an operation. An association that works in this way is an operating association.
15. Membership in an association can be voluntary or compulsory.
16. Definition: Power is the chance to enforce one's will within a social relationship even against resistance.
17. Definition: Authority is the chance to receive compliance with one's commands in a social relationship.
18. Definition: An association that subordinates its members to authority relationships is an authority association.
19. Definition: An authority association that imposes its orders successfully within a certain geographical area by threatening or applying physical force through an administrative staff is a political association.
20. Definition: An operating compulsory association that has monopolized the legitimate use of physical force for carrying out its orders is a state.
21. Definition: An association that guarantees its orders through the application of psychic constraint by granting or refusing salvation is a hierocratic association.
22. A hierocratic association that has monopolized the legitimate exercise of psychic constraint is a church.

Methodology

23. Explanations of social phenomena have to be proved according to two criteria: the adequacy of meaning and the adequacy of cause.
24. Descriptions and explanations of social phenomena have to construct ideal-types in order to single out from concrete reality those aspects on which an investigation is to focus.
25. Social science has to abstain from value judgments because it cannot answer questions of what should be. It can only answer questions of what is, why that is, what is possible, and what is not possible, and has to leave the decision on what should be done to the responsibility of the human individual.

Sociology of Religion

26. The more Western rationalism develops, the sharper the contradiction between formal and substantial rationality in culture and societal insti-

tutions of science, technology, capitalism, bureaucracy, and the legal system grows.

27. The more Western rationalism develops, the more it actively intervenes in the world in order to work on its evils and the more it creates an artificial world, which again is full of evils.

28. The more Oriental rationalism develops, the more a human being's actions will have to accommodate to the existing order of the world, so that the balance of the whole will not be disturbed, or humans will have to retreat from this world in order to gain admission to eternal order.

29. The more Western rationalism develops, the more it will be linked with an instrumental activism of mastering the world with moral universalism and individualism.

30. The more human beings experience suffering, evil, injustice, illness, and death and ask why, the more religion will develop and give answers to this question.

31. Magic is the most primitive form of answering these questions by conceiving of the perceivable world as influenced by the power of demons hidden in an unperceivable world.

32. Archaic religion is the next level of religion, exemplified in Confucianism. It conceives of the universe as hierarchically differentiated into a heavenly and a worldly order that together make up a balanced cosmos to which the human being has to accommodate in order to keep face. This leaves the world as it is including group particularism and the subordination of the individual to his or her group.

33. The Confucian accommodation to the world is shaped by the administrative spirit and the privileged position of the *literati* civil servants.

34. The ethical religions have developed a fundamental tension between a perfect divine order and an imperfect world or a perfect God and an imperfect world.

35. There are two solutions to this problem of theodicy and two paths to salvation: the world-immanent and the world-transcending solutions of the theodicy problem and the mysticist and asceticist paths to salvation, both in other-worldly and inner-worldly versions.

36. The Hindu teaching of retribution and reincarnation is an example of a world-immanent theodicy. It is connected with other-worldly and inner-worldly mysticism and other-worldly asceticism. It legitimates the caste order as it is, leaves the world as it is, and supports caste particularism and the individual's subordination to the ritual duties of the caste.

37. Buddhism explains evil as the individual's thirst for life and recommends retreat from the world in order to find entrance into the eternal peace of Nirvana: other-worldly mysticism. It, too, leaves the world as it is.

38. Judeo-Christian religion has established a world-transcending theodicy and teaches inner-worldly asceticism as the path to salvation. The world

as it is is full of evils and will come to an end when God decides that the day of judgment has come.

39. According to Jewish teachings, God dominates this world by His ethical commands and has elected His people to lead it toward a better world. His people have to obey His ethical commands, which are communicated by the ethical prophets. The result is an active intervention in this world and the carrying out of God's commands as the path to salvation. However, the confinement of the religion to the Jewish people and the domination of the group sets limits on the religion's potential for universalism and individualism.

40. The teaching of Christ opened up a universalism of love and an individualistic relationship to God.

41. The mission of the Apostle Paul founded Christianity's universalism and expansion by separating the religious from the ethnic and the national community.

42. The ancient Christian church established an accommodation between religious and worldly order.

43. Medieval scholastic teaching further developed this position in an organic conception of the universe as a hierarchically ordered cosmos. Divine and earthly order are reconciled in one cosmos.

44. The Reformation broke up the medieval reconciliation and reinstated the tension between God and this world, reinstating God's power.

45. Lutheran Protestantism made the worldly conduct of the average human being in his or her vocation the normal place to conform to God's expectations, however, in a traditionalistic sense.

46. Calvin's teaching of predestination and conception of human conduct as instrumental to the glory of God initiated a sacralization of professional work in combination with the Protestant's interest in knowing his or her status of election and with the life-world of the bourgeois carrier strata.

47. Other branches of Protestantism have developed similar forms of inner-worldly asceticism.

48. The Protestant inner-worldly asceticism is the meaning foundation for the capitalist spirit of devotion to hard work and to reliability and legality in economic exchange.

49. Ascetic Protestantism established an ethical rationalism that measures the world with absolute ethical standards, an instrumental activism of intervening in this world, and a moral universalism and individualism.

50. The secularization of the religious ethic in the Enlightenment made its ethical rationalism, instrumental activism, moral universalism, and individualism binding for everybody.

51. The secularization of the quest for meaning in the development of modern science leads to the dissolution of a binding meaningful order in the struggle between values and thus to the loss of meaning.

52. The institutionalization of modern secularized culture in the systems of capitalism, bureaucracy, and the legal system leads to the loss of freedom.

The Sociology of Economic, Legal, and Political Institutions

53. The more the development of modern economic, legal, and political institutions is shaped by the Western rationalism that emerged from Judeo-Christian religion, the more it will culminate in the contradiction between formal and substantial rationality.
54. Modern capitalism emerges as a formally rational system, which steadily increases the level of allocation of scarce resources to given needs. But it has substantially irrational consequences of making profit for its own sake, of satisfying only needs backed up by purchasing power, and of running against the individual's will and against ethical standards.
55. Modern rational-legal political authority replaces traditional and charismatic forms of authority and displays an ever higher level of formal rationality in the sense of formal control by the law, but implies substantial irrationality in the sense of growing petrification.
56. Modern rational law is formally rational in the sense of guaranteeing the rights of individuals by due process of law, but with the consequence of substantial irrationality in the sense that it constricts every sphere of everyday life by legal regulations, thus reducing the individual's freedom of choice.
57. Modern bureaucracy is formally rational in the sense of a precisely working machine that is completely predictable in its outcomes, but it is substantially irrational in the sense that it increasingly constricts any autonomy of individual decision making.
58. The more politics is organized as a democracy based on competition between charismatic leaders, the more it will work as a countervailing power against the petrifying effects of the rational-legal authority system and will keep society in motion.

Critical Assessment

Assessing Max Weber's contribution to sociology, we see it as the most forceful demonstration of the development of cultural ideas and of their effects on social action and social development ever written by a sociologist. His cultural approach provides us with insights into the basic features and contradictions of our modern society. They have not been superseded by anything written after Weber. Weber gives us an understanding of the cultural roots of urgent problems in modern society reaching far back into history.

The cultural contradiction between formal and substantial rationality constitutes the core of the problems of modern Western society. The contradictions of capitalism, bureaucracy, and the legal system are outcomes of this more basic cultural contradiction. In working out the cultural contradictions Weber reaches a much deeper level of analysis than any other classic. Marx's contradictions of capitalism, Spencer's dynamics of the industrial society, Durkheim's crisis of solidarity, and Pareto's dynamics of power systems point out features of specific institutions. Weber, however, reveals the features of our culture that are common to all these institutions and different from other cultures. Thus, what he uncovers in our culture reaches back much farther into history, covers many more areas of our lives, and reaches much farther into the future. Whereas we may change specific institutions to solve problems, it is much more difficult to change our culture. To do so involves much deeper transformations with much wider repercussions, more resistance from long-established truths, and more change in our sacred identity.

Weber's interpretation and explanation of the cultural roots of modern society is by no means one-sidedly idealistic in character. He is very conscious of the interactions of cultural development with processes of interest articulation, power struggle, and group-formation. He always relates the developmental logic of cultural ideas, in the sense of their growing systematization, codification, and generalization, to the societal position of the intellectuals who shape this development and to the interests, power, and life-world of the social strata and groups who carry these cultural ideas on in social life. In Weber's terms we cannot understand and explain Confucianism without an analysis of the *literati* and their position in the political authority system and of the social organization of ancient China. The same holds true for an understanding and explanation of Hinduism, which has to refer to the Brahmins and to the Hindu caste system, and for Buddhism, which has to refer to the Buddhist monks and their social position. It is no different for ancient Judaism, the prophets, and the political situation of the Jewish people, or for the social position of Christianity in ancient Rome and in the Middle Ages, or for that of Lutheran and Calvinist Protestantism.

Weber's comparative approach to the evolution of modern Western culture is not idealistic but synthetic in character, because it gives a central position to the interrelationship of cultural development with economic interests, political struggle, and group-formation. Nevertheless, it is an approach that concentrates on cultural systems as a dependent and an independent variable, and not to the same degree on social systems. His studies on capitalism, political authority, the legal system, and bureaucracy are overwhelmingly concerned with the cultural dimension of these institutions, with their spirit and how it is rooted in broader culture. In this respect Weber cannot deny his origination from German historical idealism, which emphasized the study of the unique spirit of a historical phenomenon against the generalizations of positivism, aiming at the formulation of laws that are valid at any place in the world.

According to Weber's roots in historical idealism, we live within a very specific culture that shapes our society and makes it different from any other society. Starting from this tradition of historical idealism Weber did not concentrate on formulating general laws. Capitalism, the legal system, and bureaucracy were social institutions that were unique to our Western culture and had to be interpreted as parts of an overall cultural system that is different from other cultural systems. However, this does not mean that Weber did not concede a place to general laws in sociological explanation. However, he made use of such general assumptions while he was writing with his historical perspective, but never made them explicitly an object of study.

Weber was convinced that our conceptual framework is unavoidably part of our broader Western cultural system and is thus historically and culturally selective in character. It throws light on those aspects of reality that are of interest within our cultural system. His own comparative studies are shaped by a Western view of world religions and by a German historical idealist view of social phenomena. However, his very knowledge of different cultures is a step toward approaching categories that are less culture-bound. His relativization of Western rationalism in the light of Oriental rationalism is a major step in this direction.

It is our task to go on with the process of approaching truly general analytical systems in the process of producing a global culture. Aiming at such general analytical systems is at least part of our scientific enterprise that we cannot give up in favor of complete relativism. Our intention to understand and to explain different cultures needs at least general instruments that allow a translation of the different languages within a general framework. In doing so we have to go beyond Weber's commitment to historical idealism.

The same holds true with regard to his value-relativism. The more we go on toward producing a global culture, the more we will do so in processes of cultural discourse, which includes discussion of moral ideas and not only of cognitive statements. We do not conceive of human and civil rights as particularistic ideas that can be questioned in light of competing ideas. We claim them to be universally valid and expect them to be realized more and more all over the world against a resistant reality. We claim that their validity can be proved in a moral discourse and that everybody would have to consent to the outcome of such a discourse.

Weber does not have any access to such a discursive grounding of moral standards. He tended rather to make them a matter of individual choice without validity reaching beyond that choice. From the point of view of a contemporary theory of discourse ethics we can therefore go beyond Weber's moral relativism. This, however, does not mean that any value-conflict addressed by Weber could be resolved by moral discourse. Much of Weber's statement on irreconcilable value-conflict applies to very specific problems where any solution has many different consequences touching different values. No general solution is possible here, but only individual choices and compromise on the political level. Here Weber's model of political competition on solving political problems remains valid.

With regard to the principle of social science's abstaining from value-judgment, Weber's position is still partially valid, because social science is a cognitive undertaking, differentiated from moral discourse. However, we can relate cognitive investigations to moral discourse in moral criticism. This is a legitimate task of a critical social science that goes beyond Weber's position. However, its task is criticism from the point of view of moral standards. It still cannot prove that any institution is absolutely valid, because this would amount to dogmatically stopping a rational discourse, which can never cease to raise doubts. It is the same as with the scientific enterprise. Whereas we can single out errors by criticism step by step, we cannot prove any theory valid in the positive sense. It is the same with normative discourse. We can criticize what is wrong with regard to universal moral standards, but we cannot prove any institution to be absolutely right in the positive sense. Here we can follow Weber, whereas we can go beyond Weber in conducting critical social science. Then again, we can well understand Weber's idea of the value-relationship and cultural relevance of social science in this updated sense, reaching beyond cultural relativism and approaching more universalizable moral points of view. In fact Weber's substantial sociology is critical social science *par excellence* when it points out the substantial irrationalities of formal rationality in modern Western culture! What we can do is update his methodological position so that it fits in with the contemporary understanding of a critical social science.

However, we can go beyond Weber in dealing with the contradiction between formal and substantial rationality. For Weber, there is no chance of escaping from this contradiction. A look at the rationalism of Oriental culture without committing oneself to a choice between the two diametrically opposed forms of rationalism, but with a conscious attempt at approaching a new synthesis, may open up future paths of development not envisaged by Max Weber.

The two types of rationalism contradict each other completely. Western rationalism destroys the balance of the cosmos, of man and nature, man and man, from the point of view of Oriental rationalism. However, Oriental rationalism leaves the world as it is, full of evils, suffering, and injustice from the point of view of Western rationalism. Inasmuch as Western rationalism has come under attack because of its contradictions and recently because of its lack of concepts for a balance between man and nature, we are now witnessing criticisms of our type of rationalism which formulate ideas similar to Oriental rationalism, ideas of balance. A neo-traditionalism often accompanies this criticism, which is a logical consequence of ideas of balance. However, we must also be aware that a complete turn of our culture toward such ideas cannot take place without a movement toward the traditionalism of Oriental culture, which dispenses with any formulation of ideas reaching beyond present or past society and leaves the world as it is with many phenomena that we would consider evil and unjust from our Western point of view.

A much richer approach would be a movement toward synthesizing both types of rationality to create holistic concepts of intervening in the world. Such an approach has to overcome isolated instrumental interventions in the world by the holistic consideration of a multiplicity of consequences and repercussions resulting from any single intervention, so that any intervention can be supplemented by a whole array of concomitant measures. In taking this approach we conceive of our intervention in the world as part of a system embracing the totality of the world, looking at the consequences for the other parts of that world. Transforming an evil society toward a better one is then the task not just of isolated interventions but of concerted actions conceptualized within a whole composed of interdependent parts. Such an approach to the world can take up critical theory's criticism of Western rationalism as purely instrumental in character and as blind for the world as a totality and may open up better paths to linking instrumental rationality — or in Weber's terms formal rationality — to a holistic concept of substantial rationality. The consequences of any single intervention for different substantial values are interpreted within a whole system of interdependent parts. In this way instrumental rationalism can be relinked to the idea of a good society on a new level; questions of formal and substantial rationality can be linked together.

Approaching such a synthesis of Western and Oriental rationalism will be the challenge of a future global culture. It will be a rationalism that actively intervenes in the world in order to make it better, but with instruments that point out the consequences and repercussions of any intervention within a global system. Approaches like systems analysis can be seen as instruments for attaining such a synthesis. Max Weber didn't formulate such ideas himself; however, he stated the contradiction between the formal and substantial rationality of Western rationalism and the contradiction between Western and Oriental rationalism in a way that makes him sociology's foremost interpreter of the modern world (see Brubaker, 1984).

Weber's preoccupation with the cultural dimension of society despite his conscious investigation of its interrelationship with processes of economic transactions, political struggle, and group formation, unavoidably implies a look at these levels of social action in terms of their relationship to cultural processes and developments and puts aside a closer look at their internal structures, processes, and development. In order to approach a full understanding of these noncultural phenomena we have to look at the contributions of other classical authors who concentrated much more on these noncultural dimensions of society. We have to complement Weber's cultural emphasis in studying modern capitalism by Spencer's liberal economic and Marx's radical economic perspectives; his cultural emphasis in studying political authority by Pareto's perspective on power and conflict in society; and his cultural emphasis in studying the legal system by Durkheim's enquiry into the transformation of systems of solidarity. Though Weber was not a narrow-minded historical idealist who did not take into account the effects of economic transactions, political struggle, and group formation, and of all the classical authors came closest to a synthetic perspective, he does not make irrelevant the contributions of these authors for approaching a truly comprehensive sociological view of social action, social organization, society, and social development.

Further Developments

The work of Max Weber has been studied by many scholars who have tried to reveal and preserve Weber's contribution to sociology. This work of interpreting and preserving Weber's work and of continuing with his approach is still going on. Indeed, it has undergone a revitalization in recent years. Because of the two basic opposing traditions that exerted their influence on Weber's work, there is a tendency to break them apart and to concentrate on one of these traditions. First of all is the idealist and historicist tradition. The major recent contributions to understanding Weber's work in this perspective came from Talcott Parsons (1937/1968), Benjamin Nelson (1949/1969, 1974), Friedrich H. Tenbruck (1975, 1985, 1986, 1989), Wolfgang Schluchter (1979, 1988), Stephen Kalberg (1980, 1990), Johannes Weiss (1975), and Werner Gephart (1990b). The author of this book did also participate in the Weber-discourse (Münch, 1982; for translation, see 1987a and 1988; 1986).

Then there is the conflict tradition. Contributions to this aspect of Weber's work are threefold. The first type of conflict interpretation is liberalist in character, the second one is conservative, and the third one is Marxist. A liberal conflict interpretation of Weber's work has been contributed by Wolfgang Mommsen (1959/1974a, 1974b/1986), Reinhard Bendix (1962, 1964, 1978), Günther Roth (1976, 1987), Gianfranco Poggi (1978, 1983), Bryan S. Turner (1974, 1981), Robert Holton with Bryan S. Turner (1989), and Cohen, Hazelrigg, and Pope (1975), and a conservative one by Wilhelm Hennis (1987). A Marxist one underlies many neo-Marxist approaches to historical sociology like those of Barrington Moore (1966), Theda Skocpol (1979), and Michael Mann (1986). We have to take into account, however, that these authors start from a specific perspective, but try to go beyond that in the same way as Weber did. Thus each author has created a complex work.

A Weberian background is also perceivable in the work of Daniel Bell. In his work *The Coming of Postindustrial Society* (Bell, 1973), Bell points out the change toward the prominence of knowledge and professional experts in the society of the future. In his work *The Cultural Contradictions of Capitalism* (Bell, 1976), he deals with the disjunction of the cultural, economic, and political spheres and the corresponding erosion of the Protestant work ethic, which he says is being replaced by a culture of the psychedelic bazaar in contemporary society. For that reason, he looks for a new religion that could guide societal development in our times.

TEN

FROM PRAGMATISM TO INTERACTIONISM: GEORGE HERBERT MEAD

GEORGE HERBERT Mead was born on February 27, 1863, and grew up in a Puritan home in Massachusetts. He graduated from Oberlin College in 1883 and went on to study philosophy at Harvard University in 1887. The next year he visited Germany to study psychology and philosophy. In 1891 he married Helen Castle, with whom he had one child, a son named Henry. In the same year Mead moved to Ann Arbor, for an appointment as instructor, where he met Charles H. Cooley, John Dewey, and James H. Tuft. In 1892 he followed Dewey to the new University of Chicago, where he taught until he died on April 26, 1931. In accordance with the concept of this new university, Mead was much involved in combining scholarly and public affairs of reform. The world's first department of sociology was founded at the University of Chicago by Albion Small in 1892. The department established *The American Journal of Sociology* in 1895, which has been a leading journal for the discipline since that time.

Intellectual Roots

What made American philosophy a distinct approach to understanding the world and the human being in that world is pragmatism (see Rorty, 1982). The leading philosophers of pragmatism, Charles S. Peirce (1839–1914), William James (1842–1910), and John Dewey (1859–1952), placed the practical-instrumental relationship of the human actor to his or her natural and social environment at the center of their investigations (see Peirce, 1934/1965; James, 1890, 1907, 1909/1968; Dewey, 1886, 1922, 1927, 1977). Knowledge and morals evolve from this practical-instrumental relationship between the actor and the environment. Truth is a question of the practical-instrumental usefulness of knowledge and morals.

James was particularly interested in the psychology of knowledge production by studying the pure stream of conscious experience. He pointed out the selectivity of perception and the dependence of attention with regard to objects on the individual's purpose. From Peirce to Dewey and Mead, however, we see more emphasis on the production of knowledge in the process of action that is embedded in collective association and social communication. For Peirce, knowledge is advanced in the process of action according to the problems that arise in the course of that action and that call for solutions. Actors start out from a base of accumulated knowledge that is sedimented in habits. When confronted with new experience together with a failure of the traditional knowledge to guide action successfully the actor looks for new solutions by playing through alternative courses of action and changes his or her habits according to the success of the new solutions.

Peirce (1934/1965: 156–57) set this pragmatic view of knowledge advancement in opposition to Descartes' advice to break completely with traditional "book knowledge" and apply doubt as a fundamental principle, from which the human being can build knowledge by pure intuition based on the first true principle of "*cogito, ergo sum*," that is, "I think, therefore I am" (see Joas, 1987: 86–87). Moreover, this whole process is not carried out by isolated individuals but by individuals who are associated collectively and who are engaged in social communication. Self-reflection and collective reflection intermesh in this process. In this way pragmatism laid the philosophical grounds for the idea of democracy as a complex web of self-governing associations and communities that are themselves mobilized by the voluntary participation of creative individuals (see Joas, 1987: 89–93). Social communication has to penetrate every sphere of society, including the economic sphere, in order to create an order that on the one hand is rooted in moral ideas and on the other hand is flexible with regard to the exigencies of the situations of action. This idea is rooted in American reality, yet it transcends this reality with more far-reaching claims. The author who contributed particularly to this idea of self-government and social communication is John Dewey (1927). It was George Herbert Mead (1934) who carried on Dewey's work. Pragmatism was a reform movement that tried to re-establish the early American tradition of individualism embedded in voluntary associations and decentralized, participatory democracy. These were displaced by the emergence of corporate capitalism, representative and centralized government, and a societal community divided into racial, ethnic, and national groups resulting from mass immigration from different parts of the world.

As pragmatism became the leading school of American philosophy toward the end of the nineteenth century, it framed the development of American sociology in the first decades of this century. The works of Charles Horton Cooley, George Herbert Mead, William I. Thomas, and Robert E.

Park, who framed American sociology to a great extent, were sociological transformations of philosophical pragmatism. Cooley taught at the University of Michigan. Thomas, Mead, and Park created what was then called the Chicago School of Sociology, which dominated American sociology until the late 1930s (Lewis and Smith, 1980; Bulmer, 1984; Joas, 1987). This school was later outranked by the Columbia University department of sociology, with Robert K. Merton and Paul F. Lazarsfeld as leading figures, and by the Harvard University department of social relations, with Pitirim Sorokin, Talcott Parsons, and George C. Homans in the lead (Wiley, 1979). Merton (1949/1968a) promoted empirical functionalism and middle range theories; Lazarsfeld advanced quantitative methodology (Lazarsfeld and Rosenberg, 1955); Sorokin (1937–1941) engaged in broader studies of social and cultural change; Parsons (1937/1968, 1951) advocated analytical functionalism and grand theory; and Homans (1961) turned to the psychological foundations of social behavior. In contrast to these later developments, the Chicago school concentrated on microsocial empirical studies with qualitative methods. Their intent was to contribute to social reform based on professional sociological work at a time when big cities were going through fundamental changes resulting from mass immigration of a growing variety of people with different national origins, and from the expansion of industrial capitalism and the growing power of the federal government. These processes changed the once relatively homogeneous communities considerably. Chicago was particularly affected by these changes.

The sociologists of the Chicago school first placed the individual, his or her relationship to the immediate social environment, small units like the family, the workplace, the neighborhood, and the local community at the center of sociological analysis. Major contributions to this approach came, for example, from Anderson (1923) on the hobo, from Trasher (1927) on criminal youth gangs, from Wirth (1928/1969) on the Jewish ghetto, and from Shaw (1930) on a juvenile criminal. Wirth's (1938, 1964) studies on the city were also of great importance. In doing this, the Chicago sociologists placed a distinct microsociological approach in opposition to the classical European sociologists' preoccupation with the macrosociological analysis of the great societal structures and transformations in the economy, polity, societal community, and culture of the whole family of modern industrial societies. The only European classical sociologist who contributed to this microsociological enterprise was Georg Simmel, who did indeed exert some influence on the pragmatist American sociologists.

Part of pragmatism in American sociology is a particular emphasis on the symbolic nature of social life. This aspect of social life, however, is studied not from above, from the great cultural systems of religion, morals, and ideologies, but from below, from the microsocial perspective of human actors involved in processes of symbolically defining their situations, their own selves, and the roles they play in social interaction. From Cooley (1902/1964, 1909/1962) we can learn how an individual's self emerges from the individual's awareness of his or her recognition in the reactions of others. The individual sees him- or herself in these reactions. This is what Cooley called the *looking-glass self.* From Thomas we have the famous phrase, "If men define situations as real, they are real in their consequences" (Thomas and Thomas, 1928: 572). This means the lines of conduct human actors choose to follow are largely determined by the definition of the situation they apply, by the perspectives, preoccupations, categories, and ideas they use for interpreting the meaning of a situation of action (Thomas and Znaniecki, 1918–1920; Thomas and Thomas, 1928; Thomas, 1937, 1972). In his classic study on the *Polish Peasant in Europe and America* (1918–1920), coauthored with Florian Znaniecki, Thomas conceptualized social change as an ongoing process of disorganization and reorganization of social life. Park has demonstrated the determination of human action by the playing of roles. He conceived of society as being composed of two types of social order: moral order, which is rooted in the common values and meanings, and biotic or ecological order, which emerges from competition for scarce resources and is represented in spatial and temporal distributions of such resources (Park and Burgess, 1921; Park, 1950–1955, 1952).

However, in retrospect, the most important contribution to the development of sociological pragmatism was made by George Herbert Mead. He developed from pragmatism what Herbert Blumer later called "symbolic interactionism," and this was to become one of the leading schools of microsociological theory.

Mead synthesized pragmatism with two other currents of his time: Darwin's theory of evolution and behaviorism, particularly as represented by the psychologist John Watson. Mead also had a respectable knowledge of classical and modern European philosophy. The tradition of German idealism that emerged from elaborating on Kant's critical philosophy was of particular importance for the shaping of Mead's work (Mead, 1934, 1936, 1938, 1959, 1964).

Mead's reading of Kant, Fichte, Schelling, Hegel, and Dilthey framed the general thrust of his approach. He tried to establish a pragmatist basis for concepts that the German idealists left to the development of the human consciousness itself. The German idealists conceived of the development of the individual and the social world as a self-realization of the spirit in objective and subjective terms, as a logic of spiritual development. Mead conceptualized this process as an interaction between the individual subject and his or her natural and social environment in pragmatist terms, guided by the pragmatic process of organizing individual and social life.

The evolutionary perspective in Mead's thought comes to light in his basic assumption that human mind, self, morals, and society evolve from the lowest forms of animal organisms' adjustment to the environment to the highest and most complex forms of human organisms' adjustment to an environment that in this case includes nature and other human beings. For example, he tries to point out how language evolves step by step from simpler forms of conversation involving gestures. This evolutionary perspective also gives special emphasis to the trial-and-error character of human learning. This perspective opposes Mead in his treatment of the evolution of social order, for example, moral order, to aprioristic approaches like that of the German philosophical tradition represented by Immanuel Kant, and after him by idealist philosophers such as Fichte, Schelling, and Hegel. According to Kant, what is morally right or wrong has to be determined *a priori*, that is, before any concrete action takes place and consequences set in. In Mead's view, conceptions of right and wrong evolve in a trial-and-error process from concrete human action and the experience emerging from looking at its consequences. To Kant's aprioristic morality he thus opposes an experimental morality (Mead, 1908, 1934: 379–89).

Mead's incorporation of behaviorism in his pragmatist social psychology turned Watson's (1913, 1914) naturalistic behaviorism into what he called social behaviorism and replaced the behavioristic refusal to study processes of the human mind, the "black box" that cannot be immediately observed, by an explicit investigation into the evolution of mind and thought (Mead, 1934: 1–41).

Mind

Behaviorism conceives of the behavior of animals and human individuals as a response to a stimulus. For example, "fire" is a stimulus that arouses the response "flight" from an animal or a human being. Social behaviorism says that a gesture made by one individual arouses a certain response in another. For example, a threatening gesture by one individual may make another individual take flight in response. What makes the difference between a gesture and a stimulus is the meaning attributed to the gesture by both the individual who makes the gesture and the other individual who recognizes it. The connection between stimulus and response may be instinctive or learned, and is direct and unambiguous in all cases. A stimulus directly and definitely arouses a specific instinctive or learned response. This direct connection between stimulus and response is interrupted if the stimulus is replaced by a gesture. What distinguishes the gesture from the stimulus is that the gesture expresses an intention; it symbolizes something beyond itself. It has meaning and needs to be interpreted in order for it to be understood and for the recipient to respond in a way that makes sense in relation to the gesture.

When two organisms meet and coordinate their conduct via gestures, there takes place what Mead (1934: 42–134) calls the conversation of gestures.

Here the gesture of one organism leads to the response of another organism, which is in itself a gesture arousing a further reaction from the first organism. Mead gives examples of three levels of the conversation of gestures: the dog-fight, the mutually related song of birds, and communication between human beings. In the dog fight, the threatening gesture of one dog leads to the same dog springing at the throat of the other; meanwhile, the gesture arouses the same response in the second dog, namely springing at the throat of the first. Here the first dog's gesture does not call forth the same response in both dogs. The first dog's threatening gesture makes its own attack more forceful; thus its response is "reinforced attack." The second dog is not reinforced in its behavior by the first dog's threatening gesture but is frightened and responds with "defense." Because of this lack of correspondence of the meaning of the threatening gesture for the two animals, it is only a preliminary form of the conversation of gestures.

A higher form of that conversation is reached by the mutually related song of birds. Here we have a conversation of *vocal* gestures. The song of one bird calls out a specific corresponding reply by the other bird. The intention of the first bird's song is to call forth the other bird's song in reply. If alone, the first bird could also sing the reply by itself. Thus the vocal gesture can arouse the same response in the first and the second bird. This is a further step toward conversation of gestures that involves the use of the so-called significant symbol. Such a conversation with significant symbols is communication with a common language, which is an evolutionary step only the human species has fully attained.

If one person at the tea-table asks another, "Would you please pass me the sugar?" the first person expresses the intention to get the sugar. If the other person responds by passing the sugar to the first person, that response corresponds exactly to the first person's intention. If the second person does not recognize what the first person wants, he or she will not respond, and the first person will try to get the sugar him- or herself. Thus, the first person responds to his or her call with the same conduct as he or she sought to illicit from the second person. Mead says at this point of the analysis: The call is a significant symbol, namely, it arouses the same response in the first and the second person. The first person is able to imagine the second person's response internally in advance.

The significant symbol is the medium of communication. The significant symbol allows mutual understanding and thus the successful coordination of action and attainment of goals. Take for example a discussion group: One participant gives another participant a sign that he or she wants to enter the discussion. Recognizing the sign, the other participant stops speaking (the intended response of the first person's sign), and the first participant implicitly anticipates that the second participant will stop talking and is therefore prepared to begin. The first participant's sign calls out the same response in both persons, overtly in the second participant and covertly in the first. Their conduct is coordinated inasmuch as the symbols they use in expressing their intentions call forth the same response in both of them.

Mead then goes on to explain the universalization of significant symbols. They become universalized insofar as the scope of social interaction grows and covers ever wider circles. In this process significant symbols tend to call forth the same response not only in two communicating actors but also in everybody who participates in or at least may enter the communication. We can say that these people speak a common language and represent a language community. The meaning of the symbols of this language is the response they call forth in both the speaking and listening actors and ultimately in each member of the language community.

This is Mead's pragmatist, evolutionary, and social behaviorist explanation of the evolution of human language. His explanation ties language to the level of practical-instrumental conduct. A symbol expresses an intention to act instrumentally with a specific goal. The meaning of a symbol also comes to light in practical-instrumental conduct. It is an overt or covert active response by actors to the symbol. This explanation of language is evolutionary in character because it sees language evolving from the simple conversation of gestures via the simple conversation of vocal gestures in the animal world to the conversation of significant symbols in the human world. It is also evolutionary because it sees language evolving from a human being's confrontation with the need to find ever more universal media of conversation in order to coordinate conduct for the sake of successful survival in an ever more complex world of widespread interdependencies in human conduct. Finally, Mead's explanation of the emergence of language is social behavioristic because it transforms the behavioristic stimulus-response perspective to the perspective of the conversation of gestures between social actors. This is social behaviorism.

Mead explains the emergence of human thinking in the same pragmatist, evolutionary, and social behaviorist way as he explains the emergence of communication and language. Thinking is internalized communication. For Mead, this means that in thinking the human individual anticipates the responses to his or her intentions expressed potentially in significant symbols. The first level at which this occurs is the technical-instrumental level. Here the actor anticipates the potential success or failure of various measures for successfully attaining his or her goal. The same is true for the internal anticipation of the responses of others to intentions that could be expressed in significant symbols.

The first step toward thinking as internal communication is when the child talks loudly to him- or herself in the voice of mother or father. The next step is such internal but explicit talk to oneself. Out of this inner talk, step by step, emerges a more abstract anticipation of possible responses to one's intentions embracing ever longer chains of possible conduct and responses. In this way the human mind evolves from social communication. This explanation of human thinking is pragmatist in character because it sees thinking as an internal anticipation of practical-instrumental, goal-oriented conduct. It is evolutionary because it perceives thinking as evolving from primitive trial-and-error conduct to self-talk and finally to the abstract anticipation of chains of conduct and responses, according to an interdependency of stronger demands for anticipation and evolving higher capacities for such anticipation. The explanation is social behavioristic because it places the origin of human thinking in the relationship between gestures and responses between social actors in social communication. And, as Mead emphasizes, the final destination of thinking as internal conversation is again social communication:

> Thinking becomes preparatory to social action. The very process of thinking is, of course, simply an inner conversation of gestures which in its completion implies the expression of that which one thinks to an audience. (Mead, 1934: 141–42)

Self

Beyond language and mind, there is a further property of the human individual that makes humans a distinctive species: the self (Mead, 1934: 135–226). This is the organizing center of the individual's experiences, thoughts, motives, and plans. It is the mediating unit between the human organism and its social environment. The self is an entity in itself, a distinctive phenomenon separate from the organism, from the body. The latter cannot relate to itself *in toto* as an object. Feelings and sense-perceptions are always particular in character, occur here and now, and relate only to parts of the organism. They lack any unity in time and space. That, however, is exactly what makes the self a distinctive entity. It can relate to itself as an object *in toto* and organizes experiences, feelings, thoughts, and ideas to make up a unity.

The human individual's organism is there from the moment of birth, whereas the self needs time to develop. It emerges from the interaction of the organism with its social environment and, in addition, develops in social communication. The individual learns to see him- or herself as a distinct person inasmuch as others respond to what he or she does. That there is someone who is responsible for what the individual does is experienced by the individual when others look at him or her, respond to him or her, and have attitudes toward him or her. The child's first steps in looking at him- or herself are replications of mother's words: "Don't cry, because boys don't cry!," "You're a brave boy," "You're a good boy, so don't annoy your mother, show some respect to your father, be good to your sister, be polite to visitors!" With the extension of the child's circle of interaction the child learns to look at him- or herself through the eyes of many other people apart from his or her mother's, and to take in the attitudes of these people, and finally of a whole group or community toward him- or herself. In this process the individual increasingly acquires the ability to view him- or herself as an object. This is what we call self-consciousness—the knowledge that one is a distinct person with specific motives, experiences, thoughts, plans, and attitudes. It results from the internalization by the individual of the attitudes that other people and groups express toward that individual. As the number of people relating to the young individual grows, the person develops many selfs as he or she communicates with others and as he or she becomes a member of different groups. The person has a multiple self. This is a stage of development in which the individual's self has still no capacity to organize the different singular attitudes of others into a whole and to shape these attitudes to form a single unity. Mead's question then is, How does such a unity emerge in the individual's self? His answer is that this unity emerges as the individual increasingly learns to recognize the organized character of the attitudes of his or her social environment, and he or she is increasingly included in ever wider communities that have ever more abstract attitudes in common.

Mead exemplifies this development from the multiple self to unity in the individual's self with his famous distinction between "play" and "game" in children's development. These represent two stages in the self's development. In the earlier stages of play, children play not in a coordinated way with each other but for themselves. They take up the roles of so-called *significant others*, for example, the roles of mother and father, and talk to themselves from the point of view of these role-models. They interact symbolically with them and internalize their attitudes toward themselves. These, however, are always "plays" with one single imagined partner, one after the other. The child does not organize their combined relationship to him- or herself and their interrelationship to form a whole. The attitudes internalized from significant others remain separate, particular standpoints. The child's self is compartmentalized in character.

Once a child becomes involved in "games" that interrelate several children in an organized way according to common rules of the game and in mutually dependent roles within teams engaged in competition with each other, the child reaches a new stage of the self's development. In a game like baseball, basketball, or football, the child cannot play with single partners one after the other, but has to relate to his or her teammates and to the opposing team at the same time and in an organized way. The child has to coordinate his or her conduct with the others and needs to know how their conduct is mutually coordinated in order to be a reliable actor for the team and the opponent. The child has to get an idea of the game as a whole, of the interrelation of all the different roles, of the unity within a team's conduct, of the mutual relationship between the opposing teams, of the rules of the game, of the unity in the performances of the two sides, and finally of the idea of the game itself. The more the child internalizes this organized unity, the more he or she relates to what Mead calls the *generalized other*. The result of such progression toward internalizing the generalized other is that the individual overcomes compartmentalization of the self and the emerging of a generalized self that reaches unity in its attitudes toward itself. This generalization of the self grows with the human individual's inclusion in ever wider groups and communities with ever wider sets of organized roles and an ever more abstract unity underlying their coordinated conduct and the rules of their games.

As Mead puts it, the generalization of the self increases its autonomy. Inasmuch as the human individual outgrows dependency upon a small set of significant others and learns the underlying unity and ideas of conduct and games of ever wider groups and communities, he or she is subordinated less and less to the judgment of single individuals and can rely more and more on standards that reach beyond any single individual or particular group. This is what makes the individual autonomous with regard to the demands of any single individual or particular group. Contributions in modern times to this widening of one's horizon and to the growing generalization and autonomy of one's self is the growing extension of social interaction with worldwide expanding markets, religious associations, scientific communities, artistic communities, and tourism.

Thus far we have talked about that aspect of the self that grows with the individual's increasing internalization of an ever wider part of his or her social environment. According to this view the self is a reflection of its social environment. This raises the question of whether the individual self merges completely with the social environment and whether there is any room for individuality that displays uniqueness. As Mead points out there is indeed room for such individuality, even though the human being's self develops in the process of internalizing its social environment. The reason for his thesis is that this process goes on as an *interaction* between the individual and his or her environment. That is, the human being is an active species that produces activities, and these activities provoke the reactions of others, which again call forth a reaction from the first person. In this process of *interaction* the self emerges with two components: the individual's spontaneous activity and his or her spontaneous reaction to the attitudes of others, and the individual's internalization of these attitudes. Mead calls the first of these the "I" and the second, the "me." The "I" stands for the spontaneous and unique individuality, the "me" for the internalized set of attitudes. Each individual experiences the attitudes of others in a unique way, in unique situations, and in a unique, historically growing perspective; he or she displays unique activities calling forth unique specifications of other people's attitudes; and he or she responds to these specifications of attitudes in a unique way.

This unique interplay between spontaneous activities, specific responses of others, and specific responses of the individual bring about a self that combines both a unique individuality and a set of internalized attitudes that are unique specifications of social attitudes. Because of this interrelated uniqueness, Mead says that "I" and "me" are two components of oneself that mutually *support* each other. Both work together in bringing about any action of the individual. According to Mead's analysis there is no contradiction between the growing individuality and growing sociality, because the individual simply needs the interaction with his or her social environment in order to develop a unique self, embracing both spontaneous activity and reaction on the one hand and specified attitudes on the other. Moreover, inasmuch as the human being needs society in order to develop his or her individuality, the human being needs the same society in order to realize his or her individuality in activity, for his or her self-realization. That self-realization is dependent on realization of the ideas about oneself in one's conduct. And this conduct relies upon the responses of others in order to initiate one's view of one's self as part of the process of monitoring whether or not the action corresponds to one's ideas about one's self. Only the continued response of others informs us about our success in self-realization. This is why Mead says the individual's self is realized in social activity.

Society

In Mead's view the individual's self emerges in its individuality from the interaction of the organism with its social environment. The other part of this perspective points to the shaping of society by its individual members (Mead, 1934: 227–336). The transformation of society also results from the interaction between the existing society as expressed in its institutions and the reactions of its members as individual entities to the social attitudes rooted in these institutions. This brings to light the social creativity of the human individual:

> As a man adjusts himself to a certain environment he becomes a different individual; but in becoming a different individual he has affected the community in which he lives. (Mead, 1934: 215)

Society is constantly being transformed by the individual reactions of each of its members to its institutions. The more society calls for the participation of its members in social life, the more it will innovate and change according to the social creativity of the members, and particularly of the spontaneous part of their selves, the "I." No society can exist without the contributions of its individual members to social life, because society *is* the coordinated activity of individuals. But societies call for this participation to a greater or smaller degree. According to Mead, the achievement of self-government in political democracy developed in paradigmatic form in the United States, where the individual's social creativity is mobilized to the highest degree. Accompanied by the expansion of social relationships and their growing interdependence, relational unity, and complexity, which is an effect of the expansion of coommunication in religion, markets, science, arts, and the public sphere, political democracy extends the individual's scope of orientation, leads his or her attitudes beyond any particular reference group and thus contributes to the universalization of associations and to the universalization and autonomy of the individual's self. A universal sense of citizenship and even humankind can develop from this process. Society then truly is an outcome of the cooperation of many individual selves who are committed to society via their "me" and who spontaneously react and enhance its innovation via their "I." Society is thus based on communication, which itself is rooted in the association of individuals.

As we can see, Mead finally formulates a theory according to which the human being develops his or her individuality in interaction with society, and society innovates via its interaction with its individual members. This is all the more true the more this interaction is intensified and expanded throughout society. In Mead's view the self-government of political democracy accompanied by increasing worldwide communication are the major preconditions for developing such a mutual support of individuality and social innovation.

Summary

Mind

1. The more the conversation of gestures progresses from the material to the vocal gesture and then to the significant symbol, the more complex the conduct that can be coordinated between organisms.
2. The wider the community in which a significant symbol calls forth the same response, the more universal is the meaning of that symbol and the more universal is the language composed of such symbols.
3. The more an individual communicates, the more his or her ability to think increases; this is internalized communication.

Self

4. The more intensive the interaction between a human organism and its social environment, the more a distinctive self will develop composed of two parts: the "I" and the "me."

5. The more the child relates to significant others in an unorganized way, the more he or she will develop multiple selves or a compartmentalized self.

6. The more the growing individual relates to a team, a group, a community, the wider the individual's scope expands, and the more he or she learns the organized set of roles, unity of conduct, rules of the game, and underlying ideas, the more the individual's self will display a unity, will be generalized and autonomous.

7. The more chances the individual has to participate voluntarily in social life, the more his or her self will combine a unique individuality based on the "I" with a generalized autonomous unity of specified attitudes based on the "me," the more the "I" and "me" will support each other, the more every action will be an outcome of their cooperation, and the more self-realization will take place in social activity.

Society

8. The more opportunities society offers for the voluntary participation of its individual members via self-government in political democracy and the more the scope of the individuals' association expands to include widespread interlocking and complex organization of social life and widespread communication, the more society will progress on the basis of its members' creativity and the more universal will become the orientation of its members.

Critical Assessment

From George Herbert Mead we learn about the dynamics of change in self and society. He points out the mutual support of growing individuality and increasingly widespread social organization, the mutual support of a spontaneous individual and a society open for the individual's participation, and the mutual support of the "I" and the "me." The human being develops an ever more general *and* autonomous attitude and an ever more unique individuality, but nevertheless is increasingly included in widespread social association and communication. This is a dynamic interaction of growing personal individuality and growing socially organized interlocking actions: Individuality and society grow and support each other.

However, this mutually related dynamic growth of individuality and social organization has specific preconditions that have to be much more explicitly stated than they are by Mead. He tends toward an unspecified overgeneralization of the mutually supportive growth of individuality and social organization, and he has often been interpreted in such an unspecified way. The qualifications of his theory must be elaborated from his arguments on self-government in society. Here it becomes apparent that the outlined growth of individuality and social organization takes place only under specific conditions: growing intensity and extensity of the individual's *voluntary participation* in social life and, along with that, an expanding scope of social association and communication. Unless these preconditions are realized the predicted consequences will not result and other types of self and social organization will occur. Mead does not tell us anything about these other types of self and social organization and their preconditions.

One such example would be the total *incorporation* of the self in society. Here society exerts its constraint on the individual and holds him or her under close control. Participation in this case is based not on free choice but on constraint rooted in the authority of society over the individual, in the solidarity of society's members and their uniform reaction to any minor deviation. Whenever the individual's attitudes incorporated in the "me" display an absolutely binding character, there must be at least something of this moral constraint of the community reflected in the individual. This is what Durkheim pointed out, and it is an insight that we cannot replace by Mead's theory of self and social organization.

There is also the *conflict* between self and society; society forces the individual's compliance by exercising its power. Once again, participation is not voluntary in character, nor is it rooted in a feeling of solidarity and obligation as in the case of moral constraint. Participation is simply enforced by external power in this case. This, however, does not call for the internalization of social attitudes by the individual. Social attitudes remain something external and alien. There is no development of a distinctive "me" in the individual, or else the "me" remains an alien element that does not unite with the "I." There is no "me" that could link the "I" to society. The result is an "I" that is in constant rebellion against society. It will either be suppressed by society or deviate from it whenever possible, or it will oppose society and reject it whenever there is a chance of articulating protest. Inasmuch as the individual's self maintains some of this power to deviate from, reject, oppose, rebel, and protest against society, there must be at least some of this conflict rooted in society's exercise of power on the individual. In order to develop a rebellious mind the individual needs chances to rebel against factually exercised power during his or her development. If there are no such objects of rebellion in the individual's development because of the absence of any source of power (for example, the power of a father), there will be no opportunity to develop a rebellious spirit. What we need in order to explain this type of relationship between individual and society is a theory of conflict that is not covered by Mead's theory. It was Simmel who provided the ground for such a theory.

The final alternative scenario is the contemplative *retreat* of the self from society. Here the individual refuses to participate in everyday social life and instead flees into an imaginary world of pure contemplation. A first step toward such retreat from society is the differentiation of religious or philosophical discourse from the practical-instrumental problems of everyday life. In this case the construction of meaning in mind and self becomes an end in itself: The mind reaches ever more abstract levels of reasoning. Discourse may even move from discourse between concrete persons toward an imaginary discourse with the great eternal figures of religious or philosophical thought, up to the extreme case of a self-contained discourse on the eternal and universal problems of human existence, including the eternal problems of morality. An individual who is on this path to eternity *retreats* from society and *moves beyond* society at the same time. He or she will develop a more abstract mind and self with much more universal ideas than any widening of concrete associations could accomplish. This level of universality cannot be reached according to Mead's suggestion of expanding worldwide social association and competition. Abstract discourse, retreat, and pure contemplation bring about a "me" that entails attitudes and ideas that reach beyond any concretely existing society and societal institution. Inasmuch as the individual lives such a retreated contemplative life, his or her individual spontaneity, the "I," merges with an all-embracing self-contained "me," becomes incorporated in such a "me," and loses its forceful capacity to decide and act. Activity disappears in a self-contained personality that has found eternal peace by not intervening in the world.

Inasmuch as an individual has at least some ability to look beyond society, to reflect from a more universal position, to have utopian ideas, and to find abstract unity even when he or she also tries to apply them to social life because of the effects of *other* relationships to society, there must be some retreat from society to engage in abstract discourse in the individual. Mead's theory does not provide access to this type of relationship between the individual and society. This is the dimension that he rejects with his criticism of Kant's aprioristic moral theory. However, we cannot completely replace such a theory by Mead's evolutionary-experimental theory, because the one does not retain the truth-content of the other. What we need in order to understand this aspect of self and its relationship to society is a theory of the self's development in moral discourse. To learn more about this we have to study the contribution of Jean Piaget and his followers from Lawrence Kohlberg to Jürgen Habermas.

Further Developments

The work of George Herbert Mead has created various forms of symbolic interactionism in American sociology. The prime example is the work of Herbert Blumer (1969), a student of Mead's and the inventor of the label "symbolic interactionism." Other versions of that approach have been worked out by Manford Kuhn (1964a, 1964b), Everett C. Hughes (1958, 1971; Hughes and Thompson, 1968), Ralph H. Turner (1962, 1968, 1976, 1978, 1979–80), Anselm Strauss (1978), Norman Denzin (1977), Theodore Kemper (1978), Sheldon Stryker (1980), and Gary Alan Fine together with Sherryl Kleinman (Fine, 1984, 1987, Fine and Kleinman, 1983, 1986). In Germany, Hans Joas (1980, for translation, see 1985; 1981, 1987) has recently reinterpreted Mead's work from the perspective of a hermeneutic-subjectivist Marxism.

BIBLIOGRAPHY

Adorno, Theodor W. 1966/1973a. *Negative Dialektik.* In: *Gesammelte Schriften.* Vol. 6, Frankfurt am Main: Suhrkamp. (Translation: 1973b. *Negative Dialectics.* New York: Seabury Press.)

Alexander, Jeffrey C. 1982–1983. *Theoretical Logic in Sociology.* 4 vols. Berkeley: University of California Press.

Alexander, Jeffrey C. 1987a. *Twenty Lectures. Sociological Theory since World War II.* New York: Columbia University Press.

Alexander, Jeffrey C. 1987b. "The Centrality of the Classics." In Anthony Giddens and Jonathan H. Turner (Eds.), *Social Theory Today,* pp. 1–57. Cambridge: Polity Press.

Althusser, Louis. 1965. *Pour Marx.* Paris: Maspero. (Translation: 1972. *For Marx.* New York: Pantheon.)

Anderson, Nels. 1923. *The Hobo.* Chicago: University of Chicago Press.

Anderson, Perry. 1974. *Passages from Antiquity to Feudalism.* London: New Left Books.

Aretz, Hans-Jürgen. 1990. *Zwischen Kritik und Dogma: Der wissenschaftliche Diskurs.* Wiesbaden: Deutscher Universitätsverlag.

Aron, Raymond. 1965. *Main Currents in Sociological Thought.* Vol. 1. New York: Basic Books.

Baran, Paul, and Paul M. Sweezy. 1966. *Monopoly Capital.* New York: Monthly Review Press.

Bell, Daniel. 1973. *The Coming of Postindustrial Society: A Venture in Social Forecasting.* New York: Basic Books.

Bell, Daniel. 1976. *The Cultural Contradictions of Capitalism.* New York: Basic Books.

Bendix, Reinhard. 1962. *Max Weber: An Intellectual Portrait.* Garden City, N.Y.: Doubleday.

Bendix, Reinhard. 1964. *Nationbuilding and Citizenship: Studies of Our Changing Social Order.* New York: Wiley.

Bendix, Reinhard. 1978. *Kings or People: Power and the Mandate to Rule*. Berkeley and Los Angeles: University of California Press.

Bentham, Jeremy. 1789/1970. *An Introduction to the Principles of Morals and Legislation*. Edited by J.H. Burns and H.L.A. Hart. London: Attslone Press.

Bernstein, Eduard. 1906. *Der Streik: Sein Wesen und sein Wirken*. Frankfurt am Main: Ruetten & Loening.

Bernstein, Eduard. 1907. *Die Geschichte der Berliner Arbeiter Bewegung: ein Kapitel zur Geschichte der deutschen Sozialdemokratie*. 2 vols. Berlin: Verlag Vorwärts.

Bernstein, Eduard. 1969. *Die Voraussetzungen des Sozialismus und die Aufgaben der Sozialdemokratie*. Reinbek/Hamburg: Rowohlt.

Bernstein, Richard. 1971. *Praxis and Action*. Philadelphia: Duckworth.

Bernstein, Richard. 1985. *Philosophical Profiles: Essays in Pragmatic Mode*. Oxford: Polity Press.

Besnard, Philippe (Ed.). 1983. *The Sociological Domain*. Cambridge: Cambridge University Press.

Blumer, Herbert. 1969. *Symbolic Interactionism*. Englewood Cliffs, N.J.: Prentice-Hall.

Bourdieu, Pierre. 1979. *La distinction. Critique sociale du jugement*. Paris: Minuit. (Translation: 1984. *Distinction: A Social Critique of the Judgement of Taste*. Cambridge, Mass.: Harvard University Press.)

Brentano, Lujo. 1901. *Ethik und Volkswirtschaft in der Geschichte*. Rektoratsrede gehalten am 23. Nov. 1901. Munich: C. Wolf & Sohn.

Brentano, Lujo. 1908a. *Die Entwicklung der Wertlehre*. Munich: Königlich Bayerische Akademie der Wissenschaften.

Brentano, Lujo. 1908b. *Versuch einer Theorie der Bedürfnisse*. Munich: Königlich Bayerische Akademie der Wissenschaften.

Brentano, Lujo. 1916. *Die Anfänge des modernen Kapitalismus*. Munich: Verlag der Königlich Bayerischen Akademie der Wissenschaften in Kommission des G. Franz'schen Verlags.

Brentano, Lujo. 1920. *Die Beamtenorganisation und ihre wirtschaftlichen Ziele*. Munich: B. Heller.

Brubaker, Rogers. 1984. *The Limits of Rationality: An Essay on the Social and Moral Thought of Max Weber*. London: George Allen and Unwin.

Bulmer, Martin. 1984. *The Chicago School of Sociology: Institutionalization, Diversity, and the Rise of Sociological Research*. Chicago: University of Chicago Press.

Burawoy, Michael. 1979. *Manufacturing Consent: Changes in the Labor Process under Monopoly Capitalism*. Chicago: University of Chicago Press.

Burger, Thomas. 1976. *Max Weber's Theory of Concept Formation: History, Laws and Ideal Types*. Durham, N.C.: Duke University Press.

Castoriadis, Cornelius. 1987. *The Imaginary Institution of Society*. Cambridge: Polity Press.

Cohen, Jere, Lawrence Hazelrigg, and Whitney Pope. 1975. "DeParsonizing Weber: A Critique of Parsons' Interpretation of Weber's Sociology." *American Sociological Review* 40:229–41.

Collins, Randall. 1988. *Theoretical Sociology*. New York: Harcourt, Brace, Jovanovich.

Comte, Auguste. 1830–1842/1969a. *Cours de philosophie positive*. 6 vols. Brussels: Culture et civilisation. (Translation: 1855. *The Positive Philosophy of Auguste Comte*. New York: Calvin Blanchard.)

Comte, Auguste. 1851–1854/1969b. *Système de politique positive*. Brussels: Culture et Civilisation. (Translation: 1968. *System of Positive Polity*. 4 vols. New York: B. Franklin.)

Comte, Auguste. 1968. *OEuvres d'Auguste Comte*. Introduction by Sylvain Pérignon. Paris: Anthropos.

Condorcet, Marie Jean Caritat Marquis de. 1795/1982. *Esquisse d'un tableau historique des progrès de l'esprit humain*. Hildesheim: Olms. (Translation: 1955. *Sketch for an Historical Picture of the Progress of the Human Mind*. New York: Noonday Press.)

Cooley, Charles Horton. 1902/1964. *Nature and the Social Order*. New York: Schocken.

Cooley, Charles Horton. 1909/1962. *Social Organization*. New York: Schocken.

Coser, Lewis A. 1956. *The Functions of Social Conflict*. New York: Free Press.

Coser, Lewis A. 1967. *Continuities in the Study of Social Conflict*. New York: Free Press.

Darwin, Charles. 1888[6]. *The Origin of Species: By Means of Natural Selection*. London: Murray.

Denzin, Norman K. 1977. *Childhood Socialization: Studies in the Development of Language, Social Behavior, and Identity*. San Francisco: Jossey Bass.

Descartes, René. 1637/1963. "Discours de la méthode." In *OEuvres philosophiques*. Vol. 1. Paris: Garnier. (Translation: 1977. *Discourse Concerning Method*. In *The Essential Writings of René Descartes*. New York: Harper & Row.)

Dewey, John. 1886. *Psychology*. New York: Harper & Row.

Dewey, John. 1922. *Human Nature and Human Conduct*. New York: Henry Holt.

Dewey, John. 1927. *The Public and Its Problems*. New York: Henry Holt.

Dewey, John. 1977. *The Essential Writings*. Edited by D. Sidersky. New York: Harper & Row.

Dilthey, Wilhelm. 1883/1968. *Der Aufbau der geschichtlichen Welt in den Geisteswissenschaften*. In *Gesammelte Schriften*. Vol. 7. Stuttgart: Teubner. (Translation: 1976. *The Construction of the Historical World in the Human Studies*. In *Selected Writings*. Cambridge: Cambridge University Press.)

Dilthey, Wilhelm. 1924/1964. *Die geistige Welt. I: Abhandlungen zur Grundlegung der Geisteswissenschaften*. In *Gesammelte Schriften*. Edited by Georg Misch. Vol. 5. Stuttgart: Teubner.

Djilas, Milovan. 1957. *The New Class: An Analysis of the Communist System*. New York: Praeger.

Durkheim, Emile. 1889/1975. "Communauté et société selon Tönnies." In *Textes*. Vol. 1, pp. 383–90. Edited by V. Karady. Paris: Minuit.

Durkheim, Emile. 1893/1973a. *De la division du travail social*. Paris: Presses Universitaires de France. (Translation: 1964. *The Division of Labor in Society*. Translated by G. Simpson. New York: Free Press.)

Durkheim, Emile. 1895/1973b. *Les règles de la méthode sociologique*. Paris: Presses Universitaires de France. (Translation: 1982. *The Rules of Sociological Method*. Edited by Steven Lukes. Translated by W.D. Halls. London: Macmillan.)

Durkheim, Emile. 1897/1973c. *Le suicide*. Paris: Presses Universitaires de France. (Translation: 1952. *Suicide*. Translated by J.A. Spaulding and G. Simpson. London: Routledge.)

Durkheim, Emile. 1912/1968. *Les formes élémentaires de la vie religieuse.* Paris: Presses Universitaires de France. (Translation: 1976. *The Elementary Forms of Religious Life.* Translated by J.W. Swain. London: Allen & Unwin.)

Durkheim, Emile. 1914/1970. "Le dualism de la nature humaine et ses conditions sociales." In *La science sociale et l'action.* Edited by J.C. Filloux. Paris: Presses Universitaires de France, pp. 314–32. (Translation: 1973d. "The Dualism of Human Nature and Its Social Conditions." In *On Morality and Society.* Edited by Robert N. Bellah. Chicago: University of Chicago Press, pp. 149–63.)

Durkheim, Emile. 1924/1974a. *Sociologie et philosophie.* Paris: Presses Universitaires de France. (Translation: 1965. *Sociology and Philosophy.* Translated by D.F. Pocock. London: Cohen & West.)

Durkheim, Emile. 1925/1974b. *L'éducation morale.* Paris: Presses Universitaires de France. (Translation: 1961. *Moral Education.* Translated by E.K. Wilson and H. Schnurer. New York: Free Press.)

Durkheim, Emile. 1950/1969. *Leçons de sociologie. Physique des moeurs et du droit.* Paris: Presses Universitaires de France. (Translation: 1957. *Professional Ethics and Civic Morals.* Translated by C. Brookfield. London: Routledge.)

Eiben, Jürgen. 1989. *Von Luther zu Kant. Der deutsche Sonderweg in die Moderne.* Wiesbaden: Deutscher Universitätsverlag.

Eisenstadt, Shmuel N., and M. Curelaru. 1976. *The Form of Sociology: Paradigms and Crises.* New York: Wiley.

Elster, Jon. 1985. *Making Sense of Marx.* Cambridge: Cambridge University Press.

Fararo, Thomas J. 1989. *The Meaning of General Theoretical Sociology. Tradition and Formalization.* New York: Cambridge University Press.

Fine, Gary Alan. 1984. "Negotiated Orders and Organization Cultures." *Annual Review of Sociology* 10:239–62.

Fine, Gary Alan. 1987. *With the Boys: Little League Baseball and Preadolescent Culture.* Chicago: University of Chicago Press.

Fine, Gary Alan, and Sherryl Kleinman. 1983. "Network and Meaning: An Interactionist Approach to Social Structure." *Symbolic Interaction* 6:97–110.

Fine, Gary Alan, and Sherryl Kleinman. 1986. "Interpreting the Sociological Classics: Can There Be a "True" Meaning of Mead?" *Symbolic Interaction* 9:129–46.

Frisby, David. 1981. *Sociological Impressionism: A Reassessment of Georg Simmel's Social Theory.* London: Heinemann.

Frisby, David. 1984. *Georg Simmel.* Chichester: Ellis Horwood.

Genov, Nikolai. 1989. *National Traditions in Sociology.* London and Newbury Park, Calif.: Sage.

Gephart, Werner. 1990a. *Strafe und Verbrechen. Die Theorie Emile Durkheims.* Opladen: Leske & Budrich.

Gephart, Werner. 1990b. *Gesellschaftstheorie und Recht.* Habilitationsschrift. Düsseldorf: University of Düsseldorf.

Giddens, Anthony, and Jonathan H. Turner. 1987. *Social Theory Today.* Cambridge: Polity Press.

Gramsci, Antonio. 1932/1975. *Letters from Prison: Antonio Gramsci.* Edited by Lynne Lawner. New York: Harper Colophon.

Gramsci, Antonio. 1971. *Selections from the Prison Notebooks.* New York: International.

Habermas, Jürgen. 1981. *Theorie des kommunikativen Handelns.* 2 vols. Frankfurt am Main: Suhrkamp. (Translation: 1984, 1987. *The Theory of Communicative Action.* 2 vols. Boston: Beacon Press.)

Hegel, Georg Wilhelm Friedrich. 1964–1971. *Sämtliche Werke.* Edited by H. Glockner. Stuttgart: Frommann Holzboog. (Partly translated in: 1974. *The Essential Writings.* New York: Harper & Row; 1972. *Hegel's Philosophy of Mind.* Freeport, N.J.: Books for Library Press.)

Heller, Agnes. 1976. *The Theory of Need in Marx.* New York: St. Martin's.

Hennis, Wilhelm. 1987. *Max Webers Fragestellung: Studien zur Biographie des Werks.* Tübingen: Mohr.

Hinkle, Roscoe. 1980. *Founding Theory of American Sociology: 1881–1915.* London: Routledge.

Hobbes, Thomas. 1651/1966. *Leviathan.* In *Collected English Works of Thomas Hobbes.* Edited by W. Molesworth. Vol. 3. Aalen, Germany: Scientia.

Hofstadter, Richard. 1959. *Social Darwinism in American Thought.* New York: Braziller.

Hofstadter, Richard. 1963. *Anti-intellectualism in American Life.* New York: Vintage.

Holton, Robert J., and Bryan S. Turner. 1989. *Max Weber on Economy and Society.* London: Routledge.

Homans, George C. 1961. *Social Behavior: Its Elementary Forms.* New York: Harcourt, Brace, Jovanovich.

Honneth, Axel, and Hans Joas. 1980. *Soziales Handeln und menschliche Natur: Anthropologische Grundlagen der Sozialwissenschaften.* Frankfurt am Main: Campus. (Translation: 1988. *Social Action and Human Nature.* New York: Cambridge University Press.)

Horkheimer, Max, and Theodor W. Adorno. 1947. *Dialektik der Aufklärung.* Amsterdam: Nijhoff. (Translation: 1972. *Dialectic of Enlightenment.* New York: Seabury Press.)

Hughes, Everett C. 1958. *Men and Their Work.* Glencoe, Ill.: Free Press.

Hughes, Everett C. 1971. *The Sociological Eye: Selected Papers of Everett Hughes.* Chicago: University of Chicago Press.

Hughes, Everett C., and Edgar T. Thompson. 1968. *Race: Individual and Collective Behavior.* Glencoe, Ill.: Free Press.

Hume, David. 1739/1978. *A Treatise on Human Nature.* Edited by L.A. Selby-Bigge. Oxford: Clarendon Press.

Hume, David. 1777/1980. *Enquiries Concerning the Human Understanding and Concerning the Principles of Morals.* Edited by L.A. Selby-Bigge. Westport, Conn.: Greenwood Press.

Israel, Joachim. 1971. *Alienation: From Marx to Modern Sociology.* Boston: Allyn and Bacon.

James, William. 1890. *The Principles of Psychology.* New York: Henry Holt.

James, William. 1907. *Pragmatism: A New Name for Some Old Ways of Thinking.* New York: Longmans, Green.

James, William. 1909/1968. *The Meaning of Truth.* New York: Greenwood.

Joas, Hans. 1980. *Praktische Intersubjektivität. Die Entwicklung des Werkes von G.H. Mead.* Frankfurt am Main: Suhrkamp. (Translation: 1985. *G.H. Mead: A Contemporary Re-examination of His Thought.* Cambridge: Polity Press.)

Joas, Hans. 1981. "George Herbert Mead and the 'Division of Labor': Macrosociological Implications of Mead's Social Psychology." *Symbolic Interaction* 4:177–90.

Joas, Hans. 1987. "Symbolic Interactionism." In Anthony Giddens and Jonathan H. Turner (Eds.), *Social Theory Today.* Cambridge: Polity Press, pp. 82–115.

Käsler, Dirk. 1984. "Flug über den Wolken. Über Niklas Luhmanns 'Soziale Systeme.' " *Der Spiegel* 38, 50 (Dec. 10):184–90.

Käsler, Dirk. 1988. *Max Weber: An Introduction to His Life and Work.* Chicago: University of Chicago Press.

Kalberg, Stephen. 1980. "Max Weber's Types of Rationality: Cornerstones for the Analysis of Rationalization Processes in History." *American Journal of Sociology* 85:1145–79.

Kalberg, Stephen. 1990. "The Rationalization of Action in Max Weber's Sociology of Religion." *Sociological Theory* 8:58–84.

Kant, Immanuel. 1781/1964a. *Kritik der reinen Vernunft.* In *Werke in sechs Bänden.* Edited by Wilhelm Weischedel. Vol. 2. Frankfurt am Main: Insel Verlag. (Translation: 1952a. *Critique of Pure Reason.* In *Great Books of the Western World 42: Kant*, pp. 1–250. Chicago/London: Encyclopaedia Britannica.

Kant, Immanuel. 1784a/1964b. "Beantwortung der Frage: Was ist Aufklärung?" In *Werke in sechs Bänden*, pp. 53–61. Edited by Wilhelm Weischedel. Vol. 6. Frankfurt am Main: Insel Verlag.

Kant, Immanuel. 1784b/1964c. "Idee zu einer allgemeinen Geschichte in weltbürgerlicher Absicht." In *Werke in sechs Bänden*, pp. 33–50. Edited by Wilhelm Weischedel. Vol. 6. Frankfurt am Main: Insel Verlag.

Kant, Immanuel. 1788/1964d. *Kritik der praktischen Vernunft.* In *Werke in sechs Bänden*, pp. 103–302. Edited by Wilhelm Weischedel. Vol. 4. Frankfurt am Main: Insel Verlag. (Translation: 1952b. *Critique of Practical Reason*, pp. 291–361. In *Great Books of the Western World 42: Kant.* Chicago/London: Encyclopaedia Britannica.)

Kant, Immanuel. 1790/1964e. *Kritik der Urteilskraft.* In *Werke in sechs Bänden.* Edited by Wilhelm Weischedel. Vol. 5. Frankfurt am Main: Insel Verlag. (Translation: 1952c. *Critique of Judgement.* In *Great Books of the Western World 42: Kant*, pp. 461–613. Chicago/London: Encyclopaedia Britannica.)

Kant, Immanuel. 1793/1964f. "Über den Gemeinspruch: Das mag in der Theorie richtig sein, taugt aber nicht für die Praxis." In *Werke in sechs Bänden*, pp. 125–72. Edited by Wilhelm Weischedel. Vol. 6. Frankfurt am Main: Insel Verlag. (Translation: 1974. *On the Old Say: That May Be Right in Theory But It Won't Work in Practice.* Philadelphia: University of Pennsylvania Press.)

Kant, Immanuel. 1795/1964g. "Zum ewigen Frieden. Ein philosophischer Entwurf." In *Werke in sechs Bänden*, pp. 193–251. Edited by Wilhelm Weischedel. Vol. 6. Frankfurt am Main: Insel Verlag. (Translation: 1972. *Perpetual Peace: a Philosophical Essay.* New York/London: Garland.)

Kant, Immanuel. 1964h. *Werke in sechs Bänden.* Edited by Wilhelm Weischedel. Frankfurt am Main: Insel Verlag.

Kautsky, Karl. 1910[13]. *Karl Marx' ökonomische Lehren.* Stuttgart: Dietz.

Kautsky, Karl. 1918[3]. *Die Befreiung der Nationen.* Stuttgart: Dietz.

Kautsky, Karl. 1922. *Die proletarische Revolution und ihr Programm.* Berlin: Dietz.

Kautsky, Karl. 1927. *Die materialistische Geschichtsauffassung.* Berlin: Dietz.

Kemper, Theodore. 1978. *A Social Interactional Theory of Emotions.* New York: Wiley.

Kilminster, Richard. 1979. *Praxis and Method.* London: Routledge.

Knies, Karl. 1853. *Die politische Ökonomie vom Standpunkt der geschichtlichen Methode.* Braunschweig: Schwetschke & Sohn.

König, René. 1962. "Die Religionssoziologie bei Emile Durkheim." In Dietrich Goldschmidt and Joachim Matthes (Eds.), *Probleme der Religionssoziologie,* pp. 39–46. Opladen: Westdeutscher Verlag.

König, René. 1978. *Emile Durkheim zur Diskussion. Jenseits von Dogmatismus und Skepsis.* Munich and Vienna: Hanser.

Kohlberg, Lawrence. 1969. "Stage and Sequence: The Cognitive-Developmental Approach to Socialization." In D.A. Goslin (Ed.), *Handbook of Socialization Theory and Research,* pp. 347–480. Chicago: Rand McNally.

Kohlberg, Lawrence. 1975. "Moral Stages and Moralization: The Cognitive-Developmental Approach." In T. Lickona (Ed.), *Moral Development and Behavior,* pp. 31–53. New York: Holt, Rinehart & Winston.

Kohlberg, Lawrence. 1981. *The Philosophy of Moral Development.* San Francisco: Harper & Row.

Kohlberg, Lawrence. 1984. *The Psychology of Moral Development. Essays on Moral Development.* Vol. 2. San Francisco: Harper & Row.

Kohlberg, Lawrence. 1987. *Child Psychology and Childhood Education. A Cognitive-Developmental View.* New York and London: Longman.

Krekel-Eiben, Elisabeth. 1990. *Soziologische Wissenschaftsgemeinschaften.* Wiesbaden: Deutscher Universitätsverlag.

Kuhn, Manford. 1964a. "Major Trends in Symbolic Interaction Theory in the Past Twenty-Five Years." *Sociological Quarterly* 5:61–84.

Kuhn, Manford. 1964b. "The Reference Group Reconsidered." *Sociological Quarterly* 5:6–21.

Lamarck, Jean B. 1815–1822. *Histoire naturelle des animaux sans vertèbres.* 7 vols. Paris: Verdière.

Lask, Emil. 1923. *Gesammelte Schriften.* Edited by Eugen Herrigel. 3 vols. Tübingen: Mohr Siebeck.

Lazarsfeld, Paul F., and Morris Rosenberg (Eds.). 1955. *The Language of Social Research.* Glencoe, Ill.: Free Press.

Lenin, Vladimir Il'ich. 1917. *From the Bourgeois Revolution to the Proletarian Revolution.* New York: International.

Lenin, Vladimir Il'ich. 1920. *Bourgeois Democracy and the Dictatorship of the Proletariat.* London: Workers Socialist Federation.

Lenin, Vladimir Il'ich. 1927. *Collected Works of V.I. Lenin.* New York: International.

Lenin, Vladimir Il'ich. 1955. *Certain Features of the Historical Development of Marxism: The Historical Destiny of the Doctrine of Karl Marx.* Moscow: Foreign Languages Publishers House.

Lepenies, Wolf (Ed.). 1981. *Geschichte der Soziologie.* 4 vols. Frankfurt am Main: Suhrkamp.

Levine, Donald N. 1980. *Simmel and Parsons. Two Approaches to the Study of Sociology.* Reprint of thesis, University of Chicago, 1957. New York: Arno.

Levine, Donald N., Ellwood B. Carter, and Eleanor Miller Gorman. 1976a. "Simmel's Influence on American Sociology—I." *American Journal of Sociology* 81:813-45.

Levine, Donald N., Ellwood B. Carter, and Eleanor Miller Gorman. 1976b. "Simmel's Influence on American Sociology—II." *American Journal of Sociology* 81:1112-32.

Lévi-Strauss, Claude. 1947. *Les structures élémentaires de la parenté.* Paris: Mouton & Co. (Translation: 1969a. *The Elementary Structures of Kinship.* New York: Basic Books.)

Lévi-Strauss, Claude. 1962. *La pensée sauvage.* Paris: Librairie Plon. (Translation: 1966. *The Savage Mind.* Chicago: University of Chicago Press.)

Lévi-Strauss, Claude. 1964. *Mythologiques. Le cru et le cuit.* Paris: Librairie Plon. (Translation: 1969b. *The Raw and the Cooked.* New York: Harper & Row.)

Lévi-Strauss, Claude. 1967. *Mythologiques. Du miel aux cendres.* Paris: Librairie Plon. (Translation: 1973. *From Honey to Ashes.* New York: Harper & Row.)

Lévi-Strauss, Claude. 1968. *Mythologiques. L'origine des manières de table.* Paris: Librairie Plon. (Translation: 1978. *The Origin of Table Manners.* New York: Harper & Row.)

Lévi-Strauss, Claude. 1971a. *Mythologiques. L'homme nu.* Paris: Librairie Plon. (Translation: 1981. *The Naked Man.* New York: Harper & Row.)

Lévi-Strauss, Claude. 1971b. *Anthropologie structurale.* Vol. 1. Paris: Plon.

Lévi-Strauss, Claude. 1976. *Anthropologie structurale.* Vol. 2. Paris: Plon.

Lewis, J. David, and Richard L. Smith. 1980. *American Sociology and Pragmatism: Mead, Chicago Sociology, and Symbolic Interaction.* Chicago: University of Chicago Press.

Locke, John. 1690/1963. *Two Treatises on Government.* In: 1823/1963. *The Works.* 10 vols. Aalen/West Germany: Scientia.

Luhmann, Niklas. 1984. *Soziale Systeme.* Frankfort am Main: Suhrkamp.

Lukács, Georg. 1923/1968. *Geschichte und Klassenbewußtsein.* 2 vols. Neuwied: Luchterhand. (Translation: 1971. *History and Class Consciousness.* Cambridge, Mass.: MIT Press.)

Lukes, Steven. 1985. *Emile Durkheim. His Life and Work: A Historical and Critical Study.* Stanford, Calif.: Stanford University Press.

Machiavelli, Niccolò. 1531/1984. *Discorsi di Niccolò Machiavelli.* Milan: Rizzoli. (Translation: 1975. *The Discourses of Niccolò Machiavelli.* London: Routledge).

Machiavelli, Niccolò. 1532/1979[11]. *Il Principe.* Torino: Einaudi. (Translation: 1976. *The Prince.* Translation, introduction, and annotation by J.B. Atkinson. Indianapolis, Ind.: Bobbs-Merrill.)

Maffesoli, Michel. 1988a. *Le temps des tribus: le déclin de l'individualisme dans les sociétés de masse.* Paris: Librairie des Meridiens Klinksieck.

Maffesoli, Michel. 1988b. "Ein Vergleich zwischen Durkheim und Simmel." In Otthein Rammstedt (Ed.), *Simmel und die frühen Soziologen. Nähe und Distanz zu Durkheim, Tönnies und Max Weber,* pp. 163-80. Frankfurt: Suhrkamp.

Mann, Michael. 1986. *The Sources of Social Power.* Vol. 1. New York: Cambridge University Press.

Mannheim, Karl. 1936/1955. *Ideology and Utopia.* New York: Harcourt Brace Jovanovich.

Markovic, Mihailo. 1968. *Dialektik der Praxis*. Frankfurt am Main: Suhrkamp.

Markovic, Mihailo (Ed.). 1979. *Praxis. Yugoslaw Essays in the Philosophy and Methodology of Social Sciences*. Dordrecht: Reidel.

Martindale, Don. 1960. *The Nature and Types of Sociological Theory*. Boston: Houghton Mifflin.

Marx, Karl. 1843/1956. *Zur Kritik der Hegelschen Rechtsphilosophie. Kritik des Hegelschen Staatsrechts. Einleitung*, pp. 201–333, 378–91. Marx-Engels Werke. Vol. 1. Berlin: Dietz.

Marx, Karl. 1844/1968. *Ökonomisch-philosophische Manuskripte aus dem Jahre 1844*, pp. 465–588. Marx-Engels Werke, Supplementary volume, part I. Berlin: Dietz. (Translation: 1971a. *The Early Texts*. Edited by David McLellan. Oxford: Blackwell.)

Marx, Karl. 1845/1969. *Thesen über Feuerbach*, pp. 5–7. Marx-Engels Werke. Vol. 3. Berlin: Dietz. (Translation: 1971a. *The Early Texts*. Edited by David McLellan. Oxford: Blackwell.)

Marx, Karl. 1852/1960. *Der achtzehnte Brumaire des Louis Bonaparte*, pp. 111–207. Marx-Engels Werke. Vol. 8. Berlin: Dietz. (Translation: 1963a. *The Eighteenth Brumaire of Louis Bonaparte*. New York: International.)

Marx, Karl. 1859/1961. *Zur Kritik der politischen Ökonomie*, pp. 3–160. Marx-Engels Werke. Vol. 13. Berlin: Dietz. (Translation: 1971b/1981. *A Contribution to the Critique of Political Economy*. Translated by S.W. Ryazanskaya. London: Lawrence & Wishart.)

Marx, Karl. 1867/1962, 1885/1963b, 1894/1964. *Das Kapital*. Vol. 1–3. Marx-Engels Werke. Vol. 23–25. Berlin: Dietz. (Translation: 1967. *Capital*. 3 vols. New York: International.)

Marx, Karl, and Friedrich Engels. 1846/1969. *Die deutsche Ideologie*, pp. 9–530. Marx-Engels Werke. Vol. 3. Berlin: Dietz. (Translation: 1947. *The German Ideology*. New York: International.)

Marx, Karl, and Friedrich Engels. 1848/1959a. *Manifest der kommunistischen Partei*, pp. 459–93. Marx-Engels Werke. Vol. 4. Berlin: Dietz. (Translation: 1959b. *The Communist Manifesto*. In L. Feuer (Ed.), *Marx and Engels: Basic Writings on Politics and Philosophy*. New York: Doubleday.)

Mead, George Herbert. 1908. "The Philosophical Basis of Ethics." *International Journal of Ethics* 18:311–23.

Mead, George Herbert. 1934. *Mind, Self, and Society*. Edited and introduction by Charles W. Morris. Chicago: University of Chicago Press.

Mead, George Herbert. 1936. *Movements of Thought in the Nineteenth Century*. Chicago: University of Chicago Press.

Mead, George Herbert. 1938. *The Philosophy of the Act*. Chicago: University of Chicago Press.

Mead, George Herbert. 1959. *The Philosophy of the Present*. La Salle, Ill.: Open Court.

Mead, George Herbert. 1964. *Selected Writings*. Edited by Andrew Reck. Indianapolis, Ind.: Bobbs-Merrill.

Meer, Simon van der. 1985. "Interview with Simon van der Meer." *Holland Herald*, January 20, 1, pp. 8–9.

Merton, Robert K. 1949/1968a. *Social Theory and Social Structure*. New York: Free Press.

Merton, Robert K. 1968b. "The Matthew Effect in Science." *Science* 159, 3810:56–63.
Mészáros, Istvan. 1970. *Marx's Theory of Alienation.* New York: Harper.
Miliband, Ralph. 1982. *Capitalist Democracy in Britain.* London: Oxford University Press.
Mill, John Stuart. 1861/1974. *Utilitarianism.* In *Utilitarianism, On Liberty. Essays on Bentham Together with Selected Writings of Jeremy Bentham and John Austin.* Edited by Mary Warnock. Westford, Mass.: New American Library.
Mommsen, Wolfgang. 1959/1974a. *Max Weber und die deutsche Politik 1890–1920.* Tübingen: Mohr Siebeck. (Translation: 1984. *Max Weber and German Politics, 1890–1920.* Chicago: University of Chicago Press.)
Mommsen, Wolfgang. 1974b/1986. *Max Weber. Gesellschaft, Politik und Geschichte.* Frankfurt: Suhrkamp.
Montesquieu, Charles de Secondat Baron de la Brède et de. 1748. *De l'esprit des lois.* Paris: Garnier. (Translation: 1989. *The Spirit of the Laws.* Translated and edited by Anne M. Cohler. Cambridge: Cambridge University Press.)
Moore, Barrington. 1966. *Social Origins of Dictatorship and Democracy: Lord and Peasant in the Making of the Modern World.* Boston: Beacon Press.
Mosca, Gaetano. 1884. *Sulla teorica dei governi e sul governo parlamentari: studi storici e sociali.* Toronto: Loescher.
Müller, Hans-Peter. 1983. *Wertkrise und Gesellschaftsreform. Emile Durkheims Schriften zur Politik.* Stuttgart: Enke.
Münch, Richard. 1982. *Theorie des Handelns. Zur Rekonstruktion der Beiträge von Talcott Parsons, Emile Durkheim und Max Weber.* Frankfurt am Main: Suhrkamp. (Translation in two parts: 1987a. *Theory of Action. Towards a New Synthesis Going Beyond Parsons.* London: Routledge; 1988. *Understanding Modernity: Towards a New Perspective Going Beyond Durkheim and Weber.* London: Routledge.)
Münch, Richard. 1984. *Die Struktur der Moderne.* Frankfurt am Main: Suhrkamp.
Münch, Richard. 1986. *Die Kultur der Moderne.* 2 vols. Vol. 1: *Ihre Grundlagen und ihre Entwicklung in England und Amerika.* Vol. 2: *Ihre Entwicklung in Frankreich und Deutschland.* Frankfurt am Main: Suhrkamp.
Münch, Richard. 1987b. "Parsonian Theory Today: In Search of a New Synthesis." In Anthony Giddens and Jonathan H. Turner (Eds.), *Social Theory Today*, pp. 116–55. Cambridge/England: Polity Press.
Münch, Richard. 1991. *Dialektik der Kommunikationsgesellschaft.* Frankfurt am Main: Suhrkamp.
Mullins, Nicholas. 1973. *Theories and Theory Groups in Contemporary American Sociology.* New York: Harper & Row.
Nelson, Benjamin. 1949/1969. *The Idea of Usury: From Tribal Brotherhood to Universal Otherhood.* Chicago: University of Chicago Press.
Nelson, Benjamin. 1974. "Max Weber's Author's Introduction (1920): A Master Clue to His Main Aims." *Sociological Inquiry* 44:269–78.
Nisbet, Robert. 1967. *The Sociological Tradition.* New York: Basic Books.
Nisbet, Robert. 1974. *The Sociology of Emile Durkheim.* New York: Oxford University Press.
Oakes, Guy (Ed.). 1984. *Georg Simmel on Women, Sexuality and Love.* New Haven: Yale University Press.

Offe, Claus. 1972. *Strukturprobleme des kapitalistischen Staates*. Frankfurt am Main: Suhrkamp.

Offe, Claus. 1984. *"Arbeitsgesellschaft": Strukturprobleme und Zukunftsperspektiven*. Frankfurt am Main and New York: Campus.

Pareto, Vilfredo. 1901. "Un'applicazione di teorie sociologiche." In *Revista italiana di sociologia*, pp. 402–56. (Translation: 1968. *The Rise and Fall of the Elites*. Totowa, N.J.: Bedminster.)

Pareto, Vilfredo. 1902–1903. *Les sytèmes socialistes*. 2 vols. Paris: V. Giard et E. Brière.

Pareto, Vilfredo. 1916. *Trattato di Sociologia generale*. 2 vols. Firenze: G. Barbera. (Translation: 1917–1919. *Traité de sociologie générale*. Edited by Pierre Boven. Lausanne/Paris: Payot et Cie; 1935. *The Mind and Society. A Treatise on General Sociology*. Edited by Arthur Livingston. 4 vols. New York: Harcourt Brace Jovanovich.

Pareto, Vilfredo. 1921. *Transformazione della Democrazia*. Milan: Corbaccio.

Park, Robert E. 1950–1955. *Collected Papers*. 3 vols. Glencoe, Ill.: Free Press.

Park, Robert E. 1952. *Human Communities*. New York: Free Press.

Park, Robert E., and Ernest W. Burgess. 1921. *Introduction to the Science of Sociology*. Chicago: University of Chicago Press.

Parsons, Talcott. 1937/1968. *The Structure of Social Action*. New York: Free Press.

Parsons, Talcott. 1940/1954a. "An Analytical Approach to the Theory of Social Stratification." In T. Parsons, *Essays in Sociological Theory*, pp. 69–88. New York: Free Press.

Parsons, Talcott. 1951. *The Social System*. Glencoe, Ill.: Free Press.

Parsons, Talcott. 1954b. "A Revised Analytical Approach to the Theory of Social Stratification." In T. Parsons, *Essays in Sociological Theory*, pp. 386–439. New York: Free Press.

Parsons, Talcott. 1954c. *Essays in Sociological Theory*. New York: Free Press.

Parsons, Talcott. 1959. "An Approach to Psychological Theory in Terms of the Theory of Action." In S. Koch (Ed.), *Psychology: A Study of a Science*. Vol. 3, pp. 612–711. New York: McGraw Hill.

Parsons, Talcott. 1961a. "An Outline of the Social System." In T. Parsons, E.A. Shils, K.D. Naegele, and J.R. Pitts (Eds.), *Theories of Society*, pp. 30–79. New York: Free Press.

Parsons, Talcott. 1961b. "Introduction to Culture and the Social System." In T. Parsons, E.A. Shils, K.D. Naegele and J.R. Pitts (Eds.), *Theories of Society*, pp. 963–93. New York: Free Press.

Parsons, Talcott. 1964. *Social Structure and Personality*. New York: Free Press.

Parsons, Talcott. 1966. *Societies. Evolutionary and Comparative Perspectives*. Englewood Cliffs, N.J.: Prentice-Hall.

Parsons, Talcott. 1967. *Sociological Theory and Modern Society*. New York: Free Press.

Parsons, Talcott. 1969. *Politics and Social Structure*. New York: Free Press.

Parsons, Talcott. 1971. *The System of Modern Societies*. Englewood Cliffs, N.J.: Prentice-Hall.

Parsons, Talcott. 1977a. "Equality and Inequality in Modern Society, or Social Stratification Revisited." In T. Parsons, *Social Systems and the Evolution of Action Theory*, pp. 321–80. New York: Free Press.

Parsons, Talcott. 1977b. *Social Systems and the Evolution of Action Theory.* New York: Free Press.

Parsons, Talcott. 1978. *Action Theory and the Human Condition.* New York: Free Press.

Peirce, Charles S. 1934/1965. "Some Consequences of Four Incapacities." In *Collected Papers*, pp. 156–69. Edited by C. Hartshorne and P. Weiss. Cambridge, Mass.: Belknap Press of Harvard University Press.

Piaget, Jean. 1932/1973. *Le jugement moral chez l'enfant.* Paris: Presses Universitaires de France. (Translation: 1977. *The Moral Judgement of the Child.* Harmondsworth: Penguin Books.)

Poggi, Gianfranco. 1978. *The Development of the Modern State: A Sociological Introduction.* London: Hutchinson.

Poggi, Gianfranco. 1983. *Calvinism and the Capitalist Spirit: Max Webers Protestant Ethic.* London: Macmillan.

Pope, Whitney. 1976. *Durkheim's Suicide: A Classic Analyzed.* Chicago: University of Chicago Press.

Popper, Karl R. 1935/1966. *Logik der Forschung.* Tübingen: Mohr Siebeck. (Translation: 1959. *The Logic of Scientific Discovery.* London: Hutchinson.)

Poulantzas, Nicos. 1968. *Pouvoir politique et classes sociales de l'état capitaliste.* Paris: Maspero. (Translation: 1968. *Political Power and Social Classes.* London: New Left Books.)

Powers, Charles H. 1986. *Vilfredo Pareto.* Newbury Park: Sage.

Prager, Jeffrey. 1981. "Moral Integration and Political Inclusion: A Comparison of Durkheim's and Weber's Theories of Democracy." *SocialForces* 59:918–50.

Quesnay, François. 1888/1965. *OEuvres économiques et philosophiques.* Edited by Auguste Oncken. Aalen, Germany: Scientia.

Rex, John. 1981. *Social Conflict. A Conceptual and Theoretical Analysis.* London: Longman.

Rickert, Heinrich. 1896–1902. *Die Grenzen der naturwissenschaftlichen Begriffsbildung. Eine logische Einleitung in die historischen Wissenschaften.* 2 vols. Tübingen: Mohr.

Rickert, Heinrich. 1910. *Kulturwissenschaften und Naturwissenschaft. Ein Vortrag.* 2nd rev. edition. Tübingen: Mohr.

Rickert, Heinrich. 1921. *System der Philosophie.* Part 1. Tübingen: Mohr.

Rickert, Heinrich. 1924. *Kant als Philosoph der modernen Kultur. Ein geschichtsphilosophischer Versuch.* Tübingen: Mohr.

Ritzer, George. 1983/1988². *Sociological Theory.* New York: Knopf.

Roemer, John E. 1982. "Methodological Individualism and Deductive Marxism." *Theory and Society* 11:513–520.

Rorty, Richard. 1982. *Consequences of Pragmatism: Essays 1972–1980.* Minneapolis: University of Minnesota Press.

Roscher, Wilhelm. 1854–1892. *Grundlagen. System der Volkswirtschaft.* Vol. 1; *Ackerbau u. verw. Urprodukt.* Vol. 2; *Handel und Gewerbe.* Vol. 3; *Finanzwirtschaft.* Vol. 4; *Armenpflege und Politik.* Vol. 5. Stuttgart: Cotta.

Roth, Günther. 1976. "History and Sociology in the Work of Max Weber." *British Journal of Sociology* 27:306–18.

Roth, Günther. 1987. *Politische Herrschaft und Persönliche Freiheit.* Frankfurt: Suhrkamp.

Rousseau, Jean-Jacques. 1762/1964. *Du contrat social ou principes du droit politique*. In *OEuvres complètes*. Edited by B. Gagnebin and M. Raymond. Paris: Gallimard. (Translation: 1973. *The Social Contract and Discourses*. Translated and introduction by G.D.H. Cole. New Edition. London: Dent.)

Runciman, Walter Garrison. 1972. *A Critique of Max Weber's Philosophy of Social Science*. London: Cambridge University Press.

Runciman, Walter Garrison. 1983. *A Treatise on Social Theory*. Vol. I: *The Methodology of Social Theory*. New York: Cambridge University Press.

Runciman, Walter Garrison. 1988. *A Treatise on Social Theory*. Vol. II: *Substantive Social Theory*. New York: Cambridge University Press.

Saint-Simon, Claude-Henri de. 1865–1878. *OEuvres de Saint Simon et d'Enfantin*. 47 vols. Paris: E. Dentu. (Translations: 1958. *The Doctrine of Saint-Simon: And Exposition, First Year 1828–1829*. Boston: Beacon Press; 1975. *Selected Writings on Science, Industry and Social Organization*. London: Croom Helm; 1976. *The Political Thought of Saint-Simon*. London: Oxford University Press; 1980. *Saint-Simon at Versailles*. London: Hamilton.)

Schleiermacher, Friedrich D.E. 1911. "Hermeneutik." In *Werke*. Vol. 4, pp. 135–206. Leipzig: Felix Meiner.

Schluchter, Wolfgang. 1979. *Die Entwicklung des okzidentalen Rationalismus. Eine Analyse von Max Webers Gesellschaftsgeschichte*. Tübingen: Mohr Siebeck. (Translation: 1981. *The Rise of Western Rationalism*. Berkeley and Los Angeles: University of California Press.)

Schluchter, Wolfgang. 1988. *Religion und Lebensführung*. 2 vols. Frankfurt am Main: Suhrkamp. (Translation: 1989. *Rationalism, Religion, and Domination. A Weberian Perspective*. Berkeley and Los Angeles: University of California Press.)

Schmoller, Gustav. 1900–1904. *Grundriss der Allgemeinen Volkswirtschaftslehre*. 2 vols. Leipzig: Duncker & Humblot.

Schmoller, Gustav. 1904. *Classenkämpfe und Classenherrschaft*. Berlin: G. Reimer.

Schmoller, Gustav. 1918. *Die soziale Frage. Klassenbildung, Arbeiterfrage. Klassenkampf*. Edited by Lucie Schmoller. Munich: Duncker & Humblot.

Schneider, Louis. 1967. *The Scottish Moralists: On Human Nature and Society*. Chicago: University of Chicago Press.

Seidman, Steven. 1983. *Liberalism and the Origins of European Social Theory*. Berkeley and Los Angeles: University of California Press.

Shaw, Clifford. 1930. *A Delinquent Boy's Own Story*. Chicago: University of Chicago Press.

Simmel, Georg. 1890. *Über Sociale Differenzierung*. Leipzig: Duncker & Humblot.

Simmel, Georg. 1892. *Einführung in die Moralwissenschaft*. Berlin: Wilhelm Hertz.

Simmel, Georg. 1900. *Philosophie des Geldes*. Berlin: Duncker & Humblot. (Translation: 1978. *The Philosophy of Money*. London: Routledge.)

Simmel, Georg. 1906/1912. *Die Religion*. Frankfurt am Main: Rütten & Loening. (Translation: 1959. *Sociology of Religion*. New York: Philosophical Library.)

Simmel, Georg. 1908a. *Soziologie. Untersuchungen über die Formen der Vergesellschaftung*. Berlin: Duncker & Humblot.

Simmel, Georg. 1908b. "Der Streit." "Die Kreuzung sozialer Kreise." In *Soziologie. Untersuchungen über die Formen der Vergesellschaftung*. Berlin: Duncker & Humblot. (Translation: 1955. *Conflict and the Web of Group Affiliations*. New York: Free Press.)

Simmel, Georg. 1911/1919. *Philosophische Kultur.* Leipzig: A. Kröner.
Simmel, Georg. 1914/1926. *Der Konflikt der modernen Kultur.* Berlin: Duncker & Humblot. (Translation: 1968. *The Conflict of Modern Culture.* New York: Teacher College Press.)
Simmel, Georg. 1917. *Grundfragen der Soziologie (Individuum und Gesellschaft).* Berlin und Leipzig: de Gruyter & Co.
Simmel, Georg. 1918. *Lebensanschauung.* München: Duncker & Humblot.
Simmel, Georg. 1971. *On Individuality and Social Forms.* In *Selected Writings.* Edited by Donald Levine. Chicago: University of Chicago Press.
Skocpol, Theda. 1979. *Social Revolutions.* New York: Cambridge University Press.
Smith, Adam. 1759/1966. *The Theory of Moral Sentiments.* New York: Bohn.
Smith, Adam. 1776/1937. *The Wealth of Nations.* New York: Modern Library.
Sorokin, Pitirim A. 1937–1941. *Social and Cultural Dynamics.* 4 vols. New York: American Book Co.
Spencer, Herbert. 1851/1970. *Social Statics.* London: John Chapman.
Spencer, Herbert. 1852/1972a. "A Theory of Population deduced from the General Law of Animal Fertility." In *On Social Evolution. Selected Writings*, pp. 33–37. Edited by J.D.Y. Peel. Chicago: University of Chicago Press.
Spencer, Herbert. 1857/1972b. "Progress: Its Law and Cause." In *On Social Evolution: Selected Writings*, pp. 38–52. Edited by J.D.Y. Peel. Chicago: University of Chicago Press.
Spencer, Herbert. 1860/1972c. "The Social Organism." In *On Social Evolution: Selected Writings*, pp. 53–70. Edited by J.D.Y. Peel. Chicago: University of Chicago Press.
Spencer, Herbert. 1862/1904. *First Principles.* London: Williams and Norgate.
Spencer, Herbert. 1873/1908. *The Study of Sociology.* London: Kegan Paul, Trench, Trübner & Co.
Spencer, Herbert. 1897–1906/1975. *The Principles of Sociology.* I–III. Westport, Conn.: Greenwood Press.
Stojanovic, Svetozar. 1973. *Between Ideals and Reality: A Critique of Socialism and Its Future.* London: Oxford University Press.
Strasser, Hermann. 1976. *The Normative Structure of Sociology.* London: Routledge.
Strauss, Anselm. 1978. *Negotiations. Varieties, Contexts, Processes and Social Order.* San Francisco: Jossey-Bass.
Stryker, Sheldon. 1980. *Symbolic Interactionism: A Social Structural Vision.* Menloe Park: Benjamin Cummings.
Sumner, William Graham. 1906/1940. *Folkways.* Boston: Ginn.
Tenbruck, Friedrich H. 1975. "Das Werk Max Webers." *Kölner Zeitschrift für Soziologie und Sozialpsychologie* 27:663–702. (Translation: 1980. "The Problem of Thematic Unity in the Work of Max Weber." *British Journal of Sociology* 31:316–51.)
Tenbruck, Friedrich H. 1985. *Die Sozialwissenschaften als Mythos der Moderne.* Cologne: Adamas.
Tenbruck, Friedrich H. 1986. *Geschichte und Gesellschaft.* Berlin: Duncker & Humblot.
Tenbruck, Friedrich H. 1989. *Die kulturellen Grundlagen der Gesellschaft.* Opladen: Westdeutscher Verlag.

Thomas, William I. 1937. *Primitive Behavior: An Introduction to the Social Sciences.* New York: McGraw-Hill.

Thomas, William I. 1972. "The Definition of the Situation." In Jerome G. Manis and Bernard N. Meltzer (Eds.), *Symbolic Interaction,* pp. 331-36. Boston: Allyn & Bacon.

Thomas, William I., and Dorothy S. Thomas. 1928. *The Child in America.* New York: Knopf.

Thomas, William I., and Florian Znaniecki. 1918-1920. *The Polish Peasant in Europe and America.* 5 vols. Boston: Badger.

Tiryakian, Edward A. 1962. *Sociologism and Existentialism.* Englewood Cliffs, N.J.: Prentice-Hall.

Tiryakian, Edward A. 1977. "Durkheim and Husserl: A Comparison of the Spirit of Positivism and the Spirit of Phenomenology." In J. Bien (Ed.), *Phenomenology and the Social Sciences,* pp. 20-43. The Hague: Nijhoff.

Tocqueville, Alexis de. 1835-1840/1986. *De la démocratie en Amérique.* 2 vols. Paris: Gallimard. (Translation: 1969. *Democracy in America.* Garden City, N.Y.: Doubleday.)

Tönnies, Ferdinand. 1887/1963. *Gemeinschaft und Gesellschaft.* Darmstadt: Wissenschaftliche Buchgesellschaft. (Translation: 1969. *Community and Society.* New York: Harper & Row.)

Trasher, Frederick. 1927. *The Gang.* Chicago: University of Chicago Press.

Troeltsch, Ernst. 1912/1922. *Die Soziallehren der christlichen Kirchen und Gruppen.* Tübingen: Mohr Siebeck. (Translation: 1931. *The Social Teachings of the Christian Churches.* 2 vols. London: Allen & Unwin.)

Turgot, Anne Robert Jacques. 1972. *OEuvres de Turgot et documents le concernant.* Glashütten/Taunus: Auvermann.

Turner, Bryan S. 1974. *Weber and Islam: A Critical Study.* London: Routledge.

Turner, Bryan S. 1981. *For Weber: Essays in the Sociology of Fate.* London: Routledge.

Turner, Bryan S. 1986. *Citizenship and Capitalism.* London: Allen & Unwin.

Turner, Jonathan H. 1985. *Herbert Spencer: A Renewed Appreciation.* Beverly Hills: Sage.

Turner, Jonathan H. 1986. *The Structure of Sociological Theory.* Chicago: Dorsey.

Turner, Ralph H. 1962. "Role-Taking: Process versus Conformity." In Arnold Rose (Ed.), *Human Behavior and Social Processes,* pp. 22-40. Boston: Houghton Mifflin.

Turner, Ralph H. 1968. "Social Roles: Sociological Aspects." In *International Encyclopedia of the Social Sciences.* Vol. 14/15, pp. 552-57. Edited by David L. Sills. New York: Macmillan, Free Press.

Turner, Ralph H. 1976. "The Real Self: From Institution to Impulse." *American Journal of Sociology* 81:989-1016.

Turner, Ralph H. 1978. "The Role and the Person." *American Journal of Sociology* 84:1-23.

Turner, Ralph H. 1979-1980. "A Strategy for Developing an Integrated Role Theory." *Humboldt Journal of Social Relations* 7:123-39.

Turner, Stephen P. 1983. "Weber on Action." *American Sociological Review* 48:506-19.

Wagner, David. 1984. *The Growth of Sociological Theories.* Beverly Hills: Sage.

Wallace, Walter. 1983. *Principles of Scientific Sociology.* Chicago: Aldine.

Wallerstein, Immanuel Maurice. 1974. *The Modern World System*. Vol. 1: *Capitalist Agriculture and the Origins of the European World-Economy in the Sixteenth Century*. New York: Academic Press.

Wallerstein, Immanuel Maurice. 1979. *The Capitalist World Economy*. Cambridge/ New York: Cambridge University Press.

Wallerstein, Immanuel Maurice. 1984. *The Politics of the World Economy*. Cambridge: Cambridge University Press.

Ward, Lester F. 1883/1902. *Dynamic Sociology*. 2 vols. New York: Appleton.

Ward, Lester F. 1903/1925. *Pure Sociology*. New York: Macmillan.

Ward, Lester F. 1906. *Applied Sociology*. Boston: Ginn.

Watson, John B. 1913. "Psychology as the Behaviorist Views It." *Psychological Review* 20:pp. 158–77.

Watson, John B. 1914. *Behavior: An Introduction to Comparative Psychology*. New York: Henry Holt.

Weber, Max. 1920–1921a/1972a. *Gesammelte Aufsätze zur Religionssoziologie*. Vol. 1. Tübingen: Mohr Siebeck. (Translations in two parts: 1976. *The Protestant Ethic and the Spirit of Capitalism*. Translated by Talcott Parsons. New York: Scribner's; 1964; *The Religion of China. Confucianism and Taoism*. Translated and edited by H.H. Gerth and D. Martindale, New York: Free Press.)

Weber, Max. 1920–1921b/1972b. *Gesammelte Aufsätze zur Religionssoziologie*. Vol. 2. Tübingen: Mohr Siebeck. (Translation: 1967. *The Religion of India. The Sociology of Hinduism and Buddhism*. Translated and edited by H.H. Gerth and D. Martindale. New York: Free Press.)

Weber, Max. 1920–1921c/1971a. *Gesammelte Aufsätze zur Religionssoziologie*. Vol. 3. Tübingen: Mohr Siebeck. (Translation: 1952. *Ancient Judaism*. Translated and edited by H.H. Gerth and D. Martindale. New York: Free Press.)

Weber, Max. 1921/1971b. *Gesammelte Politische Schriften*. Tübingen: Mohr Siebeck (Partly translated in: 1968. *Economy and Society*. 3 vols. Edited by G. Roth and C. Wittich. New York: Bedminster Press; 1974. *From Max Weber: Essays in Sociology*. Translated and edited by H.H. Gerth and C.W. Mills. New York: Oxford University Press.)

Weber, Max. 1922a/1972c. *Wirtschaft und Gesellschaft*. Tübingen: Mohr Siebeck. (Translation: 1968. *Economy and Society*. 3 vols. Edited by G. Roth and C. Wittich. New York: Bedminster Press.)

Weber, Max. 1922b/1973. *Gesammelte Aufsätze zur Wissenschaftslehre*. Tübingen: Mohr Siebeck. (Partly translated in: 1949. *Methodology of the Social Sciences*. Translated and edited by E.A. Shils and H.A. Finch. New York: Free Press; 1968. *Economy and Society*. 3 vols. Edited by G. Roth and C. Wittich. New York: Bedminster Press; 1974. *From Max Weber: Essays in Sociology*. Translated and edited by H.H. Gerth and C.W. Mills. New York: Oxford University Press; 1978. *Max Weber Selections in Translation*. Edited by W.G. Runcimann. Translated by E. Matthews. Cambridge: Cambridge University Press.

Weber, Max. 1924. *Wirtschaftsgeschichte. Aus den nachgelassenen Vorlesungen*. Edited by S. Hellman and M. Palyi. Munich: Duncker & Humblot. (Translation: 1927/1981. *General Economic History. Lecture Scripts from the Weber Estate*. Translated by F.H. Knight and new introduction by I.J. Cohen. New Brunswick, N.J.: Transaction Books.)

Weiss, Johannes. 1975. *Max Webers Grundlegung der Soziologie*. Munich: UTB.
Wiese, Leopold von. 1924–1929/1966. *System der allgemeinen Sociologie*. Berlin: Duncker und Humblot. (Translation: *Systematic Sociology*. New York: Wiley.)
Wiley, Norbert. 1979. "The Rise and the Fall of Dominating Theories in American Sociology." In William Snizek, Ellsworth Fuhrman, and Michael Miller (Eds.), *Contemporary Issues in Theory and Research*, pp. 47–79. Westport, Conn.: Greenwood Press.
Wiley, Norbert. 1985. "The Current Interregnum in American Sociology." *Social Research* 52:179–207.
Windelband, Wilhelm. 1873. *Über die Gewissheit der Erkenntnis*. Berlin: Henschel.
Windelband, Wilhelm. 1878–1880. *Die Geschichte der neueren Philosophie in ihrem Zusammenhange mit der allgemeinen Cultur und den besonderen Wissenschaften dargestellt*. 2 vols. Leipzig: Breitkopf & Härtel.
Windelband, Wilhelm. 1909. Die *Philosophie im deutschen Geistesleben des XIX. Jahrhunderts*. Tübingen: Mohr.
Wirth, Louis. 1928/1969. *The Ghetto*. Chicago: University of Chicago Press.
Wirth, Louis. 1938. "Urbanism as a Way of Life." *American Journal of Sociology* 44:1–24.
Wirth, Louis. 1964. *On Cities and Social Life: Selected Papers of Louis Wirth*. Chicago: University of Chicago Press.
Wolff, Kurt H. (Ed.). 1950. *The Sociology of Georg Simmel*. New York: Free Press.
Wolff, Kurt H. (Ed.). 1959. *Georg Simmel 1858–1918. A Collection of Essays with Translations and a Bibliography*. Columbus, Ohio: The Ohio State University Press.

NAME INDEX

Subject Index